The Best American Travel Writing™ 2011

Edited and with an Introduction
by Sloane Crosley

Jason Wilson, Series Editor

A Mariner Original
HOUGHTON MIFFLIN HARCOURT
BOSTON · NEW YORK   2011

Copyright © 2011 by Houghton Mifflin Harcourt Publishing Company
Introduction copyright © 2010 by Sloane Crosley

ALL RIGHTS RESERVED

The Best American Series® is a registered trademark of Houghton Mifflin Harcourt Publishing Company. *The Best American Travel Writing*™ is a trademark of Houghton Mifflin Harcourt Publishing Company.

No part of this work may be reproduced or transmitted in any form or by any means, electronic or mechanical, including photocopying and recording, or by any information storage or retrieval system without the proper written permission of the copyright owner unless such copying is expressly permitted by federal copyright law. With the exception of nonprofit transcription in Braille, Houghton Mifflin Harcourt is not authorized to grant permission for further uses of copyrighted selections reprinted in this book without the permission of their owners. Permission must be obtained from the individual copyright owners as identified herein. Address requests for permission to make copies of Houghton Mifflin Harcourt material to Permissions, Houghton Mifflin Harcourt Publishing Company, 215 Park Avenue South, New York 10003.

www.hmhbooks.com

ISSN 1530-1516
ISBN 978-0-547-33336-6

"My Monet Moment" by André Aciman. First published in *Condé Nast Traveler*, September 2010. Copyright © 2010 by André Aciman. Reprinted by permission of the author.

"Southern Culture on the Skids: Racetracks, Rebels and the Decline of NASCAR" by Ben Austen. Copyright © 2010 by *Harper's Magazine*. All rights reserved. Reproduced from the October issue by special permission.

"The Coconut Salesman" by David Baez. First published in *The New York Times Magazine*, June 25, 2010. Copyright © 2010 by David Baez. Reprinted by permission of David Baez.

"Venance Lafrance Is Not Dead" by Mischa Berlinski. First published in *Men's Journal*, June/July 2010. Copyright © Men's Journal LLC 2010. All rights reserved. Reprinted by permission of Men's Journal LLC.

"My Year at Sea" by Christopher Buckley. First published in *The Atlantic*, December 2010. Copyright © 2011 by Christopher Buckley. Reprinted by permission of Christopher Buckley.

"A Girls' Guide to Saudi Arabia" by Maureen Dowd. First published in *Vanity Fair*, August 2010. Copyright © 2010 by Maureen Dowd. Reprinted by permission of the author.

"The Last Stand of Free Town" by Porter Fox. First published in *The Believer*, June 2010. Copyright © 2010 by Porter Fox. Reprinted by permission of Porter Fox.

"Stuck" by Keith Gessen. First published in *The New Yorker*, August 2, 2010. Copyright © 2010 by Keith Gessen. Reprinted by permission of the author.

"Famous" by Tom Ireland. First published in *The Missouri Review*, Spring 2010. Copyright © 2011 by Tom Ireland. Reprinted by permission of Tom Ireland.

"The Vanishing Point" by Verlyn Klinkenborg. First published in *The New York Times Magazine*, March 28, 2010. Copyright © 2010 by Verlyn Klinkenborg. Reprinted by permission of The New York Times.

"Reservations" by Ariel Levy. First published in *The New Yorker*, December 13, 2010. Copyright © 2010 by Ariel Levy. Reprinted by permission of The New Yorker.

"Aligning the Internal Compass" by Jessica McCaughey. First published in *Colorado Review*, Spring 2010. Copyright © 2010 by Jessica McCaughey. Reprinted by permission of Jessica McCaughey.

"The Last Inuit of Quebec" by Justin Nobel. First published in *The Smart Set*, January 7, 2010. Copyright © 2010 by Justin Nobel. Reprinted by permission of the author. Excerpt from page 480, Volume 5, is from *Handbook of North American Indians, Volume 5: Arctic* by William C. Sturtevant and David Damas, Smithsonian (National Museum of Natural History).

"Twilight of the Vampires: Hunting the Real-Life Undead" by Téa Obreht. Copyright © 2010 by *Harper's Magazine*. All rights reserved. Reproduced from the November issue by special permission.

"A Year of Birds" by Annie Proulx. First published in *Harper's Magazine*, December 2010. Reprinted with the permission of Scribner, a Division of Simon & Schuster, Inc., from *Bird Cloud: A Memoir* by Annie Proulx. Copyright © 2011 by Dead Line, Ltd. All rights reserved.

"Moscow on the Med" by Gary Shteyngart. First published in *Travel + Leisure*, March 2010. Copyright © 2010 by Gary Shteyngart. Reprinted by permission of Denise Shannon Literary Agency, Inc.

"A Head for the Emir: Travels in Iraqi Kurdistan" by William T. Vollmann. Copyright © 2010 by *Harper's Magazine*. All rights reserved. Reproduced from the April issue by special permission.

"Miami Party Boom" by Emily Witt. First published in *N + 1*, April 23, 2010. Copyright © 2010 by Emily Witt. Reprinted by permission of *N + 1* and the author.

Contents

Foreword

Find a place. Write about it. It's the fundamental premise of all travel writing — the most basic of writing exercises, and yet arguably one of the most important. Unfortunately, many readers' introduction to travel writing begins and ends with guidebooks or service-oriented, what-to-see, what-to-do, how-much-will-it-cost articles. While these forms of writing are certainly useful and have their place, great travel writing aspires to be more than just rote information and a list of bed-and-breakfasts and restaurants. "When something human is recorded, good travel writing happens," writes Paul Theroux. Hopefully, you too will aspire to this maxim, and work to improve your powers of observation, description, and storytelling along the way.

This rather dogmatic passage is taken from the syllabus of the travel writing workshop that I teach each year at my university. As you might imagine, Travel Writing is a popular course — competing with Ballroom Dancing or Wine Tasting — and it attracts a mix of undergraduates of various majors, some who've spent intense periods of study abroad, and others who rarely leave their neighborhood in Philadelphia.

Whether they've traveled widely or not, none of the students have read very much travel writing outside of perhaps a Lonely Planet guidebook. None of them usually have heard of Paul Theroux or Pico Iyer or Simon Winchester or Bill Buford — all of whom I make them read, sometimes to their chagrin. The students who may have heard of *Eat Pray Love* or *Under the Tuscan Sun* usually know them as movies rather than books, and only a handful nod in vague recognition when I mention *On the Road*.

Most students don't take my travel writing class, then, because of the writing or because they want to be Jack Kerouac; they take it because their first travels, alone and away from home and school, just may be the most visceral experiences of their young lives so far. Writing might be one way to make sense of it. College students, lest we forget, aren't all that far removed from the "What I Did on My Summer Vacation" essays of middle school.

As we gather around the seminar table with their essays, the study-abroad students are always the boldest, sharing (often with TMI) the very recent experiences they've just returned from (only weeks ago in some cases). These are often ribald tales of hostels and drinking and romantic trysts. Often enough, though, a flicker of insight or an eye-opening moment of reflection appears. I always encourage them to think about their youthful adventures with as much distance as possible, and to fit their personal stories into the context of the place. "Why are you telling me this story?" I ask them. "What makes this your trip and no one else's?" The best of my students have a winning voice, one that makes the whole class take notice. What I ask in class, then, are the same things I ask of the essays each year as I read for this anthology.

The other students, the ones who've usually never traveled much farther than the Jersey shore, or Florida, or perhaps Cancún, usually begin with more reticence and apprehension, prefacing their essays by saying, "Well, I've never really traveled anywhere." I always try to quell their fears by saying, "Good travel writing can be about anywhere. You can write a great essay about your own neighborhood. It all depends on your approach." This, of course, is another truth I learn every year in compiling my selections of notable travel writing for the year.

So can travel writing actually be taught? Perhaps, and perhaps not.

Surprisingly, few of my students have any expectations of publishing what they write, which makes this course very different from the fiction or poetry workshops or journalism classes I've been involved with. Certainly, some do begin class by asking, "How can I get a job as a travel writer?" I quickly answer this question by explaining the shiftless, nomadic, seat-of-the-pants life that many travel writers lead (which predictably holds little appeal for this achievement-driven generation). Then I follow with the true and sad tale of how magazines are publishing less and less quality travel writing (something that makes the job of putting together this anthology harder every year). With issues of commerce out of the way, we simply write and read about one another's travels.

So why teach travel writing, then, in this age when travel writing has a declining presence? And why do students continue to take the course? Perhaps the real measure of success is whether or not these students sharpen their critical eye, learning to look for the sorts of fascinating or idiosyncratic or unexpected or profound moments and experiences that make travel (and life) more meaningful. Meaningful travel (as well as a meaningful life) is, of course, open to all of us. Writing about that travel in a way that resonates with readers? Well, that's something else altogether. But that's what we aim for in travel writing class.

And that's what this collection of fabulous writing aims for, and delivers.

The stories included here are, as always, selected from among hundreds of pieces in hundreds of diverse publications — from mainstream and specialty magazines to Sunday newspaper travel sections to literary journals to travel websites. I've done my best to be fair and representative, and in my opinion the best travel stories from 2010 were forwarded to Sloane Crosley, who made our final selections.

I now begin anew by reading the hundreds of stories published in 2011. I am once again asking editors and writers to submit the best of whatever it is they define as travel writing. These submissions must be nonfiction, published in the United States during the 2011 calendar year. They must not be reprints or excerpts from published books. They must include the author's name, date of publication, and publication name, and must be tear sheets, the complete publication, or a clear photocopy of the piece as it originally appeared. I must receive all submissions by January 1, 2012, in order to ensure their full consideration for the next collection.

Further, publications that want to make certain their contributions will be considered for the next edition should be sure to include this anthology on their subscription list. Submissions or subscriptions should be sent to Jason Wilson, Drexel University, 3210 Cherry Street, 2nd floor, Philadelphia, PA 19104.

Working with the talented Sloane Crosley this year was wonderful and refreshing. Her choices make a unique book that will take fans of the series down fascinating new paths. I am also grateful to Nicole Angeloro and Jesse Smith for their help on this, our twelfth edition of *The Best American Travel Writing*.

JASON WILSON

Introduction

TEN YEARS AGO, *This American Life* devoted an entire episode to "kid logic." From start to finish, it featured more adorable moments per square inch than the state of Wisconsin has cheese wheels. A spiffed-up-for-the-NPR-audience version of *Kids Say the Darndest Things,* the episode went a bit deeper in exploring how children view and process the world around them. Included is a brief interview with a child psychologist that doesn't amount to more than a minute of airtime, but you can see why Ira Glass included it then and, I hope, why I include it here now. See, there's this four-year-old girl on her first flight ever. As the plane takes off, she turns to the woman next to her and says, with the utmost sincerity: *When do we get smaller?* Until that moment, her only experience of airplanes was watching them disappear into the sky. I remember listening to this in my car as I pulled up to visit my parents, who still inhabit my childhood home. I turned the radio off and cut the engine. I looked out over our modest square suburban yard, recalling how unexotic I found Westchester to be as a child. Most of me was charmed by the *This American Life* story as I was meant to be charmed—but I felt a twinge of melancholy upon hearing it as well. Not because of the poignant moments in which children learn about the world, moments that come barreling at them through space like meteors of reality. But because sometimes imagination comes from a place not of pure delight but of pure boredom. At least that's what suburbia was for me. People with oceans and deserts and wild streams for backyards were surely better off. They had the luxury of spending less time conjuring and more time befriending actual whales.

Furthermore, I assumed that Westchester dully pulsated with this blandness for everyone, visitor or native. Then one day during high school an old camp friend from New Zealand paid me a visit. She pointed to the perfectly boring tree under which I had just parked my car, alongside our perfectly boring driveway, and screamed at the top of her lungs, "Oh my God, what is that *thing?*"

Surely, I remember thinking, they have trees in New Zealand.

"That!" She pushed her finger harder into the air.

There was a squirrel pinned, mid-chase with another squirrel, to the side of an oak tree. Its squirrel talons clung to the bark, its black tail fluffed up and protruded at a right angle toward the two of us. The thing of it is, she actually *was* witnessing something rare: black squirrels exist in limited pockets in the Northeast and Midwest. My parents' front yard happens to be located in one of those pockets. But it was this whole new animal that awed her. She had never seen anything like it, and yet it certainly wasn't on her list of "things to explore in America." She stealthily exited the car and began taking pictures.

This is why we travel. Oh yes, that's right: to see rats with fluffy tails. We travel to discover what we don't know, to get away from what we know too well. We seek out the unexpected. That's the deal we made when we asked our neighbors to take in the mail and headed for the airport. These days we also travel with the hope of leaving our phones unanswered and our e-mail logged out of. With so much thorough planning, so many suggested trip highlights and firsthand accounts available at our fingertips, the unexpected is of greater value than ever. It's a pure shot of experience.

As we grow up, most real experience is increasingly hindered by two factors. One is the infamous prism of our own perspective (the real terrain of exploration is seldom external). I would argue that the second, equally intuitive but less discussed obstacle has to do with a kind of virginity of the mind. We can only learn something —I mean really be introduced to it—once. Hence the incredible shrinking airplanes and the black squirrels. Hence the explorers and the travel guides and the carefully allotted weeks of vacations to places we've never been and likely will never go again. I will say now that I have been to Puerto Rico three times in my life and won't be returning. Because Puerto Rico is a terrible place? Well, it ain't Bali, but no, that's not why. It's because of the other 30 percent of the planet Earth covered in landmass. I have the one life and the one brain to match it, and I'd rather not waste either on knowing a foreign locale like the back of my hand unless the front of my hand is signing a lease there.

Perhaps this seems fickle or limiting or just rings false. If we were discussing people instead of places, no one in their right mind would suggest that a series of casual friendships are more ideal than a handful of deep relationships. To get the most out of any relationship, I have to take off my coat and stay a while. But travel is different. I have seen other humans before. I get the general idea of what one might look like. But I have never spent a year at sea like Christopher Buckley (coat required, a warm one) or journeyed to the wild and endangered terrain of Australia's "Top End" like Verlyn Klinkenborg. And I have *really* never gone on a bowhead whale hunt in Quebec with Justin Nobel. That I think I would have remembered.

In reading the nearly one hundred essays narrowed from the numerous excellent pieces of travel writing published last year, I found myself most drawn to those whose authors, simply put, went because I couldn't. This is not a prerequisite for the foreign or the expensive — I suppose if I really wanted to visit Bristol Motor Speedway and try to explore the decline of NASCAR like Ben Austen in "Southern Culture on the Skids," I could give it a shot. But there's no way I'd make it around the track with the same brand of skillful insight unique to Austen. So there I sat in my armchair (no, really, it's blue and has a throw pillow), where I relied on him and seventeen other literary witnesses to be my eyes and ears. The tales of their experiences were so intoxicating because I felt as if I were *with* them, along for the ride as they employed a combination of cultural absorption and opinion. They opened up new means of thinking in their own brains and dragged me through the portal with them. There is much to be said for staking out a foreign spot as your own, but like I said: the nature of the world is that it will provide that valuable introductory course only once. Each of these essays reads like a remarkably successful social experiment, an answer to the question of what happens when you take a handful of the country's most talented writers and show them something they don't know.

It is to the original assigning editors' credit that many of these explorers were perfectly matched to their destinations from the start. Many of the accounts featured here are less unknown chem-

istry experiments and more cases of hydrogen + fire = explosion.
Harper's Magazine is no dummy. It knew what it was doing when it
sent William T. Vollmann to Kurdistan, just as *Vanity Fair* knew what
it was doing when it sent Maureen Dowd to Saudi Arabia, just as
Travel + Leisure knew what it was doing when it sent the instinctively funny Gary Shteyngart to eat and drink his way through a
Russian neighborhood in Tel Aviv. The results are predictably,
transportingly phenomenal. In Vollmann's case, they are eye-
opening as well. In "A Head for the Emir," a title that becomes
quickly and disturbingly relevant in Vollmann's narrative of traveling across checkpoints within Kurdistan, the "air smelled of manure from the cattle that came grazing there, human urine, and
sweat: of the many people all around, the closest man, in sandals
and striped shirt, squatting."

Other selections are no less rewarding—some might say even
more so—for the gamble their publications took on an unknown
kid. Emily Witt's account of two very neon years in Miami, chroni-
cling her struggle between gluttony witness and gluttony partici-
pant for $N + 1$, is so artfully crafted one wonders how anyone else
could dare to write about the city after she's through with it.

There seems to be a stylistic choice among travel writers: Do they
become the doctors making their rounds or the patients being ex-
perimented on? The point of travel writing is not always to exhaust
a subject, to record everything so that the next person won't have
to. The writer runs the risk of sucking the life out of a place. But
it's a risk that pays off wonderfully for Witt, and she is actually part
of a two-woman cleanup crew. I assume she won't mind terribly if I
suggest that she has a kindred spirit here in Annie Proulx. "A Year
of Birds," about Proulx's summer spent meticulously documenting
Wyoming eagle nests, is a rare bird itself. True, it's hard *not* to include an essay on bald eagles in a book with *American* printed on
the cover. But you really have to be as grossly talented as Annie
Proulx to write thirteen thousand words on birds—and birds only.
It's like saying, "I'm going to do this and you're going to sit there
and enjoy it because it's just that good." And of course she's right. I
imagine that reading her piece is not unlike being an actual bald
eagle, dipping up and down and playing in the wind. Behold: "Days
of flailing west wind, strong enough to push its snout under the
crust of the fallen snow wherever hares or I had left footprints,

strong enough to then flip up big pancakes of crust and send them cartwheeling east until they disintegrated in puffs. Eagles love strong wind. It is impossible to miss the joy they take in exhibition flying. The bald pair were out playing in the gusts, mounting higher and higher until they were specks, then splitting apart. After a few minutes of empty sky the unknown big dark bird flapped briefly into view before disappearing in a snow squall."

Proulx also quotes from Aldo Leopold's *Sand County Almanac,* which points out that "books on nature seldom mention wind; they are written behind stoves." Leopold makes a solid point: 2010 was not without its dramas, but the more perennial unsung adventures of travel rarely get, well, sung. There is so much world to see, why dwell on the minutiae of how we get from point A to point B? After all, the play's the thing. Not the drive to the theater. Which is precisely why, in our GPS-reliant reality, Jessica McCaughey's "Aligning the Internal Compass" is of note. In what sounds like a personal nightmare for most travelers, McCaughey intentionally engages in the lesser-known sport of "orienteering." See also: getting lost in the woods on purpose. With unexpected twists and turns, literal and metaphorical alike, it's an endearing but never precious exploration of an otherwise unglamorous subject —getting there. When one is publishing one's travel writing in a periodical, there is an unspoken competition for relevancy. The essay that opens with the traveler being catapulted into a secret bay by a lost tribe of Mongolian shamans wins, right? An essay such as McCaughey's is not flashy. It may not be a frontrunner for Most Newsworthy Travel, but it has a happy home in the Most Eternal Travel category.

Actually, "getting there" was a general problem all over the globe in 2010. Even when a writer was already stationed at the "there" in question. To sit with Keith Gessen, sipping on overpriced coffee at a café, watching his sister sit in traffic just feet away, trapped in Moscow's infamous gridlock, is to be frustrated along with him. "Stuck" is a cultural history of Moscow via its abysmal traffic loops. Thanks to Gessen, we see a gridlock so persistent that it presents an alternate form of human contact. There's the voice, the touch, the written word, and now the hostile merging of lanes. It is a frustration known only too well in America to those who have foolishly attempted to drive from New York City to Long Island on a summer weekend. "To get to the Hamptons, just east of Manhattan," explains Ariel Levy in "Reservations," "you must sit on the Long Island Expressway—the biggest parking lot in the world, as they say —for hour upon hour of overheated immobility." But of course tourism and travel can (and probably should, if at all possible) be two different things. Levy's exploration of the Shinnecock tribe's financial and cultural survival goes deeper than the question of outsider traffic in a way that is, ironically, transporting. And who can resist its featured star, the memorable Lancelot Gumbs? He is a character reminiscent of *The Orchid Thief*'s John Laroche.

The mix of exotic drama and good old-fashioned human drama is what makes many of these essays sparkle. As I read, I found that both qualities could be traced to the initial impetus for writing the essay. Having gone through the same process myself, I will cop to its being a bit formulaic. The magazine pitch goes something like this: (1) writer has the notion of a location in his or her head, (2) writer travels to said location, where upon arrival the notion is (2a) corrected or (2b) confirmed, (3) magazine, hopefully, prints piece. The result is many travel pieces that revolve around falling in love with the idea of a place prior to arrival. Thankfully, in this year's selections the ideas themselves are anything but formulaic. Sometimes the idea manifests itself literally. (See, for example, Porter Fox's essay, "The Last Stand of Free Town," about the micronation of Christiania, a state within a state in Copenhagen and a temporary autonomous zone built on utopian ideals.) Sometimes the idea is more of a fixation. In Tom Ireland's "Famous," the author develops an almost Capote-like obsession with the two terrorists responsible for the 2008 killing spree at Mumbai's Victoria Terminus. And sometimes it's just a beautiful thought. In André Aciman's "My Monet Moment," the author travels to Bordighera, Italy, to track down the exact spot where his favorite painting was painted.

"I like not knowing," admits Aciman. "Knowing anything about the painting would most likely undo its spell. But I can't help myself."

Though one of the lighter pieces here, Aciman's account does touch on another theme in travel writing, and that is the idea of taking our world for granted. Of recognizing common misimpressions and issuing correctives through writing. Aciman had casually ogled a print of Monet's painting for years before he decided to do something about it. It's always fascinating to watch gifted writers leave town to explore the lives they're already living. Téa Obreht's "Twilight of the Vampires" starts with the much-heeded superstitions of her native land, which did not strike her as unusual as a child. But her essay soon becomes an eerie account to end all eerie accounts when she returns to Serbia to hunt for real-life vampires.

Here is a place where people do not so much fall in love with ideas as obey their every whim. A road trip outside Belgrade drives us through a country where ritual reigns high above religion. Though it's not all menacing descriptions of open graves, 1970s horror films, and dried goat meat. Obreht's piece also contains the single most amusing image in the pages of this book: "Among numerous indignities through history, the Roma suffered the obscure nuisance of vampire watermelons."

If the superstitions of Serbia overwhelm any religion, so does Haitian folklore overwhelm any earthquake. Mischa Berlinski's love letter to a devastated country is something special indeed. In "Venance Lafrance Is Not Dead" there are enough descriptions of a Haiti you've never seen to correct the images you might have if you have been mainlining CNN only. When the January 2010 earthquake hits, Berlinski and his wife are stationed "only about 125 miles from Port-au-Prince but remote, like an island off the coast of Haiti . . . There were more coffin makers in Jérémie than restaurants, more donkeys than cars, and the paved roads petered out at the edge of town . . . In the mornings, merchants came down from the hills past our front gate with baskets of fruit balanced on their heads, and at night in bed under the mosquito net when the moon was silver and big, we heard voodoo drums and strange, spooky singing. I don't know if I've ever liked a place more in my life." It is an epic, heart-wrenching essay about hope, and these emotions are delivered in such a way that I don't feel the least bit silly in using clichéd adjectives to describe them. I became so immersed in the narrative and was so wracked with worry about the fate of Berlinski's friend Venance, I nearly forgot the title of the essay.

I've noticed that the best travel writing doesn't have real resolutions. Instead of providing a sense of closure, which normally comes when the last word is typed and the writer and reader agree to part ways, the most memorable essays here feel like a beautiful mess at the end. This is because it's impossible to tie them up neatly. The places and the people who inhabit them still exist. Their stories go on. It's what makes travel writing so unusually difficult. All writing revolves around choices, around killing your darlings and the like. But if that's true, it means that travel writers have it harder than anyone else. How do you choose what goes and what stays when everything is new and of note? What about when it's assaulting all of your senses simultaneously? Some adventures would register to anyone as more significant than others, but the moment the writer takes leave of his or her normal life, everything falls under the purview of new experience. Nothing is safe from examination, including the writer. "It was quite fair," says Annie Proulx of the eagles that watched her like, well, hawks. "I peered at them through binoculars, they peered back."

The *This American Life* broadcast moved on to the next adorable story after the interview with the psychologist. It made no mention of the woman's response to the little girl on the airplane. Endeared as this woman must have been, there was a pair of wide eyes staring back at her, waiting for a reply to a perfectly reasonable question. *No, really: When do we get smaller?* I wonder what she said. Perhaps the little girl was encouraged to look out the window and down at the landscape below. Look at all those new places! Imagine how many kinds of lives are being lived down there right this minute. And how incongruous for the human brain that it all fits in a tiny rounded window. Whole cities! Whole oceans! Whole countries! And it's all right there, laid out for our viewing. Ready to be examined. Of course, therein lies the little girl's answer. We never do get smaller. It's just that the world gets bigger.

SLOANE CROSLEY

The Best American
Travel Writing 2011

ANDRÉ ACIMAN

My Monet Moment

FROM *Condé Nast Traveler*

THE ROMANCE BEGINS FOR ME with a picture of a house by
Claude Monet on my wall calendar. More than half the house is
missing and the roof is entirely cropped. All one can see is an
arched balcony with hints of another balcony on the floor above.
Outside, wild growth and fronds everywhere, a few slim trees—
palms mostly, but one agave plant stands out—and beyond, along
a wide, unpaved road, four large villas and a dappled sky. Farther
out in the distance is a chain of mountains capped with what could
be snow. My instincts tell me there is a beach nearby.

I like not knowing anything about the house or the painting. I
like speculating about the setting and imagining that it could easily
be France, Italy, possibly elsewhere. I like thinking that I'm right
about the wide expanse of seawater behind the house. I stare at the
picture and fantasize about the torpor hanging over old beach
towns on early July days, when the squares and roads empty and
everyone stays out of the sun.

The caption, when I finally cheat and find it at the bottom of the
calendar, reads "Villas in Bordighera." I've never heard of Bordighera before. Where is it? Near Lake Como? In Morocco? On Corfu?
Somewhere in Asia Minor? I like not knowing. Knowing anything
about the painting would most likely undo its spell. But I can't help
myself, and soon I look up more things, and sure enough, Bordighera, I discover, lies on the water, on the Riviera di Ponente in
Italy, within sight of Monaco. Further research reveals the villa's
architect: Charles Garnier, famed for building the Opéra de Paris.
Finally, the year of the painting: 1884. Monet, I realize, was still a
few years away from painting his thirty views of Rouen Cathedral.

I know I'm bit by bit demystifying the house. As it turns out, the Internet reveals more paintings of gardens and palm trees in Bordighera, plus one of the very same house. It is a copy of the image on my wall calendar, painted by Monet, not in Bordighera but later that same year in Giverny and meant as a gift for his friend the painter Berthe Morisot. As always, Monet liked to paint the same scene again and again. Sometimes nothing at all changes—just the transit of light spells the difference between impressions of morning and noon.

Monet went to visit Bordighera for the light. His intended visit of a couple of weeks ended up lasting three laborious months in the winter of 1884. He had come the previous year with the painter Renoir for a brief stay. This time he was determined to come alone and capture Bordighera's seascapes and lush vegetation. His letters were filled with accounts of his struggles to paint Bordighera. They were also littered with references to the colony of British residents who flocked here from fall to early spring each year and who transformed this fishing and agrarian sea town famed for its lemons and olive presses into an enchanted turn-of-the-century station for the privileged and happy few. The Brits ended up building a private library, an Anglican church, and Italy's first tennis courts, to say nothing of grand luxury hotels, precursors of those yet to be built on the Venice Lido. Monet felt adrift in Bordighera. He missed his home in Giverny and Alice Hoschedé, his mistress and later wife; and he missed their children.

As far as he was concerned, Bordighera promised three things: Francesco Moreno's estate, containing one of Europe's most exotic botanical gardens; breathtaking sea vistas; and that one unavoidable belfry with its dimpled, onion cupola towering over everything. Monet couldn't touch one of these without invoking the other two. Lush vegetation, seascapes, towering belfry—he kept coming back to them, painting them separately or together, shifting them around as a photographer would members of a family who were not cooperating for a group portrait.

If he was forever complaining, it may have been because the subject matter was near impossible to capture on canvas, or because the colors were, as Monet liked to say in his letters, terribly difficult —he felt at once entranced, challenged, and stymied by them. But it was also because Monet was less interested in subject matter and colors than he was in the atmosphere and in the intangible and, as he called it, the "fairylike" quality of Bordighera. "The motif is of secondary importance to me," he wrote elsewhere. "What I want to reproduce is what lies between the subject and me." What he was after hangs between the visible and the invisible, between the here and now and the seemingly elsewhere. Earth, light, water are a clutter of endless, meaningless things; art is about discovery and design and a reasoning with chaos.

Many years after seeing the reproduction on my wall calendar, I finally happen upon Monet's third painting of that very same house at an exhibition in the Wildenstein gallery in New York. Same missing back of the house, same vegetation, same sky, same suggestion of a beach just steps away, except that the third floor, which is absent in the first two canvases, is quite visible here; one can almost spot the balusters lining the balcony. And there is another variation: in the background looms not the snowcapped mountains but Bordighera Alta—the *città alta,* the oldest part of the city—which like so many old towns in Italy is perched on top of a hill and predates the Borgo Marino on the shore. This inversion is also typical of Monet. He wanted to see how the scene looked from the other side.

I want to be in that house, own that house. I begin to people it with imaginary faces. A plotline suggests itself, the beach beckons ever more fiercely. Like a fleeing cartoon character painting escape routes on a wall, I find my own way into this villa and am already picturing dull routines that come with ownership.

Then one day, by chance, I finally find the opportunity to visit Bordighera and to see it for myself. I have to give a talk on Lake Como, so rather than fly directly from New York to Milan, I decide to fly to Nice instead and there board a train to Italy. The bus from the airport to the train station in Nice takes twenty minutes, purchasing the train ticket another fifteen, and as luck would have it, the train to Italy leaves in another fifteen. Within an hour I am in Bordighera. The train stops. I hear voices on the platform. The door opens and I step down. This is exactly what I expected. Part of me is reluctant to accept that art and reality can make such good partners.

I don't want a taxi, I want to linger, I want to walk to my hotel. Before me, leading straight from the small train station and cutting its way through the heart of the town, is a palm-lined avenue called the Corso Italia, once known as the Via Regina Elena. I've arrived, as I always knew I would, in the very early afternoon. The town is quiet, the light dazzling, the turquoise sea intensely placid. This is my Monet moment.

I've come to Bordighera for Monet, not Bordighera—the way some go to Nice to see what Matisse saw, or to Arles and St.-Rémy to see the world through the eyes of Van Gogh. I've come for something I know doesn't exist. For artists seldom teach us to see better. They teach us to see other than what's there to be seen. I want to see Bordighera with Monet's eyes. I want to see both what lies before me and what else he saw that wasn't quite there, and which hovers over his paintings like the ghost of an unremembered landscape. Monet was probably drawing from something that was more in him than out here in Bordighera, but whose inflection we recognize as though it's always been in us as well. In art we do not see, we recognize. Monet needed Bordighera to help him see something he'd spot the moment he captured it, not before; we need Monet to recognize what we've long sought but know we've never seen.

My first stop, I tell myself, will be the house on the Via Romana, my second the belfry, and my third the Moreno gardens. Luckily, my hotel is on the Via Romana too.

As I walk, I cannot believe what I am seeing: plants and trees everywhere. The scents are powerful and the air pure, clean, tropical. Right before me is a mandarin tree. Something tells me the potted lemons are false. I reach out through a fence and touch them. They are real.

I force myself to think positively of the hotel I booked on-line. I even like the silence that greets me as I arrive and step up to the front desk. Upstairs, I am happy to find I have a good room, with a good-enough balcony view of the distant water, though the space between the hotel and the sea is totally obstructed by a litter of tiny brick houses of recent vintage. I take out clean clothes, shower, and, camera in hand, head downstairs to ask the attendant where I can find the Moreno gardens. The man at the desk looks puzzled and says he's never heard of the Moreno gardens. He steps into the back office and comes out accompanied by a woman who is probably the proprietress. She has never heard of the Moreno gardens either.

My second question, regarding the house painted by Monet, brings me no closer to the truth. Neither has heard of such a house. The house is on the Via Romana, I say. Once again, the two exchange bewildered looks. As far as they know, none of the houses here were painted by Monet.

Monet's Bordighera is gone, and with it, most likely, the house by the sea. On the Via Romana, I stop someone and ask if she could point me in the direction of the town's belfry. Belfry? There is no belfry. My heart sinks. Minutes later I run into an older gentleman and ask him the same question. Shaking his head, the man apologizes; he was born and raised here but knows of no campanile. I feel like a Kafkaesque tourist asking average Alexandrians where the ancient lighthouse stands, not realizing that nothing remains of the ancient Greek city.

From the Via Romana, I make my way back to the train station, where earlier I had spotted a few restaurants on the long seaside promenade called Lungomare Argentina, probably because Eva Perón loved it. Yet along the way—and I barely have time to realize it—there it is: the belfry I've been searching for. It looks exactly as in Monet's paintings, with its glistening, mottled, enamel rococo cupola. The name of the church is Chiesa dell'Immacolata Concezione, built by none other than Charles Garnier. It's probably the tallest structure in town. How could anyone not know what I was referring to when I kept asking about a campanile? I snap pictures, more pictures, trying to make the photos look like Monets, exactly as I did twenty minutes earlier when I stumbled upon a public garden with leafy dwarf palms that resemble those Monet painted in Moreno's garden. An old lady who stops and stares at me suggests that I visit the *città alta,* the town's historic center. It's not too far from here, she says, impossible to miss if I keep bearing left.

Half an hour later, I'm on the verge of giving up on the *città alta* when something else suddenly comes into view: a small hill town and, towering above it, another belfry with a bulbous cupola almost identical to the one I spotted on the *chiesa* by the shore. I can't believe my luck. Bordighera, I realize, has not one but two steeples. The steeple in Monet's paintings is not necessarily that of Garnier's church by the marina but probably another one that I didn't even know existed. Coastal towns always needed towers to warn of approaching pirate ships; Bordighera was no exception. A steep, paved walkway flanked by old buildings opens before me; I'll put off my visit to the historic center and walk up to the top of this minuscule town instead. But this, it takes me yet another delayed moment to realize, is the *città alta* I came looking for. My entire journey, it appears, is made of uninformed double takes and inadvertent steps.

Bordighera Alta is a fortified, pentagon-shaped medieval town full of narrow, seemingly circuitous alleys whose buildings are frequently buttressed by arches running from one side of an alley to the other, sometimes creating vaulted structures linking both sides. Laundry hangs from so many windows that you can scarcely see the sky from below. The town is exceptionally clean — the gutters have been covered with stones, and the clay-tiled paving is tastefully inconspicuous. Except for a televised news report emanating from more than one window lining the narrow Via Dritta, everything here is emphatically quiet for so packed a warren of homes. As I make my way around the square, I see the Santa Maria Maddalena's clock tower again, and to my complete surprise, once I step into a large courtyard that might as well be a square behind the main square, another belfry comes into view. Then a post office. A church. A barber. A baker. A high-end but tiny restaurant, a bar, an *enoteca*, all tucked away serendipitously so as not to intrude on this ancient but glitzified town. A few local boys are playing *calcetto*, or pickup soccer. Others are chatting and leaning against a wall, all smoking. A girl, also smoking, is sitting on a scooter. I can't decide whether this town is inhabited by working-class people stuck on this small hill all year or whether the whole place has been refurbished to look faux-rundown and posh-medieval. Either way, I could live here, summer and winter, forever.

Once again, through an unforeseen ascent of a hill, I've stumbled upon something perhaps far better than what I came looking for. I find myself suspecting that the humbling, intrusive hand of Providence is arranging events which couldn't seem more random. I like the idea of a design behind my desultory wanderings around Bordighera. I like thinking that perhaps this is how we should always travel, without foresight or answers, adventitiously, with faith as our compass.

As I'm making my way through a maze of narrow lanes, I finally come to an open spot that looks out toward a huge expanse of aquamarine. Straight below me is a marina. I decide to head back down to the Lungomare Argentina and am beginning to leave Bordighera Alta. Because I am already planning my return trip to Bordighera in six months, I stop at what looks like a picturesque two-star hotel. I walk inside and start by asking the man at the desk for the price of a double. Then, as though my next question follows up on the previous one, I ask if he can tell me something about the Moreno gardens. Once again I am given the same story. There are no Moreno gardens. "But Monet—" I am about to interrupt. "Moreno's land was broken up more than a century ago," says a portly man who had been chatting with the hotel's owner and was sitting in the shade. Francesco Moreno, he continues, came from Marseille and, like his father before him, was a French consul in Italy—he owned almost all of Bordighera and was in the olive and the lemon trade. He imported all manner of plants from around the world, which is why Monet tried everything he could to be allowed inside the garden. The estate, however, was sacrificed to build the Via Romana.

Moreno, it appears, did not put up a fight with the city planners, even though he was the wealthiest landowner in sight. He died, probably a broken man, in 1885, one year after Monet's visit. The family sold their land, gave the rest away, then his widow moved to Marseille. The Morenos never returned. There is scarcely a trace of the Moreno mansion or its grounds—or, for that matter, the Moreno family. For some reason no one wants to talk about them.

It's only then, as I leave the hotel and take a steep path to the Church of Sant'Ampelio by the sea, that I finally spot a white house that might very well be the house, or something that looks just like it, though I could, of course, be wrong. A rush of excitement tells me that I have found it all on my own—yes, adventitiously. Still, I could be wrong. It is a gleaming-white construction; Monet's house is not so white nor does it have a turret. But then, I've seen only cropped versions of it. I walk down the path and head right to the house. There is no doubt: same balconies, same stack of floors, same balusters. I approach the villa with my usual misgivings, fearing dogs or a mean guardian or, worse yet, being wrong.

I brace myself and ring the buzzer by the metal gate. "Who is it?"

asks a woman's voice. I tell her that I am a visitor from New York who would give anything to see the house. "*Attenda,* wait," she interrupts. Before I can compose an appropriately beseeching tone in my voice, I hear a buzzer and the click of the electric latch being released. I step inside. A glass door to the house opens and out steps a nun.

She must have heard my story a thousand times. "Would you like to see the house?" The question baffles me. I would love to, I say, still trying to muster earnest apology in my voice. She asks me to follow and leads me into the house. She shows me the office, then the living room, then what she calls the television room, where three old women are sitting in the dark watching the news. Is this a nunnery? Or a nursing home? I don't dare ask. She shows me into the pantry, where today's menu is written in large blue script. I can't resist snapping a picture. She giggles as she watches me fiddle with my camera, then shows me to the dining room, which is the most serene, sunlit dining room I have seen in ages. It is furnished with separate tables that could easily seat thirty people; they must be the happiest thirty I know. The room is impeccably restored to look its age, its century-old paintings and heavy curtains bunched against the lintel of each French window. The house must cost a fortune in upkeep.

Would I like to take a look at the rooms upstairs? asks the nun. Seriously? She apologizes that her legs don't always permit her to go up and down the stairway but tells me I should feel free to go upstairs and look around, and must not forget to unlock the door leading to the top floor on the turret. The view, she says, is stupendous. We speak about Monet. She does not think Monet ever stepped inside this villa, but he must have spent many, many hours outside.

I walk up the stairs gingerly, amazed by the cleanliness of the shining wooden staircase. I admire the newly corniced wallpaper on each floor. The banister itself is buffed smooth, and the doors are a glistening enamel white. What timeless peace these people must live in. When I arrive at the top floor, I know I am about to step into a view I never thought existed, and will never forget. And yet there I was, minutes earlier, persuaded that the house was turned to rubble or that they weren't going to let me in. I unlock the wooden door. I am finally on the veranda, staring at the very same balusters I saw in Monet's painting in the New York gallery, and all around me is . . . the sea, the world, infinity itself. Inside the turret is a coiling metal staircase that leads to the summit. I cannot resist. I have found the house, I have seen the house, I am in the house. This is where running, where searching, where stumbling, where everything stops. I try to imagine the balcony a hundred years ago and the house a century from now. I am speechless.

Later, I come down and find the nun in the kitchen with a Filipina helper. Together, the nun and I stroll into the exotic garden. She points to a place somewhere in the far distance. "There are days when you can see the very tip of Monte Carlo from here. But today is not a good day. It might rain," she says, indicating gathering clouds.

Is this place a museum? I finally ask. No, she replies, it's a hotel, run by Josephine nuns. A hotel for anyone? I ask, suspecting a catch somewhere. Yes, anyone.

She leads me back into an office where she pulls out a brochure and a price sheet. "We charge thirty-five euros a day." I ask what the name of this hotel is. She looks at me, stupefied. "Villa Garnier!" she says, as if to imply, what else could it possibly be called? Garnier built it, he died here, and so did his beloved son. The widow Garnier, unlike Moreno's, stayed in Bordighera.

It would be just like me to travel all the way to Bordighera from the United States and never once look up the current name of the villa. Any art book could have told me that its name was Villa Garnier. Anyone at the station could have pointed immediately to it had I asked for it by name. I would have spared myself hours of meandering about town. But then, unlike Ulysses, I would have arrived straight in Ithaca and never once encountered Circe or Calypso, never met Nausicaa or heard the enchanting strains of the Sirens' song, never gotten sufficiently lost to experience the sudden, disconcerting moment of arriving in, of all places, the right place. What luck, though, to have found the belfries and heard the sad tale of the Moreno household, or to have walked into an art gallery in New York one day and seen the other version of a painting that had become like home to me, and if not home, then the idea of home—which is good enough. I tell her I'll come back to the Villa Garnier in six months.

But the nun has one more surprise in store for me.

Since I've come this far for Monet, she suggests, I should head out to a school on the Via Romana that is run by other nuns and is called the Villa Palmizi, for the palm trees growing on what was once Moreno grounds. The school, which is totally restored, she tells me, contains part of the old manor house.

We say good-bye and I head out to the Villa Palmizi, eager to speak to one of the nuns there. The walk takes five minutes. The end of one search has suddenly given rise to another. I knock, a nun opens. I tell her why I've come. She listens to what I have to say about Monet, about the Villa Garnier, then asks me to wait. Another nun materializes and takes her place. Then another. Yes, says the third, pointing to one end of the house that has recently been restored, this was part of the Moreno house. She says she'll take me upstairs.

More climbing. Most of the schoolchildren have already gone home. Some are still waiting for their parents, who are late picking them up. Same as in New York, I say. We climb one more flight and end up in a large laundry room where one nun is ironing clothes while another folds towels. Come, come, she signals, as if to say don't be shy. She opens a door and we step onto the roof terrace. Once again, I am struck by one of the most magnificent vistas I have ever seen. "Monet used to come to paint here as a guest of Signor Moreno." I instantly recognize the scene from art books and begin to snap pictures. Then the nun corrects herself. "Actually, he used to paint from up there," she says, pointing to another floor I hadn't noticed that is perched right above the roof. *"Questo è l'oblò di Monet."* "This is Monet's porthole." I want to climb the narrow staircase to see what Monet saw from that very porthole.

The story of Monet's *oblò* is most likely apocryphal, but I need to see what Monet might have seen through this oblong window just as I needed to come to Bordighera to see the house for myself. A sense of finality hovers in my coming up here to see the town through Monet's window. Same belfry, same sea, same swaying palms, all staring back now as they did more than a century ago, when Monet first arrived.

I begin to nurse an eddy of feelings that cannot possibly exist together: intense gratitude for having witnessed so much when I was so ready to give up, coupled with the unsettling disappointment which comes from knowing that but for luck and my own careless-ness, I would never have witnessed any of this, and that, because luck played so great a part in things today, whatever I am able to garner from this experience is bound to fade. Part of me wishes to make sense of all this, only to realize in a flash of insight as I'm standing in Monet's room, that if chance — what the Greeks called *tyche* — trumps meaning and sense every time, then art, or what they called *techne,* is itself nothing more than an attempt to give a tone, a cadence, a meaning to what might otherwise be left to chance.

All I want, all I can do is retrace my steps and play the journey over again. Stumble on the image of a house on my wall calendar, spot the same house in a gallery, arrive by train, know nothing, see nothing, never sight the old *città alta* until I come upon it, see the town "with" and "without" the belfry, with and without the sea, with and without the chopped-up quarter of Moreno's house, and al-ways, always chance upon Garnier's home last. I want to restore this moment, I want to take this moment back with me.

Stepping out of Monet's tiny room, I am convinced more than ever that I have found what I came looking for. Not just the house, or the town, or the shoreline but Monet's eyes to the world, Mo-net's hold on the world, Monet's gift to the world.

BEN AUSTEN

Southern Culture on the Skids

FROM *Harper's Magazine*

THE BRISTOL MOTOR SPEEDWAY, its silver grandstands tower-ing 220 feet above a half-mile track, is often compared to the Ro-man Colosseum. Measured in seating capacity, the comparison is if anything belittling: the Colosseum could accommodate 55,000 spectators; Bristol has room for three times that number. But unlike the streets of ancient Rome, the rural byways of Sullivan County, in northeastern Tennessee, offer nothing else close in terms of scale. Arriving at the track feels like moseying up to a fa-vorite fishing spot and seeing at the dock the *Queen Mary* 2. For NASCAR diehards, the speedway is a national shrine, a destination whose very specialness inspires tautological koans that are uttered there reverently and yowled there drunkenly and stenciled there on many a T-shirt and cap: *"Bristol is Bristol." "That's Bristol, baby." "It's Bristol, fuck it."*

On a Friday night in March, two days before a big Sprint Cup race, I wandered among several thousand NASCAR lovers on the grounds outside this colossus. The crowds had come to hear a free concert and watch their favorite drivers play Wii video games and to pose for photographs with people dressed as Tony the Tiger, or as Snap, Crackle, and a walking Ding Dong. The fans shook hands with the proud drivers from minor racing leagues, women and children and older men who sat at foldout tables in front of their variously sized and styled race cars. They nodded admiringly at the muscle cars that locals had souped up themselves and driven over to the track for display.

Near two Hooters girls, *I* ♥ *HOOTERS* stickers adhered to their décolletage, I watched a man's eyes widen into full ovals and his lips form a silent "Oh shit" as he realized he was standing beside Kerry Earnhardt, son of the late Dale Earnhardt Sr. (once NASCAR's most beloved driver), and half brother of Dale Earnhardt Jr. (currently the sport's most popular star). Gail and Bill Long, a couple who had driven seven and a half hours from Alliance, Ohio, told me that they had been to the Bristol race four years in a row and were even married at the track. "I told Bill I wanted to get married on 8/8/08," Gail said—8 and 88 being Dale Jr.'s former and current car numbers. "And he said, 'Let's do it at Bristol.' We ended up doing it 8/23/08."

Bruton Smith, the owner of Bristol as well as several other tracks on the NASCAR circuit, addressed the multitude from the main outdoor stage. "The only jokes I have Obama supporters wouldn't like, and we're all bipartisan here," he said with a chuckle. Later that weekend Congress would vote health care reform into law, but on Friday the bill's passage remained a long shot. Smith playfully worked his audience, asking whether health care was going to pass and eliciting in response a roaring "No!"

Smith called to the microphone his director of children's charities, retired Air Force major general Tom Sadler. The general picked up the battle cry, telling those gathered that they were "the lone pole in the tent. You're the greatest patriotic sports fans in all of sports. Don't worry about it, folks. This country is far too great for a few people to run it into a hole. It's because of people like you. God bless you. God bless this country!"

Amid the many testaments of fealty, it was easy to forget that the ranks of the NASCAR faithful were dwindling.

Competitive stock-car racing, with its fabled moonshine-running roots in the Prohibition-era South, burst into mainstream prominence a decade ago. It was then that NASCAR signed a multibillion-dollar consolidated TV rights deal. By 2003, after losing its longtime chief sponsor, R. J. Reynolds Tobacco Company, and replacing it with the less controversial Nextel, NASCAR had become the second-most-watched sport on television, behind football, boasting a fan base of 75 million. Pretty soon NASCAR plotlines began appearing in Hollywood blockbusters— *Herbie: Fully Loaded*, *Talladega Nights: The Ballad of Ricky Bobby*, the Pixar movie *Cars*—part of the cross-marketing deals worked out by the sport's new Los Angeles office. Races at time-honored tracks in the South were removed from the schedule; ones at new, larger facilities in southern California and Las Vegas were added. There were even plans to open a track in New York City. And to avoid displeasing its growing list of Fortune 500 sponsors, officials fined drivers when they tussled or cursed. In 2006, near the height of the sport's popularity, NASCAR president Mike Helton pronounced, "The old southeastern redneck heritage that we had is no longer in existence."

But since then attendance at races has steadily fallen. NASCAR leadership attributes the decline in ticket sales to the miserable economy, yet television viewership has also plummeted, corporate sponsors have been pulling out, and the publicly traded company that manufactures NASCAR collectibles has tottered near bankruptcy. To fill the stands at the 2010 Daytona 500, NASCAR's biggest race, the speedway had to cut the price on many tickets by half, remove seats, and reduce what it charged for concessions and merchandise. During the actual race, a giant pothole formed on the track, twice sidelining the cars for a total of more than two hours. Increasingly, NASCAR seemed like a clunker.

For their part, fans complained that the drivers had become too corporate and bland, that the racing itself was boring, that the newly standardized race cars — redesigned for safety and closer competition — no longer looked anything like the Fords and Chevys and Dodges that they parked in their own driveways. Stock-car racing is currently dominated by Jimmie Johnson, the skilled non-conflict driver, a clean-cut Californian whose race team, Hendrick Motorsports, seemingly had all the resources and character of a Mercedes-Benz plant. Victory at the track now appeared to be in the hands of the technicians in the lab, rather than in those of the shade-tree genius mechanics or the gutsy drivers. At a time when the rest of America was forced to reckon with a "NASCAR demographic," NASCAR itself seemed to lose touch with its presumptive base.

During its sixty-two-year history, NASCAR has been run as a somewhat benevolent dictatorship by the sport's founding family, the Frances, who over three generations have unilaterally amended rules and regulations as they saw fit. So it was all the more surprising when the association of stock-car racing reacted to its woes by implementing an array of changes demanded by fans. NASCAR officials widened restrictor plates on engines to allow the vehicles to generate more power and speed. They scrapped the rear wing, regarded by purist gear-heads as a sign of Formula One's nefarious influence, and returned to the rear spoiler, which is what you saw on Chargers and Camaros anyhow. They relaxed rules against "bump-drafting," a dangerous maneuver in which a driver, tailgating at 120 miles per hour, knocks the back end of the car in front of his and is drawn forward in its wake. Having pushed the Sunday start times to late afternoons and early evenings in hopes of attracting larger television audiences, officials now moved most of them back to 1 P.M., when traditional fans were just coming home from church. And, desperate to reconnect the sport with its rebel roots, they said to the guys on the track, "Boys, have at it," a bit of vernacular signaling that drivers would now be free to police themselves and to show more down-home personality — never mind that home for all but a handful of the top racers was now somewhere north of the Mason-Dixon line or west of Texas.

In Atlanta, two weeks before my trip to Bristol, one of the "boys" heeded the call. A driver named Carl Edwards, more than 150 laps off the lead, decided to exact a little old-school vengeance on a young racer named Brad Keselowski, who had collided with him the previous season. At speeds of about 190 mph, Edwards intentionally steered into Keselowski's car, which spun out, flipped, hovered airborne for a harrowing moment, then landed, nose first, pile-driving into the ground. Although Keselowski was pulled from the wreckage without injury, the sight of a car airborne in proximity to the stands exceeded even the ordinarily sanguinary predilections of the NASCAR set. "That's not stock-car racing. That's carnage. That's demolition derby," Liz Clarke, a sportswriter for the *Washington Post* and the author of the NASCAR history *One Helluva Ride,* told me. "Fans want to see a wreck, not a blood sport. The mandate to 'have at it, boys,' it's a very debasing way of treating a sport in order to sell tickets and drive ratings."

Long known as the hottest ticket in NASCAR, Bristol had sold out fifty-five straight races, with a season-ticket renewal rate of over 90 percent. But in the days before the race it appeared that, for the first time since 1982, the speedway would be nowhere near full. The local hotels were reporting steep drops in reservations, and

on the neighboring campgrounds—normally blanketed by monster RVs—much of the land remained vacant. The track's management decided against lowering ticket prices—which started at $93
a seat—opting instead to "add value" as a way to draw walk-up
ticket buyers. One of the added-value features was a thirty-five-lap
"legends race," a competition featuring twelve of NASCAR's most
beloved former drivers. Rounding the second turn on lap thirty,
fifty-six-year-old Larry Pearson slid into the outer wall and aimlessly
drifted back down along the track, into the path of Charlie Glotz-
bach, age seventy-one, whose throwback stock car hurtled into
Pearson's sidelong vehicle, plowed it into the infield wall, and
erupted in flames. An unconscious Pearson had to be cut out of
his car. Over the next twelve days he would undergo six surger-
ies to treat two broken legs, a shattered pelvis, two broken ribs, a
broken ankle, and a broken right hand. So much for resurrecting
NASCAR's fabled past.

Having only recently moved to Nashville from Brooklyn, I was new
both to the South and to stock-car racing. When Mike Helton
learned that Bristol would be my first race, he said, "Any fan sam-
pling NASCAR today who felt it like I first felt in 1963, they're going to stick around in the sport just like I did." We were sitting in a
trailer parked on Bristol's chockablock infield. Helton, who grew
up in a nearby county, said that this track embodied NASCAR's
core values—values, he admitted, from which the sport had
veered. "We were so busy growing that our respect and proudness
of our heritage got overshadowed. What you've seen in the last
couple of seasons are moves that NASCAR is making to remind us
of that heritage, of what made NASCAR what it is."
    To help me feel NASCAR as he had first felt it, Helton offered to
arrange a ride in Bristol's official pace car, a Ford Mustang painted
in a checkered-flag motif. I thanked him but said there was no
need; the guys at Ford Racing had already extended the same invitation. When I arrived, as instructed, at 7:30 A.M., the empty sta-
dium felt like the inside of a Coca-Cola can, the metal bleachers
rising up on all sides, a stripe of red running along the top. I folded
my six-foot-three-inch self into the Mustang's back seat. Nestled
back there with me was a writer from *Time* magazine, also tall, also
a Yankee new to the track. Riding shotgun was Claire B. Lang, a

petite reporter from Sirius NASCAR Radio. She waved a microphone in front of our driver, Brett Bodine, a former Cup Series racer in his fifties whose job it now was to pilot the pace cars at NASCAR events. "Have at it, buddy. Step on it," Lang said. And Bodine did.

The Ford rocketed to 80 mph, which on the short track felt like twice that, the car careering into the next turn almost as quickly as it came out of the last one. Since its dramatic 30-degree banking allows for more speed than at other short tracks, Bristol has long called itself the "World's Fastest Half-Mile." This superlative proved insufficiently exciting: in the run-up to this race Bristol's marketers rebranded it "the half-mile of havoc," airing ads that replayed the radio call of the Edwards-Keselowski crash followed by a narrator ominously intoning, "The one question on everybody's mind is: What is going to happen at Bristol?"

There, in the pace car's back seat, the question on my mind was much the same. On the corners, Bodine skimmed the walls and then, on the straightaways, slung us down for an extra burst of speed. As we screeched around in that tight oval, I struggled just to remain seated upright. The exertions of the engine and the shifting gears made it sound as though the undercarriage was being torn apart. I could see almost nothing of the track in front of us, nor could I see the stands looming overhead, nor the pit, nor the infield. The only thing I had a clear view of from my backseat perch was the wall to my right, which, with every turn, leaped out, a concrete blur only inches from the door.

Bodine spoke casually into the microphone, narrating his actions for Lang while fiddling with a transmitter. "Here's a hard brake to get into turn one. Put the throttle down in the middle of one and two. Now we're accelerating down the back straightaway."

Unlike athletes in other professional sports, a NASCAR driver is blessed with no conspicuous physical gifts—neither great height nor strength nor explosive quickness. The thing he does so well most of us do every day on highways and back roads. The car he drives even looks like a sedan, like the cars we drive. So it's less of a stretch for fans to imagine that they could be a race car driver than, say, a guard for the Chicago Bulls or an Olympic gymnast. And over the years, the diehards regularly showed up or tuned in because of that easy identification with the drivers, that alluring mix of rever-

ence and familiarity. Richard Petty, known as "The King," would
sign autographs for hours and was said to have the "common
touch." Dale Earnhardt Sr., for all his success as a driver and a
brand, was always thought of as working class. By contrast, a recent HBO documentary meant to reveal the real Jimmie Johnson,
who has now won the sport's top prize an unprecedented four
straight years, showed him flying on his private jet, drinking healthy
smoothies, and hanging with his wife, a former model, in the
kitchen of their largely vacant mega-mansion.

Between turns one and two, to demonstrate how our speed had
offset the gravitational effects of the track's steep banking, Bodine
brought the car to a full stop.

"I'm standing on my head! I'm falling out of my seat belt here!"
Claire B. Lang said, her voice rising animatedly at the end of each
word. Instinctively I leaned in the opposite direction, as if to keep
us from tipping over. After Bodine got the Ford whipping around
the track again, he reminded us that in a race forty-two other cars
would be fighting us for position. One of the most repeated sayings
around NASCAR tracks, a phrase coined in the 1990 Tom Cruise
film *Days of Thunder,* is "rubbin' is racin'." Although specially designed for high speeds, stock cars have fenders and are meant to
"trade paint." Bodine said to try to imagine those other cars bump-
ing and pushing us around a bit. Although I'd like to say that I was
able to envision myself as a badass NASCAR driver, that the only
thing separating Brett Bodine and me was where we sat in the Mustang, I couldn't entertain the thought of a single car driving within
twenty feet of us—not without seizing up.

NASCAR has always been defined by its wrecks, by thrown helmets
and thrown fists. Indeed, NASCAR's wider popularity beyond the
South and Midwest can be traced to a fistfight at the conclusion of
the 1979 Daytona 500 between Cale Yarborough and the Allison
brothers, Donnie and Bobby, that was caught live on national television. And the crash that killed Dale Earnhardt Sr., on the very
last turn of the 2001 Daytona race, not only ushered in NASCAR's
more stringent safety regulations but also propelled the sport into
pop culture ubiquity. With all the added attention, new fans flocked
to NASCAR, chasing an icon and an experience that were already
gone.

Humpy Wheeler, one of NASCAR's most illustrious promoters and recently the president of Charlotte Motor Speedway, explained to me that this craving for violence was actually embedded in NASCAR's backwoods Southern DNA. Whenever he speaks to young drivers at NASCAR's annual rookie seminar in Florida, he always recommends that they read Senator Jim Webb's book about the Scots-Irish, *Born Fighting*. "If they can understand what makes that culture different and interesting—the meanness in it, why fellas love to fight, how they 'turn red' and completely lose it—then they'll understand the South, country and western music, and stock-car racing," Wheeler said. Darrell Waltrip, who in his prime in the 1970s and 1980s won eleven times at Bristol, now was a broadcaster on Fox and owned a car dealership not too far from my home in Nashville. He told me there was no denying that the sport was "blue-collar, Middle-America, shotgun-in-the-back-window. That's our fan base. You can't make a dog meow."

But even as NASCAR was making every effort to satisfy these "traditional" fans, it was also trying to become more inclusive and reach new demographics—to coax other sounds out of that figurative dog. Its Drive for Diversity program was developed six years ago to put more people of color behind the wheels of race cars, with the hopes that fans of more varied backgrounds would fill the grandstands once they saw drivers that looked like them. Currently no African Americans race in any of NASCAR's top series, and Wendell Scott remains the only black driver ever to win a Cup Series event, a feat he accomplished back in 1963. A woman, Danica Patrick, did come over to NASCAR from Indy racing this season, with great fanfare, but only to enter a handful of lower-level races. Apart from Juan Pablo Montoya, a Colombian and former Formula One driver, everyone in NASCAR's top Sprint Cup series was a white guy. Drive for Diversity included eleven young drivers, all of whom competed in the equivalent of Single-A and ten of whom trained together as part of an independently owned team called Revolution Racing. Marcus Jadotte, NASCAR's managing director of public affairs, didn't think there was any conflict between the several diversity efforts he headed up for NASCAR and the sport's attempts to return to its "roots." "NASCAR isn't rolling anything back," Jadotte asserted. "The language of 'boys, have at it' speaks solely to the rules on the racetrack. It's about increasing competitiveness and modifying driver behavior. It's not about who's watching in the stands."

Max Siegel, a former sports and entertainment lawyer who once ran a major gospel label, is the primary owner of Revolution Racing. Siegel recently had the idea of turning the trials and triumphs of the drivers on his team into a reality television show, a series he sold to Black Entertainment Television. The first episodes of *Changing Lanes* appeared on BET this summer, and Siegel told me that a sneak preview shown to NASCAR executives, corporate sponsors, and groups of students brought in from historically black colleges was a hit. He knew that the sport's perception and history were huge obstacles, but he believed they could be overcome. When he was hired to be president of global operations at Dale Earnhardt, Inc., the race team owned by Dale Sr.'s widow, he was the organization's first black employee. "I started looking at the sport, saying, 'Okay, what do I have in common with these people? How do we break down barriers and move forward?' If you grew up in the trailer park or the projects, like me, there's a lot that's the same." I asked him whether I would be surprised by the amount of diversity at Bristol. He paused for a moment, as if picturing the track and its environs. "If your expectation is no people of color, and you look very carefully at the pit crews, the officials, and the fans, you'll see some participation. You might see more if you were at the tracks in Atlanta or Chicago."

I did look carefully, and still I spotted far more Confederate flag bandanas at Bristol than black and Hispanic people. The speedway employed a hype man named Jose Castillo, whose job it was to talk animatedly to fans during lulls on the track, the exchanges shown live on the Jumbotron planted in the center of the infield. He said he had never come across any racism there. "I'm Jose," he added, pointing to the name stitched into his shirt pocket, "and no one ever said a thing to me. Don't get me wrong, the fans are rednecks. But that's not a socioeconomic thing. Guys worth millions could be camping out next to people who scrape for this one trip."

According to Humpy Wheeler, someone like Dale Earnhardt Sr. was so appealing to the core audience because he was a "John Wayne character, a kind of Civil War hero, a Confederate soldier." But Wheeler also agreed that the sport could gain traction in the big urban markets if it fielded a diverse group of drivers. He ran down an imagined lineup of multicultural all-stars, envisaging diversity as an ensemble cast in a Hollywood caper—an immigrant ex-cabbie from Long Island or Queens, an Italian driver from Chicago, a Hispanic kid from East L.A., with tattoos, a ring or two in his nose, who had been caught speeding forty-nine times in his rice rocket but was now sating his need for speed on the racetrack. What NASCAR really could use, Wheeler insisted, was a dramatic new star pitted against someone who was his opposite. He cited one of the young drivers on Max Siegel's Revolution Racing team, a New Jerseyan of Syrian descent named Paul Harraka. Then he had me consider the potential in setting Harraka—an Arab American, a northerner, a student at Duke, which Wheeler called "the wrong part of the South"—against an up-and-comer named Jordan Anderson. Anderson was a dirt-track racer from South Carolina, still a kid, whom Humpy Wheeler liked to call "Preacher" for his ability to quote anything from the Bible, Old Testament or New, but who in an instant could turn "Scots-Irish red, absolutely vicious." Wheeler said, "See, the contrast creates the rivalry."

Max Siegel said that NASCAR's decentralized ownership model actually made it less exclusive than other professional sports. There was no league, no franchises, no old boys' club barring entry. Anyone with the $30 million or so to own and operate a car could start a team and enter a race. He felt minority-owned businesses and black professionals needed to look very closely at NASCAR simply for the economic opportunities it offered. In North Carolina alone, motor sports had a $5-billion-a-year impact.

We were speaking by phone, and Siegel suddenly interrupted himself. "Right now I'm at the barbershop in Indianapolis," he said, "at Fresh Kutz, on Sixtieth and Michigan Road, where I grew up in the 'hood. And there's a dude getting out of a car right next to me—the guy's got on an M&M's NASCAR jacket. It's just ironic."

Ricky Stenhouse Jr. would not lead the rebel yell or rise up as NASCAR's fiery new star. He was a chubby-cheeked twenty-two-year-old from Olive Branch, Mississippi, who started racing when he was six—first go-carts and then open-wheel cars on dirt tracks for his dad—and he answered just about every question with a "Yes, sir" or "No, sir." "When I raced up north, in Indiana and Ohio,

I always got that I was polite. That's just the way I am. That's how my dad taught me," he said. Ricky Stenhouse Sr. built race-car engines for a living. He worked on customers' cars during the day and then stayed up through the night to build engines for his son. Racing is an incredibly expensive pursuit for a kid, costing around $10,000 a year for anyone serious about it, but the father's job made the burden a little more tolerable. Ricky Jr. grew up playing baseball and football and riding skateboards, but he stuck with motor sports, winning the go-cart races and getting noticed on the circuit. In 2007 Roush Fenway Racing, one of the sport's top teams, signed him to run Fords for them. It was Ricky's first time racing stock cars, and now he was in his first full season in the Nationwide series, the JV to the Sprint Cup's varsity.

For Saturday's Nationwide race at Bristol, I sat on the "box," the perch overlooking a team's pit area, in a chair directly behind Ben Leslie, Ricky's crew chief. While Ricky and the other forty-two drivers on the track followed the pace car for their parade laps, Leslie looked past me to see that his spotter, Mike Calinoff, was in position, binoculars in hand, atop the track's roof. It was the spotter's job to guide the driver, to explain what was happening on the track around him. "When he says there's a hole," Ricky told me later, "you gotta get in it. Things happen so quickly."

I was wearing headphones tuned to the communications between Ricky, Leslie, and Calinoff, an ongoing conversation concerning strategy and car condition that was available to any fan via scanners they could purchase at the track for $110. Leslie told his driver, "Protect yourself. Protect your equipment. Race hard. Race smart."

"Yes, sir, got it. Race hard. Race smart," Ricky repeated. And the cars were off, zipping around the track, the entire crew watching Ricky pass in front of them and then in unison craning their necks to see the big monitor displaying the cars speeding down the front stretch, then turning back around to see him pass again before their eyes, each revolution completed in fifteen seconds.

Bristol was only Ricky's thirty-second stock-car race, and his goals for the day were modest: to avoid getting hung up in a wreck and to gain as much "seat-time" experience as possible. Fifty-five laps into the three-hundred-lap race, Leslie decided to bring Ricky's Ford in for a pit stop, sooner than most other cars on the track.

The vehicle was driving loose, its back end sliding sideways as it came around each turn. Leslie announced that the car would get four new tires, the gas would be topped off, and the car's track bar, which adjusted its suspension, would be tightened a notch. The seven members of the pit crew, in fire suits, knee pads, and helmets, waited with legs flexed against the top of the short wall separating them from pit road. They were all basketball tall and lean and broad-shouldered. Although they are called upon only two or three times over the course of a race, pit crews practice their highly choreographed routine dozens of times each week. It might take twenty laps for a driver to pass a car in front of him, but that same position can be gained in the pit by sending a vehicle back out onto the track a second faster.

The men pounced over the wall and onto pit road, jumping and sliding around to the passenger side, the car lifting, tools whirring. Old tires were flung off, new ones secured. A man carrying a seventy-five-pound swan-necked gas can inserted it into the tank, while another crew member ripped a plastic screen from the windshield. Ricky dumped the clutch, hit the gas, and was gone, leaving discarded tires, scattered lug nuts, and splashed gasoline in his wake.

Ninety laps in, a wreck halted the race, and when it started again ten minutes later, Ricky Stenhouse Jr., previously stuck in the middle of the pack, had moved into fourth place. Later, after Leslie pitted the car a second time, Ricky reentered the track in eighteenth place. But Leslie could see that Ricky had fresher tires than all but one car in front of him and was running each lap faster than most of the competition. With nearly 150 laps to go, Leslie told Ricky to follow the No. 3 car, which, he said, would win the race and Ricky would come in second. "You're doing a whale of a job. You're handling it like a man," Leslie said.

Another yellow caution prompted several cars with less fuel and older tires to enter pit road. Suddenly Ricky—the rookie from Olive Branch, Mississippi, who was angling only for a decent amount of seat-time—was in the lead. Leslie's pit strategy had paid off. Everyone on the team perked up as the cars, in a double-file line, prepared for the restart. The green flag was waved and the cars took off. But Ricky shifted into third gear too quickly, then tried to compensate by letting off the brake entirely on a turn, almost hitting the wall. In a few seconds he had dropped to seventeenth, then eighteenth, then twenty-third. At lap 250, Ricky tried to maneuver around the No. 15 car, passing underneath it, and his front end hit the other car's back bumper. Ricky's Ford ricocheted off the top wall. Leaking water and needing a new radiator, the car was sent to the infield, where the crew tried desperately to repair it.

During the race season, Ricky rents an apartment in Charlotte, a three-hour drive from Bristol. He didn't get home from the Nationwide race until 2:30 A.M., so late, he told me when I called him, that he missed church the next morning. Sunday afternoon he headed over to a friend's house, where they watched supercross, the Sprint Cup race, and bull riding. On Monday he had a 7 A.M. workout at Roush Fenway. He didn't have many days off, and he raced more than thirty-five weekends a year. It was a job, he said, but at least it left him time to play golf and listen to country music and even take the occasional vacation. Soon he would go snowmobiling in Jackson Hole, Wyoming. He wasn't too beat up about the Bristol race, about the wreck that busted his radiator. "The spotter felt the 15 came off the wall more than he had to," he said. "It's not that big of a deal. I was just trying to gain a position, and he was trying to keep a position. That's just racin'."

Early on Sunday morning, the day of the Sprint Cup race, the teams were working on their cars out on pit road, portable lights set up around them and generators whirring. Groups of five hovered beside the cars, one or two with a head under the hood, others polishing tires and doors or measuring dimensions or pouring gasoline or standing a few feet back drinking coffee or leaning against the pit wall smoking, looking like they could be just about anywhere. There was no sense of panic. The men consulted sheets of paper affixed to the cars' windows, checking off the list of things to inspect and glue and ratchet. Grills were already fired up in the infield, behind the team haulers, and men ate breakfast burritos and yogurt with fruit.

I wandered onto pit road, walking up and down the line of parked race cars, transfixed by their cartoon colors. They looked almost like township art, aluminum cans taken apart and reshaped into boxy metallic toys, each one emblazoned with its chief sponsor's name and corporate colors. There was the Energizer car, the

Cottonelle, the TaxSlayer, the ExtenZe, the Denver Mattress, the
U.S. Census, the Prilosec, the Kleenex, the Little Debbie ("AMER-
ICA'S FAMILY BAKERY FOR 50 YEARS" read the ad on the side
panel). Dozens of other insignias from secondary sponsors also
decorated each car like a smattering of bad tattoos. In their press
conferences, some drivers shilled for their patrons. Jeff Gordon,
PEPSI writ large on his chest, held a Pepsi can in his hand, logo
facing out. Asked how he spent the week between races, Kurt Busch
did not neglect to mention that he enjoyed a couple of ice-cold
Miller Lites, and he raved about the Dodge Challenger, "the best-
looking car out there." It has long been known that NASCAR fans
are among the most brand-loyal of consumers, that they are said to
be five times more likely to buy products advertising with the sport.
Officials from Ford told me on several occasions that of all the people planning to buy new cars in the next year, 40 percent are race
fans, and 84 percent of them follow NASCAR. In these lean times,
Ford, Chrysler, Dodge, and Toyota all told me they maintained racing programs to sell cars, period.

On pit road, I inched up to the No. 48, the Lowe's-sponsored
Chevy driven by the vanilla superstar Jimmie Johnson. Despite fans'
numerous frustrations with NASCAR and with Johnson's domi-
nance, everyone I spoke to about the recent decline in popularity
firmly believed that the actual racing on the track was better now
than it had ever been. In the past, races were won by laps; now they
are won by seconds, with each contest including dozens of lead
changes and at least as many different possible winners. In the era
everyone now romanticized, five, maybe at most ten drivers had a
real chance of entering Victory Lane. Like Southern identity itself,
NASCAR was overrun with nostalgia: its fans and participants pined
for bygone days that—at least in recollection—now seemed so
much more alive and fulfilling. So even while detailing the superi-
ority of today's competitive races, the people I interviewed slipped
into reveries for a truer time of Southern aggression and defining
peril. After praising Jimmie Johnson, Darrell Waltrip couldn't help
but compare the present crop of drivers with his cohort. "We were
just tough guys," he said, suddenly solemn. "We could take it and
dish it. There's no way we'd fit in today, with all the rules and restrictions. Back in the day, men were men."

I leaned in closer to Johnson's blue and white car and saw that a crew member was applying duct tape to the inside of the front bumper. As high-tech and pristine as Johnson's operation was, his team employed the sort of garden-variety solution I might use. I moved in for a better look. Suddenly the car burst to life, its 900-horsepower engine thundering so loud that the ground actually quaked.

Fifteen minutes before the start of the race, I saw drivers accosted by autograph- and photograph-seekers who had paid a bit extra for the freedom to wander about Bristol's crowded infield. No other big-league sport makes its stars available to the public in this way. Fans positioned themselves just behind pit crews, within arm's reach of the stacks of Goodyears, the hundreds of thousands of dollars in equipment. Some fans lingered beside the vehicles lined up for their final inspection, while others simply cut between the queuing cars on their way to different infield sites. As 4Troops, an a cappella group of former military personnel, sang the national anthem, drivers stood stoically beside their vehicles, their wives or girlfriends accompanying many of them in these final moments before they would don helmets and slide behind the wheel. I was on pit road as well, just three feet in front of a solitary Mark Martin, who leaned against his No. 5 Chevy, squinting nobly into the distance, his fifty-one-year-old face creased and weathered. He looked like a wizened jockey from a Hemingway story, a grayed hero unwilling or unable to quit, and all the more so because he was outfitted in a fluorescent lime-green jumpsuit with the name of his sponsor, GoDaddy.com, splashed across his abdomen.

At Bristol, drivers made their dramatic entrances by stepping out from a cupola of sparkling pyrotechnics and onto the flatbed of a Ford F-150 pickup truck that then slowly circled the track. With all the access afforded fans, I didn't think it too bizarre when I was given a seat in the bed of one of these F-150s. My sole companion back there, a young Wisconsin woman named Karen, had paid $1,900 in a charity auction for the privilege of riding in the truck with her favorite driver, Kasey Kahne. I asked what she liked about Kahne, who hailed from Washington State, and Karen explained that she had been a fan of the legendary driver Rusty Wallace, but when Wallace retired in 2005 she started looking for someone new. "I'm a Dodge person. And Kasey drove a Dodge then. He's also young and brash. And he looks a lot like a neighbor of mine. After I saw that he shares my birthday, that was it." When Kahne finally joined us in the Ford, waving beauty pageant–style to the grandstands above, Karen turned to me with a look of shock and said, "I'm going to shit."

We rounded the track, the fans lined up on the lowest steps of the bleachers, waving back, yelling, banging on the fencing. Viewed from the bottom of the bowl, the stands seemed to rise into the heavens, an arena of Babel echoing with the din of a hundred thousand screams. Karen handed over her camera, asking me to snap a few shots of her and Kahne. Side by side astride the ambling F-150, they were like the king and queen of the parade. Karen beamed, her two grand well spent.

When our trip around the track ended in the infield, the MC was already talking up the impending race. "Who thinks we're going to see some retaliation today? What do you think, guys? Are we going to see some retaliation?" He drew out the last word heavy-metal style, enunciating every syllable in a kind of lascivious battle cry. *Ree-tal-ee-ayyy-shun!* Ron Ramsey, the most conservative of the three Republicans then running for governor of Tennessee (during the campaign, he suggested that religious freedoms did not apply to Muslims living in the United States), delivered a plea to the "God-fearing, NASCAR-loving, red-blooded Americans" in attendance. He asked them to vote for him and to spend lots of money at the track. Kahne and the other drivers hopped out of the truck beds and headed to their cars, some of the classier ones stopping to shake hands with the drivers of the F-150s, all employees from nearby Ford dealerships. I went to help Karen down from the truck, reaching over to release the tailgate. She dropped a heavy hand on my shoulder, shunted me aside, and, with surprising nimbleness, swung her body out and over to the ground below, landing with a solid dismount. She walked off, pausing only to look partly over her shoulder and spit out, "I have a truck at home, buddy."

I watched some of the racing from one of Bristol's 179 skyboxes. At that height, the cars appeared to revolve in a single band of multicolored light. The effect was beautiful, a bit hypnotizing, and abstract. When I spoke to Freddie Hayter, a local who had been to every NASCAR race in Bristol's forty-nine-year history, he said he didn't like the skybox suites. "A race fan needs to be in the middle of the crowd. He needs the sound, the smell. The people in the suites are not true race fans; they're corporate people. That's not a place for someone who has been to ninety-nine races in a row." Hayter was certainly an authority, so I descended to the grandstand, to a spot midway up a section named for Darrell Waltrip, just above turn three.

Officially, Bristol announced that the speedway had fallen 22,000 tickets short of selling out. But that figure was likely far greater. Following the race, a headline in *Sporting News* would ask, "Empty Seats at Bristol a Sign of NASCAR's Apocalypse?" And in the ensuing weeks, almost every track experienced its lowest turnout in years. At the Dover race entire sections of the grandstand were closed off and covered in giant advertising banners. Although some 140,000 fans showed up for July's Brickyard 400, in Indianapolis, twice that number had attended the race three years ago.

The fans who sat in pairs and groups around me stirred a bit when a driver attempted a pass, or they lifted their beers together in a salute and drank each time a favorite driver rounded the track. But only when there was an accident of some sort would they stand up and cheer. While the race was under green, I could *feel* the rumble of the forty-three engines, even from my seat hundreds of feet from the track, and it was far too loud to carry on a conversation. Besides, almost everyone wore headphones, either listening to a radio call of the race or using a scanner to tune in to a team's transmissions. Others, like me, had stuffed foam plugs deep into their ears.

Sitting in the row in front of me, four guys in their late twenties were smoking cigarettes and drinking Bud tall boys, occasionally casting what seemed suspicious glances my way. The one closest to me, with a wispy goatee and greasy black hair, gave me a quick, unsmiling nod. Finally, during a caution—a car bounced off a wall and two other cars barreled into it—as the race slowed to a lighter roar, my neighbor turned to face me.

"Where'd you get that?" he demanded, pointing to the press pass that hung from a strap around my neck. I held up my credentials, dumbly inspected them, and explained that I was a reporter. He was interested not in the press pass but in the lanyard that held it.

"I'd trade ya'," he said. All fans wore their tickets necklace-style, but the lanyard issued to the general ticket buyer, I now saw, was a black and yellow band with the word NASCAR repeated along it. Mine was red and white and had BRISTOL running along its elastic material. I could think of no reason why I'd want to keep the artifact, why my children would prefer it to the NASCAR one, and I was nearly certain that it had no or little monetary value. So I swapped him. He rubbed his new strap between a thumb and two fingers, then passed it down the line to his admiring friends. "Man, you don't know how much this means to me," he told me. "Thank you."

He and his friends had driven in that morning from Georgia, about eight hours away, and they would head home after the race. The tickets belonged to his boss, who couldn't use them. He told me he was a Tony Stewart fan, big time, and so were his friends, except one of them, who pulled for Dale Jr. Then he asked me where I went to school for reporting, and whether he might have seen me on TV earlier in the race, and who my favorite driver was. I had actually anticipated being asked this last question, and so had tried to figure out the best response. Over the weekend I had heard each of the top drivers speak during their press conferences, spent half an hour with the veteran Jeff Burton in his trailer, spoken to Jack Roush about his Ford team, and seen the drivers practice and interact with their crews. But under the Georgian's gaze, I could think of no reply that would properly elevate me in his eyes. I told him Juan Pablo Montoya. At least the Colombian looked like a comic book supervillain in his red car and red jumpsuit adorned with the Target bull's-eye logo. My new friend stared at me, seeming to consider my choice. "Yeah, Montoya brings a little more color to the sport, a different flavor," he said.

When he inquired where I was from, because he could tell that it wasn't the South, I told him I was living in Nashville but was originally from Chicago. He used to party in downtown Chicago, he said. Then he offered up his review of northern cities: "Detroit—shitty city; Chicago—great city." He said his mother was from Dayton, Ohio. Which meant he was not like the other guys. He motioned toward his three Georgia buddies. "Yankees," he said, holding up his hands, palms out, in an expression of nonviolence. "They're okay with me."

Kurt Busch, from Las Vegas, led for 278 of the 500 laps of the race, but then with just seventeen remaining, a late caution gave Jimmie

Johnson the opportunity to pit and take four new tires. On the re-start, he somehow catapulted from sixth place to first in just three quick turns around the track and then nosed ahead of Tony Stew-art to win the race by .89 seconds. (Montoya, for what it's worth, finished twenty-sixth.) It was Johnson's third victory of the young season, the fiftieth win in his career, and his first triumph at Bristol. I looked in the papers the next day, at all the write-ups of this stun-ning come-from-behind finish, both to understand how it could happen and to see what poetry it might inspire. There was none. Most accounts simply described the race as a failure, Johnson's vic-tory coupled with the lackluster attendance a double loss for the sport.

At the race's conclusion, the track announcer tried to put a smile on things, saying to the crowd that this would be the last Sprint Cup event with the much-derided rear wing. "Fans, you do make a difference. And NASCAR hears you. You didn't like the wing, and we got rid of it." I tuned in to the drivers' post-race interviews.

Greg Biffle: "I'm just so proud of everything. I'm just so proud to have the U.S. Census on this car."

Tony Stewart: "I just want to thank Office Depot and Old Spice."

But Kurt Busch may have best captured the general mood among the fans at the track, and among those at home. When a mic was thrust in front of him just moments after his last-minute defeat, he said, "To lose to the 48 sucks. I'm sure everyone here wanted any-one but the 48."

By the middle of August, the Sprint Cup season would see a to-tal of eleven different drivers claim victory, with Denny Hamlin, a twenty-nine-year-old Virginian, winning as many races as Jimmie Johnson, and Kevin Harvick leading in overall points with the most top-ten finishes. It was, however, a season that was doing little to reverse NASCAR's fortunes; restoring the devotion of fans would require something far more elusive than rear spoilers and revised start times. NASCAR hoped to inject into the sport not only more action but also a greater sense of authenticity. Gaining speed on such slippery ground would not be easy. The New NASCAR, like the New South, is less culturally distinct from the rest of America than its votaries would like to believe. The sport still delivers on horsepower, but as a costume drama set in some imaginary Dixie, it is no longer as pleasing, or convincing, as it used to be. Every performance leaves the audience longing for some golden era when *The Dukes of Hazzard* played on prime time and the stars of the track were better stand-ins for the stand-ins for Southern manhood who had come before them.

At Bristol, wandering about the grounds outside the track, I joined some tailgaters in a couple of rounds of cornhole, the beanbag-toss game. The rear window of the car they were tailgating behind displayed both the Red Sox insignia and the number of Jeff Gordon's race car. The owner, busy manning his portable grill, had moved from Boston to Charlotte years earlier, his accent still thick as a Kennedy's. He dropped his *r*'s, broadened his *a*'s. He went to about a dozen races a year, he told me, and had seen the steady declines in attendance everywhere. "The South built this sport," he said, pronouncing "sport" as two syllables and gazing wistfully at the giant billboards on the speedway's façade, one showing a snarling Dale Earnhardt Sr., another shoots of E-Z Seed grass sprouting from the center of a potted race tire. "It is regional. That's what it's all about. It started to go wrong with the races up North."

DAVID BAEZ

The Coconut Salesman

FROM *The New York Times Magazine*

THE COCONUT SALESMAN appears every morning in front of
the tourist hotel in Jinotepe, Nicaragua. He stands there with his
cart full of coconuts, his machete to hack the tops off, and his bag
of straws. He is in his fifties, with a pronounced belly that strains
the fabric of the old T-shirts he wears, and dark, wet eyes.

Last year, unable to find work in the U.S., I came to Nicaragua to
stay with a relative. Shortly thereafter I started drinking so much
that I checked myself into rehab here for eight weeks. When I got
out some months ago, I used to run into the coconut salesman
near the market, and he would try to get me to buy coconut milk. I
never really liked the taste, yet he was persistent, so one day I asked
him why I should spend money on a drink that I didn't like very
much. He told me coconut milk has a multitude of health benefits;
that it cleans out the kidneys, for example. I asked him if it would
therefore be good for a person who had a long history of drinking,
and he said yes. So I decided I would try to drink coconut milk
every morning. He sold it for 30 cents.

Not long after, I came to live in the hotel in exchange for volunteer work. And so I saw him every day. One day he told me that he
wanted to paint his cart red as a way of attracting more clients. His
cart was functional, but some of the wood had rotted away, and the
wheels were almost as close to square as they were to round. When
I asked him if he really thought it would help, he just crouched
down and pantomimed painting the cart with quick sidelong
strokes, and smiled.

He told me that the paint would cost 95 córdobas (about $5), but that he had only 40. He showed me the 40 córdobas. He was asking me for a loan. I told him that I had very little money. He said that if I gave him the money, he would bring me coconut milk every day until he had given me an amount of equal value. So I gave him 50 córdobas and told him I was looking forward to seeing the freshly painted cart.

The next morning the coconut salesman did not show up, and once evening came, nobody had seen him all day. I just figured that I had lost about $2.50, and that I could learn some sort of lesson from it.

The following day, when the coconut salesman saw me, he immediately grabbed a coconut, hacked the top off, stuck a straw inside, and handed it to me. I drank the milk and asked him why his cart was the same sorry green it was before. He told me that on the day I gave him the loan, a pickpocket stole all his money. I decided that whatever happened, the coconut salesman was making good on the deal we'd made.

The next morning the coconut salesman came again, gave me my coconut, and told me he had a problem. I drank my coconut milk and told him I wasn't surprised. He told me that one of his sons wanted a Bible but that he didn't have the money. I told him that the managers of the hotel were Evangelical Christians and might be happy to give him one. He asked me if I would go in for him. I said sure, and went in and got him a Bible.

The next day the coconut salesman told me he had another problem. I told him I wasn't surprised. He told me that his son was very happy with the Bible, but now his other son wanted one, too. He wanted me to go into the hotel and get a second Bible. I said: "I'm pretty sure there's a passage somewhere in the Bible about the concept of sharing. Maybe they could read that together." The coconut salesman listened to me, then went inside the hotel himself and got another Bible.

About a week after that I noticed that the coconut salesman had placed a coconut on top of his cart as a way of advertising his product, and was selling his coconut milk in a much more energetic manner than usual. A couple of hours later, he was still there, and I asked him if his newfound promotional zeal had made him any money. He reached in his pocket and took out 60 córdobas. I encouraged him to continue with this kind of advertising and promotion. He told me that since he now had 60 córdobas, he only needed 35 to buy the paint for his cart. Could he borrow it from me, since he was now so close to his goal? I told him I would think about it. In early sobriety, and especially in Nicaragua, hasty decisions are rarely advisable. And so I went inside the hotel to take a nap.

MISCHA BERLINSKI

Venance Lafrance Is Not Dead

FROM *Men's Journal*

A COUPLE OF WEEKS after the earthquake, the werewolves came down from the hills.

"It's serious!" one man said.

He was talking about the loup-garou, a distant cousin of the werewolf. In Haitian lore the loup-garou was a kind of sorcerer who had learned to transform himself into an animal—a cat, a goat, or even a cow. Thus disguised, the loup-garou went out into the night to feast on the blood of small children. Two or three days after such a visitation, children would sicken and die. Now, with so many people in Port-au-Prince sleeping in the open air, the loups-garous were believed to present an exceptional danger.

He told me that not here but farther up on the mountain the werewolves had already killed a number of small children. This was the way the loup-garou story always went—not here, but not far away, the loups-garous were prowling. Another man told me that a *brigade vigilance* was formed to keep an eye out. Our baby's nanny later said that the police in her neighborhood had instituted a policy of zero tolerance for looters and loups-garous: both were killed on sight.

We were in the hills of Carrefour Feuilles, a neighborhood above Port-au-Prince. Before the quake small cinder-block houses had been stacked steeply one upon the next, climbing the bowls of the mountain, the inhabitants maneuvering through tiny alleyways. When the quake came, one house took down the next, leaving the entire hillside a smear of concrete and rubble and fallen satellite dishes.

"But why do loups-garous want to suck children's blood?" I
asked.

The question provoked discussion. One man proposed it was
a vice, like a taste for whiskey or smoking. Another man just
shrugged. But a third man said, "*Le loup-garou — c'est le mal absolu.*"
The loup-garou is absolute evil. I suppose, thinking it over now,
that it was easier to stay awake at night watching for werewolves
than it was to stay on guard for lethal aftershocks.

The earthquake was still recent enough that every passing truck
gave me the shivers. Very early one morning, my phone rang, but
when I answered it, the caller abruptly hung up. This pattern irri-
tatingly repeated itself perhaps five or six times. This was Venance
Lafrance's way of saying he was not dead.

I had met Venance three years earlier, shortly after my wife and I
moved to Haiti. She had found a job in the justice section of the
United Nations peacekeeping mission here, working with judges,
prosecutors, and lawyers to reform the Haitian legal system. I had
just published my first novel, and I figured that I could avoid writing a second one as easily in Haiti as anyplace else; in this I would
eventually be proven completely correct. Cristina was initially assigned to the town of Jérémie, only about 125 miles from Port-au-
Prince but remote, like an island off the coast of Haiti, fifteen
hours of bad road between us and the capital. There were more
coffin makers in Jérémie than restaurants, more donkeys than cars,
and the paved roads petered out at the edge of town. We rented an
old gingerbread house flanked by a quartet of sturdy mango trees.
In the mornings merchants came down from the hills past our
front gate with baskets of fruit balanced on their heads, and at
night in bed under the mosquito net when the moon was silver and
big, we heard voodoo drums and strange, spooky singing. I don't
know if I've ever liked a place more in my life.

Everywhere I went in Jérémie, people asked me for money. Out
front of the Internet cafe, a woman who was almost obese looked
up from her breakfast and told me she was hungry. At the market,
on the beach, in the streets, people would throw up their palms
and say, "*Blan, ba'm cinq gourdes*" — White, give me five gourdes. I've
been in other places as poor as Jérémie — the slums of Calcutta,
the highlands of northern Thailand — but I've never seen more

persistent and aggressive begging. There is a Creole proverb: *"Degagé pa peché"*—Getting by isn't a sin. Asking someone who had money for money was just another way of getting by.

Venance Lafrance asked me for money just a few days after I got to Jérémie. I was walking to the beach—think goats, chickens, cows, pigs, and wild turkeys; mud huts; a strip of white dirt road snaking along high cliffs diving down to a postcard sea—when a young man with a bag of sweet potatoes on his head accosted me and told me in broken French after some conversational preliminaries that he wanted to be an artist. He was seventeen at the time but looked about twelve. He looked a little like a space alien, with very big eyes, a wide, tall forehead, and high, prominent cheekbones tapering down to a narrow, angular chin. He was wearing a T-shirt that read LIFE IS SHORT. EAT DESSERT FIRST. He was very skinny. I don't remember how he began the conversation, but the upshot was this: he was a student; he had no money; his mother had no money; his little brothers were hungry; and he wanted to be an artist. He had a terrific smile—chiefly what the good Lord gave him in exchange for all his troubles was this smile like an exploding sun. He asked me for money to feed his little brothers and I gave him the change in my pocket—about a buck fifty. I wouldn't have been sad if I never saw him again.

A few days later, Venance presented himself at the front gate of our house. Jérémie is a small place, and Venance, going from neighborhood to neighborhood and door to door, had found me. This was a degree of persistence and hard work that Venance would never again display in my presence. He had a look on his face as he waited for me of patient, fragile hopefulness. I invited him in, where he drank a glass of orange juice. Much later I learned that he was so excited to see me that he hadn't slept the night before. That's exactly the look he had on his face as he sipped his orange juice, like he couldn't quite believe that he, Venance Lafrance of Carrefour Prince, Haiti, was sitting there on my terrace drinking orange juice. Like it was all too good to be believed.

In the weeks and months thereafter, no pretty lady has ever been courted by such an animated and constant suitor as I was courted by Venance Lafrance. He came by the house all the time. He was unshakable. My wife and I tried many schemes to convince Venance to leave us alone. I told him that he was allowed to visit only every third day. Every third day without fail he showed up at our door. We asked him to visit only between five and six in the evening, with the result that we had a standing appointment with Venance Lafrance at 5:01 P.M. We told him not to visit us at all. *Ha!* He was resistant to hints, oblivious to suggestions. What did he want? Not *just* to ask for money, but also to say hello, or to eat a meal, or to hang around, or to ask a question. After I had known him a week, he told me that he loved me like a brother; after I'd known him a month, that he loved me like a father. What he wanted more than anything, I think, was to sit with us out on the terrace in the evening and *belong*.

In the end Venance wore me down. I came to like him. It was hard to be mean to somebody so young who wanted so badly to be liked. He was the kind of kid you could horse around with. He was always up for kicking around a soccer ball, or taking a trip to the beach. You could send him up the mango tree and he'd come down with a half-dozen fresh, juicy pieces of fruit. He had an easy laugh. You could read a book around him and he'd amuse himself, or you could tease him about girls and he'd laugh. After a couple of months in Jérémie, it got to be an accepted fact of life that two or three or five days a week, Venance Lafrance would show up at our house and hang around until we told him that he had to leave.

Brilliant smile aside, Venance wasn't very handsome. He had terrible body odor, and his hair was reddish at the roots, a sign of protein deficiency. He asked me for money to buy deodorant and shoe polish, which he rubbed on his head. Though he said he wanted to be an artist, I never saw him actually make art. He was functionally illiterate. He was one of the laziest people I've ever met—and I say this as someone who is quite lazy himself. He had been admitted to a free school of ironwork, which he often didn't bother to attend. We would later hire Venance and his younger brother to sweep our yard on Saturday mornings. His brother would arrive on time and work diligently. Venance would show up late, work halfheartedly, and leave early.

Venance Lafrance had only one real asset in life—but it was considerable. Despite every disadvantage that he suffered, despite every self-inflicted wound, Venance was nevertheless making his way in the world with radiant, unwavering optimism. One day he bought a hen whom he named Catalina. This was to be the start of

a chicken-breeding empire. Then his family got hungry and ate
Catalina. Venance was undismayed. He asked me for money to buy
another starter chicken. If you gave Venance 50 gourdes, he'd give
half to the kids on the street to buy candy—Venance saw himself as
somebody who could afford to be generous. When he told us he
wanted to be an artist, I think he chose the word almost at random from a list of grand words that to Venance were synonymous
with hope. He would tell me later that he wanted to be a preacher,
a doctor, an engineer. Step by step he went forward toward an
opaque future that he was sure—absolutely, unquestionably sure
—would one day be glorious.

In the meanwhile, he got by.

Walking around Port-au-Prince after the quake and talking to people, I learned all sorts of ways to describe in Creole just how a building fell down. A house that had held was said to have *kembé,* or
hung tight, thank God. This was the case with my own house, in
which not even the wineglasses had broken. A house with a crack
or two or a hundred was *fissuré,* generally considered to be alarm-
ing depending only on the depth of the crack or its location. Sometimes a crack could be so wide as to admit sunlight and rain. Still
more severe was a house that was *fracturé,* or fractured. This was the
case with our immediate neighbor's house, whose walls split open
to reveal the steel skeleton buried in the reinforced concrete. Some
houses split in two—half the house coming down completely, the
other half perfectly intact, leaving little windows into the occupants' lost worlds: a table still set for meals, books on bookshelves,
a toilet. Even more dramatic than the fractured house was the
house that was *penché,* or tilted. We saw such oddities all over town
—houses that had suffered little or no apparent damage but were
now tilting at extreme angles to the horizontal. The gravest category of destroyed home was said to have been *krazé,* or wiped out.
If you wanted to add emphasis, you'd say that the house had been
krazé net—the word *net* in this case meaning 100 percent, down
to the ground, nothing left whatsoever but a pile of cement and
twisted rebar.

The Lafrance family had not always been poor. Venance's mother
had once been a successful merchant. When Venance was twelve,
his little brother Frandi got into a fight with a neighborhood bully.

The other child was the son of a prominent Jérémie sorceress. Madame Lafrance and this other lady got to words. The other lady said, "Evelyne, you're too rich! You won't have money again!" Various magical curses were thus effected, and after that Venance's mother no longer had the strength to go to the market. That's how the Lafrance family fell on such hard times.

A couple of months after we met Venance, his mother came to visit us. Madame Lafrance was a slender, pretty woman in an ankle-length skirt who never smiled—she looked a little like she was suffering at all times from a very bad stomachache. She wanted, she told us, to start a little business buying vegetables wholesale off the boat from Port-au-Prince, then reselling them in the market, and she asked if we would be willing to invest in her enterprise.

Was she, I asked, still afraid of the effects of the magic curse?

"Oh, no!" she said. That was all finished.

We gave her the money, but things didn't work out as well as we had hoped: Madame Lafrance invested half her funds in the lottery and the remainder in a large stock of garlic. Madame Lafrance did not win the lottery. The garlic failed to move in the market and then rotted. When we asked her what happened, she explained that her enemies had—*once again!*—used black magic to curse her and her market stall.

We kept trying to help the Lafrances. There is only one upside to living on 50 cents per day: it shouldn't be that hard to reach $1.50 per day. That's the difference between the bitterest poverty and what Haiti's former president Jean-Bertrand Aristide called "dignified poverty." We were willing to try most anything short of giving them a large wad of cash. What follows is a nonexhaustive list of various schemes we employed to help them:

Venance wanted to sell coconut water on the beach, at the big party the local population held every August to celebrate Jérémie's patron saint. I fronted Venance the capital to acquire the coconuts, but he forgot to bring his machete. When he went back home to get his machete, people stole all his coconuts.

. . . And then there was the time Madame Lafrance wanted to sell clothes on the street at Christmas. This scheme, too, was a failure, as Madame Lafrance bought ugly clothes. Also, we later learned, she gave away half the clothes to her relatives.

. . . And then there was the time my wife and I came back from

New York with a suitcase stuffed with merchandise that we'd found in a dollar store in Chinatown—a dozen toothbrushes for a dollar; children's toys; little clocks; cheap cosmetics; and so on. Madame Lafrance and Venance got to squabbling about just whom this merchandise was intended for. Both insisted that the other would waste the profits: Venance told us that his mother would spend the money on the lottery and magic; Madame Lafrance predicted that Venance would buy himself new clothes. Venance eventually dropped out of school to sell the merchandise himself. All the stock was sold at a loss, and Venance never went back to school, although he did acquire a nice wardrobe.

This last failure was what convinced us to leave the Lafrances to their own destiny. Our small experiment in social engineering had done more harm than good, and the Lafrances were as poor when we were done as when we started.

Port-au-Prince after the quake abounded in conspiracy theories. Many people were convinced that the United States military had caused the quake, using advanced high-technology weapons. Apparently such weapons had once been featured on the Discovery Channel. The earthquake was said to be either the result of an experiment gone awry, or the prelude to an invasion. *Why would you want to invade Haiti?* I asked. *Who wants this place?* It seemed I was naive: people told me that Haiti possessed vast mineral wealth and untapped oil reserves. All this jibed nicely with a central facet of the Haitian worldview—namely, that the great nations of the world all yearned to dominate plucky little Haiti.

A cartoon in the standard fifth-grade textbook, *Histoire de Mon Pays,* illustrates the thesis nicely. Haiti is shown not as a small island in the Caribbean, but as a huge and swollen territory sprawling from the reaches of the North Pole to the equator. Four figures, ostentatiously white and with rapacious grins, stretch from the four corners of the globe to lay huge hairy hands on Haitian soil. They are labeled France, the United States, England, and Germany.

If all the world were conspiring against Haiti, then your neighbor was probably conspiring against you. Truckloads of fifty-five-pound sacks of rice were being given away every day throughout Port-au-Prince after the quake, a program organized by the World Food Program, working with a consortium of international NGOs.

These NGOs were staffed by foreigners and relied on the cooperation of Haitian staff to decide who should receive assistance and
who shouldn't. It was a commonplace of tent-city life that the Haitian staff had rigged the game: they were giving out rice only to
their own families, or they were demanding kickbacks for the ra-
tion cards. People took me aside to level accusations at their neighbors, who were said to have counterfeited their card; or sold their
rice on the black market at exorbitant prices; or feigned extreme
poverty to receive aid, but were secretly wealthy.

The mood of suspicion was contagious: after a little while, I got
suspicious too. People everywhere asked me for help. In the claus-
trophobic camp on the Route de l'Aeroport, one woman insisted
that she had never received rice because she had been a parti-
san of the deposed President Aristide. Sitting inside her house in
plain view were two full bags of rice. When I pointed them out,
the little crowd around us began to laugh appreciatively. Nobody
thought this lady had done anything wrong. Neither did I. Getting
by isn't a sin.

About a year after I met Venance, he moved to Port-au-Prince. He
was eighteen years old, and he went without so much as a gourde
in his pocket.

In Venance's way of thinking, the world was like a series of concentric circles, the absolute center of which was Carrefour Prince,
the village where he was born and where his grandmother still
lived. You might not eat as much in Carrefour Prince as you'd like,
but you'd always have something: there was (almost) always breadfruit from the breadfruit tree. But you were absolutely trapped.
Life today was like life yesterday and like life tomorrow. The next
circle outward was Jérémie. This was the life journey his mother
had made: to leave the countryside. Venance had explored every
narrow alley of the town and gotten nowhere. He had discovered
only the world of his mother—small, provincial, mistrustful, and
suspicious. This was a world in which the best you could aspire to
was just scraping by, in which either your enemies were plotting
against you or you were plotting against your enemies; a world
dominated by the fear of magic. But Port-au-Prince—that was the
outer circle of this particular human being's universe. It was the
place to go in Haiti if you were young and excited about life.

Port-au-Prince was the only place in all of Haiti commensurate with Venance Lafrance's ambitions—to live decently, to eat copiously, to dress sharply, all without having to work very hard.

Shortly after Venance left Jérémie, my wife and I moved to Port-au-Prince also.

Venance was no longer a daily fixture in our life, but he made a point of staying in contact with us. He'd call every week or two, and from time to time we saw each other. A call from Venance Lafrance is a unique act of telephonic communication, because Venance, having no money to make a telephone call, will call—and hang up—until you call him back. There is no relenting and no choice. He might continue to call—and hang up—for an hour. Then he will take a break, perhaps to play dominoes or take a nap. He will then begin to call—and hang up—all over again, until finally you call him back. Venance is, above all, patient.

My Port-au-Prince was behind high walls and tinted windows: I shopped in a supermarket surrounded by a twenty-foot wall topped with barbed wire, and a squad of shotgun-toting toughies patrolled the parking lot. Venance's Port-au-Prince ran parallel to mine and was there always, but without Venance was invisible to me. Venance could hardly walk a block downtown without slapping hands with another acquaintance. He knew how everyone on the street earned their living, every scam, dodge, and swindle. Venance could tell me the latest jokes (I never found them very funny) or the latest Creole slang. He told me gossip from Cité Soleil, the slum where he lived: apparently the president of Haiti, René Preval, had spent an evening there not long before, drinking rum on the stoop. Every time I left Venance, I gave him a few bucks, and I considered the money well spent.

Venance was getting by in Port-au-Prince. He had scraped together the money to buy a portable telephone, and he wandered the city selling phone calls—anyone who wanted to make a call could use Venance's phone. Half of the young men in Port-au-Prince have the same job, but Venance was unusually good at it: Venance was social and knew everyone, and people liked to use Venance's phone. In the course of a long day strolling the city, he might make a hundred gourdes—about $2.50. This is why Venance had come to the big city. His job took him all over town: he could walk over to the sprawling neighborhood of Carrefour

on the south side, with its narrow twisting lanes heaped high with
garbage—he had family there—or he could park himself on the
Champ de Mars out front of the National Palace. He could just sit
on the corner with his buddies playing dominoes.

Venance's hold on the city, though, was tenuous at best. He was
robbed at gunpoint and lost his phone and income. Then the
cousin he was staying with evicted him from his shack and Venance
was forced to mooch off a succession of different, more distant relations, who tolerated him for a short time, then got tired of feeding his perennially hungry mouth. At one point he thought he
found a job as a houseboy: a childhood acquaintance had become
a police officer and needed somebody to watch over his car and
dogs. This fell through when the police officer was transferred to
the northern city of Cap Haitien. The last of Venance's relatives
was sick of him. Venance had just about exhausted his options in
Port-au-Prince when he met Cousin Maxo.

Venance met Maxo Pierre on the Champ de Mars. Maxo made a
living selling barbecued chicken there in the evening. It turned
out that Maxo came from Chambellan, not far at all from Jérémie.
Both Venance and Maxo were proud sons of the Grand'Anse province, so there was a bond between them. Thereafter, on seeing
Maxo, Venance always asked after Maxo's bad foot, a kindness
Maxo noted. Sometimes Venance passed all day with Maxo down
on the Champ de Mars telling stories. This was about the time
when Venance was out of a job and home, and he opened his heart
to the bearded older man. Maxo said, "Venance, barbecue business
is good business. Tomorrow if you want you can become a big barbecue entrepreneur. Keep it up. Venance, stay with me for a long
time. That way you can get ahead."

Chicken was a good business for Venance, not only on account of
the fact that it suited his temperament and he was a good chicken
cook, but also because he was observant and a fast runner. You
needed to run fast if you were going to make it in the chicken game
—the police would impound the barbecue of anyone caught grilling out on the Champ de Mars. That's why Venance was so useful
to Cousin Maxo: Maxo had the bad foot, but when the police came
down, Venance could grab that 'cue and *fly*. Together they made a
good team, Venance and Cousin Maxo—Cousin Maxo teaching
the young man the secrets of the Champ de Mars BBQ game, show-

ing him the special Maxo chicken sauce; Venance protecting the BBQ from the police; the two of them sociable fellows, flirting with the ladies and grilling up the birds and laughing and joking until the early hours of the morning.

Not only did Maxo bring Venance into his business, but he invited this lanky kid off the street into his home, giving him a place to sleep right on the floor with his own kids. That's when Venance started calling Maxo "Cousin Maxo," as a sign of respect and affection. Venance appreciated the fact that Cousin Maxo treated him like a man, but treated him like family, too, showing him kindness, never telling him what to do, just letting him be.

In Maxo, Venance found something he'd been looking for all his life. His father had been a sorcerer named Destiné Paul. Destiné Paul quarreled with an unsatisfied client. The client swore he would take his revenge on Destiné Paul. Which he did—Venance's father died, a victim himself of magic, when Venance was just five months in the womb.

Each morning Maxo would give Venance a little money for coffee and bread. Venance saved a bit of that every day and soon was able to invest in a chicken breast or two, which he put on the grill. The profit was his own, and he turned it around into more chickens. What he was looking forward to and working toward was the day he could buy himself a whole case of chicken. Break up the birds, boil 'em. Rent refrigerator space. Get himself a barbecue of his own. Buy cabbage and bananas and manioc. Go out on the Champ de Mars at night, pay to plug a light bulb into the generator, and call himself a chicken man, too.

Venance had been out every day with Cousin Maxo for about six months, selling chicken and earning, when Venance got it into his head that he wanted to spend the hot month of August back home in Jérémie. He had a little cash in his hand and he wanted to flaunt it, show the girls back home the success he was making of himself in Port-au-Prince. Cousin Maxo told Venance that this was a poor idea, that if he had a good thing going, he should stick with it. But Venance ignored Cousin Maxo and went home.

The National Palace had been a source of considerable pride. I was standing in front of its vast, very white edifice when a young man approached and asked me if it was true that the National Palace, before its collapse, had been the most beautiful building in the world, as he had learned in school.

"It was *very* beautiful," I said, looking for a diplomatic answer.

The conversation attracted, as often happens in Haiti, a crowd of kibitzers, all wanting to throw in their own two cents. Two Haitians can converse, but three is an argument. Some maintained that the presidential palace was the most beautiful building in the world; others that it was the most beautiful presidential palace in the world. The argument was not about aesthetics but about the precise recollection of a fact that had been memorized in a schoolbook. The conversation got quite heated, and in the end one man had to be taken away before he slugged somebody.

In a city of remarkable piles of rubble, the presidential palace rubble was particularly spectacular. In its collapse it looked as if it had been constructed originally with Legos, then smashed by the hand of a very large child. It was somewhere between *fracturé* and *krazé*—it all depended on whether one looked to the wings, which were almost intact, or to the center. Certain portions of the rubble expanse could even be described as *penché*.

A large tent city had cropped up directly in front of the gates of the palace, and then metastasized to the palace's flanks. Each of Port-au-Prince's tent cities had its own character, as any small town will, and here the mood was surlier and more aggressive than in other refugee camps. I asked somebody why the mood in this particular camp was so rough, and was told that it was due to the presence of the many escapees from the National Penitentiary, which was just a few blocks from here—although I found this explanation unlikely. Surely if anyone had cause to rejoice these days, it was the escapees.

Just three days before the world came to an end, Venance Lafrance slunk back into Port-au-Prince like a beaten dog. His return to Jérémie had been disastrous. His mother had gotten sick. His brother had gotten sick. And then he'd gotten sick too. He had almost died. All the capital he had accrued in the chicken game sweating over a hot barbecue, he had lost. He'd gone home to Jérémie to show off what a big man he'd become. But now, just to get back to Port-au-Prince, Venance had visited a local politician and agreed to sell her his vote in the upcoming parliamentary elec-

tions in exchange for a place on the big Trois Rivières, the weekly
ferry to the capital.

The next morning, Venance made his way on foot (not even a
gourde to take a bus) up to Cousin Maxo's little concrete house in
Bel Air.

"Venance, I didn't know you were coming!" Cousin Maxo said,
happy to see him.

Cousin Maxo wasn't just happy to see Venance on account of Venance being Venance, but also because Cousin Maxo *needed* Venance Lafrance. Madame Cousin Maxo gave Venance some bread
and coffee, and then Cousin Maxo told Venance the bad thing that
had happened in his absence. It was just a couple days back. Madame Maxo had been out grilling on the Champ de Mars when the
police had come round. She wasn't fast enough. The police had
seized the family barbecue and all the chicken on the grill, too.
She had gotten away with just a bowl of raw bird.

Cousin Maxo sent Venance out to buy some water for the house.
Venance came back with five five-gallon buckets. After he had
bathed, Venance lay down on the floor of the house and went to
sleep for the rest of the morning.

Venance was finally home. Venance was finally needed.

The Rue Dalencourt winds down then up the steep valley between
the Avenue John Brown and Canapé Vert. Before the quake, this
had been a shady street of small houses and apartment complexes.
The largest of these apartment complexes, a homicidal five-story
monster, had come down. A few surviving relatives—a young
woman, her brother, some friends—had hired a group of young
men to do the dangerous work of pawing through the rubble. I sat
outside and watched the diggers for a few minutes. Not far from
us on the ground was a charred spinal cord and skull. The smell
of decomposing flesh was quite strong in the air. Later, the diggers came up with the body of the young woman's sister—a large
woman, to judge by the six men needed to carry her. Haiti is a
country where women take pride in their voluptuous displays of
grief—there exists an entire profession of paid mourners, whose
copious tears and loud wailings are taken as a tribute to the qualities of the departed. I had been at a funeral not long before the
quake where distant lady friends of the deceased had attempted to

throw themselves bodily into the coffin. Now this young woman walked over, identified her sister, and walked back with a cool smile on her face.

This was like another country than the one I thought I knew.

On Tuesday, January 12, in the late afternoon, Venance Lafrance was playing dominoes out front of his friend Alfred's house. The board was balanced on the players' knees. They'd been slapping the bones for hours—days even. There was a big crowd around the board waiting to get in on the game. The board started shaking. The tiles started sliding. One of the fellows said, "Who's shaking the board?" Another fellow said, "Not me." Then the bricks started falling— *ka-choo, ka-choo, ka-choo!* Venance heard a noise like ten thousand trucks roaring up a steep hill. The street itself started making waves. Some of the fellows who'd been waiting to play dominoes started running—but Venance didn't run; he just stood his ground, watching the houses shaking and the street swinging up and down like a rubber hose, rolling up, down, left, and right. The dominoes that had been on the board were on the ground, clattering like they were dancing. Right in front of Venance a two-story brick house leaned over on its side in a big cloud of dust, like it was tired and needed a break— *penché.*

When the ground stopped shaking, Venance's first thought was Cousin Maxo. He ran home through the streets. He passed collapsed house after collapsed house; the entire population of Port-au-Prince was in the streets.

Cousin Maxo's two-story house lay on a little alley. The cinder-block walls had given way and buckled outward. The first floor had come down, exploding massively as it made contact with the concrete foundations. Then the roof had come down also, staying largely intact. The house that had been two stories, or about twenty feet tall, was now just concrete slab on a waist-high pile of rubble. *Krazé net.*

Madame Maxo was outside. She was showing up at the house just as Venance was getting there. She was saying, "Where's Maxo?" Then she was saying it all over again: "Where's Maxo?" And again, "Where's Maxo?" Venance knew where Cousin Maxo was. When Venance had left to play dominoes earlier that afternoon, Maxo had gone upstairs to take a nap.

"Maxo's inside," he said.

"Are you sure?" Madame Maxo said. "Is it true?"

Venance thought a second. But he knew Maxo had been sleeping. He was sure of it.

"Yes," he said.

"Then he's dead," she said.

Venance Lafrance stood with Madame Maxo out front of the rubble that buried the body of Cousin Maxo. She began to cry. Now the neighbors were drifting out front of the collapsed house. Madame Maxo collapsed into their arms. All that evening and night, Madame Maxo lay on the sidewalk on a cardboard box out front of her collapsed house with her head in Venance Lafrance's lap. She didn't know yet—nobody knew—that the city was destroyed; she thought it was just her house that had collapsed. Venance ran his hand through Madame Maxo's hair to calm her. The radio announced that there would be another quake in the night, and the radio was correct: there were aftershocks all through the night. In the distance there was the sound of sirens.

Venance stayed with Madame Maxo for two days in front of the ruined house. For two days he didn't sleep. Neighbors cooked and passed around food—only Madame Maxo didn't eat. Venance had never been responsible for anyone before. Now he washed the children and made sure they ate, and kept far from the rubble, and stayed far away from the burning bodies. When Madame Maxo cried, he consoled her, as best he could. Madame Maxo had a little money in her pocket when the quake hit—that's what kept the family going. Venance himself didn't cry for Cousin Maxo. The tears wouldn't come. He felt light in his head—like he had been transported to some strange new world.

Behind the Église Sacré-Coeur—*krazé*—there was a little garden, with benches and a small statue of the Madonna. Both a school and a rectory had collapsed here, and many priests had died, their bodies decomposing not far from where we stood. A middle-aged man with a trim beard and spectacles approached me and asked in French if I had noticed the amazing particularity of the Madonna.

"No," I said. The Madonna had neither fallen nor was it weeping.

He looked at me a long time, as if I couldn't possibly be as dense as I seemed.

"*She's turned to the east,*" he finally said.

"To the east?"

"To the east."

The Madonna, on further examination, had shifted slightly, several degrees off the horizontal.

The man went on to claim that *all* of the Madonnas of Port-au-Prince had shifted to the east. He had gone around and examined them, he said. I asked him what was the significance of this unusual fact.

"This could not be an accident," he said.

Venance Lafrance, wearing sandals, stepped on something soft and squishy—a lady's arm, just lying out on the Champ de Mars. Venance Lafrance, whose fast feet had made him a natural in the chicken game, sprinted off. Bodies. Bodies starting to smell, bodies rotting in the sun. Fat dead people. Skinny kids. Big strong corpses, corpses built from lifetimes of lifting, toting, and hauling. Bodies of families. Bodies of naked old ladies. Bodies of naked old men. All the bodies puffy and gray. A guy saying, "You got to see this," then a big crowd watching a couple of dead kids having sex in a hotel room on the Grand Rue. More bodies. Some covered. Some not covered. Bodies in flames—the smell of meat cooking. Still more bodies. A tractor loading up bodies, scooping the bodies into a dump truck. Venance figured, based on the numbers of bodies he saw in the streets, that most all of Port-au-Prince was dead. That's what Venance saw on the way from Cousin Maxo's house in Bel Air to my house. When he got to my house, it was closed, locked, and empty. Then Venance kept walking, all across town, to his niece's house in Carrefour. On the way he saw two young men, handcuffed, splayed out on the ground, sticky blood running river-like from their heads. Shot by the police. The folks watching them called them *voleurs*—thieves. When Venance got out to his niece's house, it was gone, collapsed, like all the others.

On the radio they had announced that the government of Haiti had arranged free transport to the provinces by all available means. Venance left Madame Maxo and her children on the street beside the rubble of the house they had occupied: he was just another mouth to feed. Cousin Maxo's body still lay trapped under the crushed cement—a few days later he would be pried out and burnt on the street. Venance left Port-au-Prince with nothing but the clothes that were on his back when the quake struck.

The return to Jérémie was not easy. Others had the same idea as Venance, and the Wharf Jérémie was packed. The wharf was not large, and great nervous crowds jostled for position. There was no place to stand or sit. Venance heard snippets of conversation: "Let me go! Let me pass! I didn't die on Tuesday, I'm not going to die in Port-au-Prince!" People carried what possessions remained to them in huge bundles on their heads and in suitcases. Venance spent almost three days trapped on the wharf. The pier itself had collapsed, and access to the Trois Rivières was only by private canoe or dugout: those who could pay found a place onboard. Venance had no money; the big boat left; and he waited. He didn't eat. Water was his priority. He found some.

By the time the ferry returned, barges had been stacked to create a makeshift dock. He found a place on the boat—nobody knows just how many were onboard, but every available inch of the boat was packed: the aisle, the stairs, the decks. The mood was tense. A large aftershock hit, and from the boat you could see the city rise and fall. The passengers began to stampede back to solid ground. Venance shouted, "You're on the boat, you're on the sea! Why are you running? If you run on the ground, you could die!" But nobody listened. When the ground calmed down, they came back on the boat.

Then, finally, the boat set sail, and Venance Lafrance watched Port-au-Prince recede into the distance.

Venance's story has an epilogue, of sorts.

When Venance called me very early in the morning, it meant that he was alive—and that he wanted money.

He told me that he had big plans: he wanted to start his own business barbecuing chicken in Jérémie, and he was looking for an investor. I gave him a hundred dollars. Later, I learned that he spent it on a couple of pairs of jeans and some shoes. When I remonstrated with him, he explained that nobody wants to buy chicken from a chicken man who looks like a bum.

Where there's life, there's hope; and where there's hope, there's life.

Long live Venance Lafrance.

CHRISTOPHER BUCKLEY

My Year at Sea

FROM *The Atlantic*

CALL ME WHATEVER. I went to sea in 1970, when I was eighteen, not in Top-Siders, but in steel-toed boots.

I was deck boy aboard a Norwegian tramp freighter. My pay was $20 a week, about $100 today. Overtime paid 40 cents an hour, 60 on Sundays. Not much, I know, yet I signed off after six months with $400 in my pocket. My biggest expense was cigarettes ($1 a carton from the tax-free ship's store; beer was $3 a case). I've never since worked harder physically or felt richer. The Hong Kong tattoo cost $7 and is with me still on my right shoulder, a large, fading blue smudge. Of some other shore-side expenses, perhaps the less said, the better.

The term *gap year* wasn't much in use then, but I've never thought of it as a gap year. It was the year of my adventure. I was "shipping out," and there was romance in the term. I'd read Conrad and Melville at boarding school. It's tricky—or worse, boring—trying to explain an obsession. Mine had something to do with standing on the ice out on Narragansett Bay, watching the big ships making their way through the ragged channel toward open sea. Maybe it makes more sense just to quote from the first paragraph of *Moby-Dick:*

> Whenever it is a damp, drizzly November in my soul . . . then, I account it high time to go to sea . . . If they but knew it, almost all men in their degree, some time or other, cherish very nearly the same feelings towards the ocean with me.

I went around the world. Our itinerary wasn't fixed—a tramp freighter goes where the cargo is. The *Fernbrook* ended up taking me from New York to Charleston, Panama, Los Angeles, San Francisco, Manila, Hong Kong, Bangkok, Singapore, Sumatra, Phuket (then still an endless white beach with not a building on it), Penang, Port Swettenham, India, and, as it was still called, Ceylon.

The final leg—Colombo to New York, around the Cape of Good Hope—took thirty-three days, longer than expected owing to a Force 10 gale in the South Atlantic. I remember the feeling of barely controlled panic as I took my turns at the helm, the unwelcome knowledge that thirty-one lives depended on my ability to steer a shuddering, heaving 520-foot ship straight into mountainous seas. When the next man relieved me, my hands were too cramped and shaky to light a cigarette. Even some of the older guys, who'd seen everything, seemed impressed by this storm: "Maybe ve sink, eh?" one winked at me, without detectable mirth.

They were Norwegian, mostly, and some Germans and Danskers (sorry, Danes). The mess crews were Chinese. I was awoken on the first cold (November, as it happened) morning by a banging on my cabin door and the shout "Eggah!" It took me a few days to decipher. Eggs. Breakfast.

This was long before onboard TVs and DVD players. Modern freighters, some of which carry up to twelve passengers, come with those, plus three squares a day, plus amenities: saunas, pools, video libraries. If I embarked today as a passenger aboard a freighter, I'd endeavor not to spend the long days at sea—and they are long—rewatching *The Sopranos*. I prefer to think that I'd bring along a steamer trunk full of Shakespeare and Dickens and Twain. Short of taking monastic vows or trekking into the Kalahari, a freighter passage might just offer what our relentlessly connected age has made difficult, if not impossible: splendid isolation.

You can't tell what's aboard a container ship. We carried every kind of cargo, all of it on view: a police car, penicillin, Johnnie Walker Red, toilets, handguns, lumber, Ping-Pong balls, and IBM data cards. A giant crate of those slipped out of the cargo net and split open on the deck as we were making ready to leave San Francisco. A jillion IBM data cards, enough to figure out $E = mc^2$. It fell to me to sweep them into the Pacific. I reflected that at least they made for an apt sort of ticker tape as we left the mighty, modern U.S. in our wake and made for the exotic, older-world Far East.

The crossing took three weeks. I didn't set foot onshore in Manila until four days after we landed. As the youngest man onboard,

I had drawn a series of cargo-hold watches. My job, ostensibly, was to prevent the stevedores from stealing, a function I performed somewhat fecklessly. On the last day in Manila, after I'd stood a seventy-two-hour watch, another huge crate slipped its straps and crashed to the deck. Out poured about five thousand copies of *The Short Stories of Guy de Maupassant* intended for Manila's public schools. The stevedores seemed confused as to whether these were worth stealing. By now I was beyond caring. I yawned and told the foreman, "Good book. Go for it."

At sea in those latitudes, temperatures on the ship's steel decks could reach 115 degrees. During lunch breaks, I'd climb down the long ladder to the reefer (refrigerated) deck at the bottom of Number Two Hold. There were mounds, hillocks, tons—oh, I mean *tons*—of Red Delicious apples from Oregon. I would sit on top in the lovely dark chill, munching away, a chipmunk in paradise. One day I counted eating eight. I emerged belching and blinking into the heat, picked up my hydraulic jackhammer, and went back to chipping away at several decades of rust and paint.

I remember standing in the crow's nest as we entered the misty Panama Canal, and the strange sensation as the four-thousand-ton ship rose higher and higher inside the lock. I remember dawn coming up over the Strait of Malacca; ragamuffin kids on the dock in Sumatra laughing as they pelted us with bananas; collecting dead flying fish off the deck and bringing them to our sweet, fat, toothless Danish cook to fry up for breakfast. I remember sailing into Hong Kong harbor and seeing my first junk; steaming upriver toward Bangkok, watching the sun rise and set fire to the gold-leafed pagoda roofs; climbing off the stern down a wriggly rope ladder into a sampan, paddling for dear life across the commerce-mad river into the jungle, where it was suddenly quiet and then suddenly loud with monkey-chatter and bird-shriek, the moonlight lambent on the palm fronds.

Looking back, as I often do, these ports of call seem to me reachable only by freighter. Mine was a rusty, banged-up old thing, but I suppose there's no reason a shiny new container ship wouldn't do the trick.

MAUREEN DOWD

A Girls' Guide to Saudi Arabia

FROM *Vanity Fair*

I WANTED TO KNOW ALL ABOUT EVE. "Our grandmother Eve?" asked Abdullah Hejazi, my boyish-looking guide in Old Jidda. Under a glowing Arab moon on a hot winter night, Abdullah was showing off the jewels of his city—charming green, blue, and brown houses built on the Red Sea more than a hundred years ago. The houses, empty now, are stretched tall to capture the sea breeze on streets squeezed narrow to capture the shade. The latticed screens on cantilevered verandas were intended to ensure "the privacy and seclusion of the harem," as the Lebanese writer Ameen Rihani noted in 1930. The preservation of these five hundred houses surrounding a souk marks an attempt by the Saudis, whose oil profits turned them into bling addicts, to appreciate the beauty of what they dismissively call "old stuff."

Jidda means "grandmother" in Arabic, and the city may have gotten its name because tradition holds that the grandmother of all temptresses, the biblical Eve, is buried here—an apt symbol for a country that legally, sexually, and sartorially buries its women alive. (A hard-line Muslim cleric in Iran recently blamed provocatively dressed women for earthquakes, inspiring the *New York Post* headline SHEIK IT!) According to legend, when Adam and Eve were evicted from the Garden of Eden, they went their separate ways, Adam ending up in Mecca and Eve in Jidda, with a single reunion. (Original sin reduced to friends with benefits?) Eve's cemetery lies behind a weathered green door in Old Jidda.

When I suggested we visit, Abdullah smiled with sweet exasperation. It was a smile I would grow all too accustomed to from Saudi men in the coming days. It translated into "No f—ing way, lady."

"Women are not allowed to go into cemeteries," he told me.

I had visited Saudi Arabia twice before, and knew it was the hardest place on earth for a woman to negotiate. Women traveling on their own have generally needed government minders or permission slips. A Saudi woman can't even report harassment by a man without having a *mahram,* or male guardian, by her side. A group of traditional Saudi women, skeptical of any sort of liberalization, recently started an organization called My Guardian Knows What's Best for Me. I thought I understood the regime of gender apartheid pretty well. But this cemetery bit took me aback.

"Can they go in if they're dead?" I asked.

"Women can be buried there," he conceded, "but you are not allowed to go in and look into it."

So I can only see a dead woman if I'm a dead woman?

No wonder they call this the Forbidden Country. It's the most bewitching, bewildering, beheading vacation spot you'll never vacation in.

Hello — Good-Bye!

Saudi Arabia is one of the premier pilgrimage sites in the world, outstripping Jerusalem, the Vatican, Angkor Wat, and every other religious destination, except for India's Kumbh Mela (which attracts as many as 50 million pilgrims every three years). Millions of Muslims flock to Mecca and Medina annually. But, for non-Muslims, it's another story. Saudi Arabia has long kept not just its women but its very self behind a veil. Robert Lacey, the Jidda-based author of *The Kingdom* and *Inside the Kingdom,* explains that only when revenues from the hajj pilgrims fell drastically, during the Depression, did the Saudis allow infidel American engineers to enter the country and start exploring for oil.

Before 9/11, Saudi Arabia was in fact gearing up to welcome, or at least accept, a trickle of non-Muslim visitors, dropping a handkerchief to the world. Crown Prince Abdullah — now the king — was a radical modernizer by Saudi standards. He wanted to encourage more outside contact and to project an image other than one of religious austerity (with bursts of terrorism). The Saudis had already cracked open the door slightly for some degree of cultural tourism. Leslie McLoughlin, a fellow at the University of Exeter's

Institute of Arab and Islamic Studies, led tours to the Kingdom in 2000 and 2001, and both groups included affluent and curious Jewish men and women from New York. But on 9/11 the passageway narrowed again as Saudi Arabia and the United States confronted the reality that Osama bin Laden and fifteen of the nineteen terrorist hijackers were Saudi nationals.

The news cut to the very character of the Saudi state. Back in 1744, the oasis-dwelling al-Saud clan had made a pact with Muhammad bin Abdul Wahhab, founder of the Wahhabi sect, which took an especially strict approach to religious observance. The warrior al-Sauds got religious legitimacy; the anhedonic Wahhabis got protection. To this day the Koran is the constitution of Saudi Arabia, and Wahhabism its dominant faith. The royals doubled down on the deal when Islamic fundamentalists took over the Grand Mosque, in Mecca, in 1979. Now, with bin Laden's attacks, the bargain the royals struck with the fundamentalists — allowing anti-Western clerics and madrassas to flourish and not cracking down on those who bankroll al-Qaeda and terrorism — had borne its poison fruit.

Three years after 9/11, in 2004, the Kingdom decided to give the tourism business another try, this time hiring a public relations firm to get things rolling. The website of the resulting Supreme Commission for Tourism was "a disaster," one Saudi official abashedly recalls, shaking his head. The site noted that visas would not be issued to an Israeli passport holder, to anyone with an Israeli stamp on a passport, or, just in case things weren't perfectly clear, to "Jewish people." There were also "important instructions" for any woman coming to the Kingdom on her own, advising that she would need a husband or a male sponsor to pick her up at the airport, and that she would not be allowed to drive a car unless "accompanied by her husband, a male relative, or a driver." Needless to say, there would be no drinking allowed — Saudi officials even try to enforce no-drinking rules on private jets in Saudi airspace, sometimes sealing the liquor cabinets. Finally, belying the fact that Arabs consider hospitality a sacred duty, there was the no-loitering kicker: "All visitors to the Kingdom must have a return ticket." After New York congressman Anthony Weiner kicked up a fuss, the anti-Semitic language on the website was removed.

Now, six years later, the Saudis are trying yet again. But they aren't opening their arms unless (with a few exceptions) you are part of a special tourist group. "No backpacking stuff," says Prince Sultan bin Salman, the tall and chatty former astronaut who is the president and chairman of the Saudi Commission for Tourism and Antiquities. "You know, high level," he goes on, and involving only "fully educated" groups.

You still have to accept all the restrictive rules. And it won't be easy getting in. Visas these days for Westerners are so scarce that even top American diplomats have a hard time obtaining them for family members. The Kingdom recoils at the thought of the culture clash that could be caused by an invasion of French girls in shorts and American boys with joints. A sign at the airport warns: DRUG TRAFFICKERS WILL BE PUT TO DEATH.

Saudis fret that the rest of the world sees them as aliens, even though many are exceptionally charming and welcoming once you actually breach the wall. They are sensitive about being judged for their Flintstones ways, and are quick to remind you of what happened to the shah of Iran when he tried to modernize too fast. Not to mention their own King Faisal, who was assassinated in 1975 (regicide by nephew) after he introduced television and public education for girls. This prince-and-pauper society has always had a Janus face. Royals fly to the South of France to drink, gamble, and sleep with Russian hookers, while reactionary clerics at home delegitimize women and demonize Westerners. Last winter, a Saudi prince found himself under arrest for allegedly strangling his servant in a London hotel. (He has pleaded not guilty.) The Kingdom didn't have widespread electricity until the 1950s. It didn't abolish slavery until the 1960s. Restrictions on mingling between unrelated members of the opposite sex remain severe. (Recently, a Saudi cleric advised men who come in regular contact with unrelated women to consider drinking their breast milk, thereby making them in a sense "relatives," and allowing everyone to breathe a sigh of relief.) Today, Saudi Arabia is trying to take a few more steps ahead—starting a coed university, letting women sell lingerie to women, even toning down the public beheadings. If you're living on Saudi time, akin to a snail on Ambien, the popular eighty-six-year-old King Abdullah is making bold advances. To the rest of the world, the changes are almost imperceptible.

"Lots of Attentions"

The idea of seeing Saudi Arabia with the welcome mat out was ir-
resistible — even when the wary Saudis kept resisting. I made plans
for a Saudi vacation, knowing that the only thing more invigorat-
ing than ten days in Saudi Arabia would be ten days there as a
woman. Actually, it would be two women: joining me was my in-
trepid colleague and trip photographer Ashley Parker. I was a little
squeamish about boarding a Saudi Arabian Airlines flight with a
cross on my forehead. (It was Ash Wednesday.) Some Saudi flights
embark with an Arabic supplication, in the words of the Prophet
Muhammad. The flight attendants — who are not Saudi, because it
would be dishonorable for the airline to employ Saudi women —
bring around baskets of Saudi newspapers. A glance at the headlines underscored the fact that we were in a time machine hurtling
backward. One article in the English-language *Arab News* was titled
"Carrying Dagger a Mark of Manliness." Another warned, "Women
lawyers are not welcome in the Kingdom's courts." It was startling
to see a thumbnail portrait of a female columnist — my counter-
part — in which only her eyes were not concealed by a veil. Reading the airline magazine is like the moment in *The Twilight Zone*
when you sense there's something slightly off about that picture-
book town. The magazine is called *Ahlah Wasahldn,* meaning "Hello
and Welcome," but the welcome seems to be to Versailles, Provence,
and Belize. There's no hint that Saudi Arabia itself might be a destination.

The in-flight movies offer a taste of things to come. If you order
The Proposal, you get a blurry blob over Sandra Bullock's modest
décolletage, and even her clavicles, and the male stripper scene
and the erection joke have vanished altogether. A curtained partition goes up so that Saudi women can nap without their abayas.
There's no alcohol onboard, although some veteran business travelers en route to the Kingdom order vodkas at the airport bar and
pour them into a water bottle for sustenance along the way. At the
airport in Riyadh, the gender segregation ratchets up. There's a
Ladies' Waiting Room and a Ladies' Prayer Room. If there hadn't
been a Saudi majordomo to come and collect us, we would have
been in limbo — a pair of single women wandering the airport with
no man to get them out, trapped forever like Tom Hanks in *The
Terminal.*

In America, you get chocolates in your hotel room. In Riyadh, you might get a gift bag from your hosts in the Kingdom with something to slip into for dinner — a long black abaya and a black headscarf that make you look like a mummy and feel like a pizza oven. And even then they'll stick you behind a screen or curtain in the "family" section of the restaurant. The big Gloria Steinem advance in recent years is that women now wear abayas with dazzling designs on the back (sometimes with thousands of dollars' worth of Swarovski crystals) or Burberry or zebra-patterned trim on the sleeves.

I respect Islam's mandate for modest clothing. But I don't see why I have to adopt a dress code, as Aaron Sorkin put it on *The West Wing*, that makes "a Maryknoll nun look like Malibu Barbie." Needless to say, Barbie herself was banned in Saudi Arabia, though I did see Barbie paraphernalia for sale in a Riyadh supermarket and a Barbie-like doll, accessorized with headscarf and abaya (and of course not in a box with Ken), in the National Museum gift shop. As for *Hello!* magazine, a recent import to the Kingdom, Saudi censors paste small white squares of paper on the models' glossy thighs.

Soon after our arrival I asked Prince Sultan bin Salman, the tourism minister, about the dress code for foreigners. "Well, the abaya is part of the uniform," he said. "It's part of enjoying the culture. I've seen people who go to India dress up in the Indian sari." Najla Al-Khalifah, a member of the prince's staff in the female section of the tourist bureau, offered another analogy: "You can't wear shorts for the opera. You must dress for the occasion. If you don't like it, don't go." Fair enough, but if you do wear shorts to the opera, you won't get arrested by the roving outriders of the Commission for the Promotion of Virtue and Prevention of Vice — that is, the *mutawa,* or religious police.

Being in purdah pricks more deeply when you're dealing with American-owned enterprises — it's as if your own people are in sexist cahoots with your captors. In 2008, covering President Bush's trip to the Middle East, I was standing next to ABC's Martha Raddatz at the desk at the Riyadh Marriott when she angrily pressed the clerk about getting into the gym. He gave her The Smile. How about never, lady? On this trip, at Budget Rent a Car, the man at the counter explained to me that women could rent cars only if they paid extra for a driver. (And, to boot, it would be dishonorable for a woman to sit in the passenger seat unless a male relative were driving.) When I said I could drive myself, the man's head fell back in helpless laughter. I enlisted Nicolla Hewitt, a gorgeous, statuesque blonde New Yorker on business in Saudi Arabia, to join me in a brief sit-in at the men's section of Starbucks in the upscale Kingdom Centre mall. Her head was swirling with lurid news accounts of a Western woman who had been dragged from a Starbucks for committing the crime of attempted equality. "If I see the bloody *mutawa*," she said, gripping her latte nervously, "I'm hoofing it."

At various establishments I began amusing myself by seeing how long it took for male Cerberuses to dart forward and block the way to the front sections reserved for men. At McDonald's, dourly observing my arrival, a janitor barred the door with a broom in two seconds flat. At the posh Al Faisaliah Hotel, in Riyadh, I was asking the maître d' why I couldn't sit with the businessmen when he suddenly caught sight of an elegant woman sashaying through the men's section. He made a Reggie Bush run to knock her out of bounds before turning back to thwart my own entrance with a Baryshnikov leap. I did manage a moment of Pyrrhic triumph in the deserted men's section in the lobby café of the Jidda Hilton, ordering a cappuccino, but then the waiter informed me that he couldn't serve it until I moved five feet back to the women's section.

Hotel desk clerks would warn me to put on my abaya merely to walk across the lobby, even when I was wearing my most modest floor-length navy dress, the one reserved for family funerals. "You will get lots of attentions—not good attentions," one clerk said. Not wearing an abaya can be hazardous—but so can wearing one. Signs on the mall escalators caution women to be careful not to get their cloaks caught in the moving stairs. (A Muslim woman was recently choked to death by her hijab while on holiday in Australia; it had gotten caught in a go-cart at high speed.) You soon become paranoid, worrying that if you open the door for room service wearing a terry-cloth robe, you'll end up in the stocks. But the top hotels are staffed by foreign men—something I realized must be the case when my butler at the Al Faisaliah folded my underwear unprompted. If I were buttled by a Saudi, we'd probably be shut-tled to Deera Square—or Chop Chop Square, as it's better known —where the public beheadings occur. It's the one with the big drain, which the Saudis claim is for rain.

Sunny Side of Repression

The first time I traveled to Saudi Arabia was in the aftermath of the 9/11 attacks: Prince Saud al-Faisal, the foreign minister, had in-vited me to come over and see for myself that not all Saudis are terrorists. On that trip, I was more heedless and cavalier. I wore a hot-pink skirt, with fringe, to go to an interview with the Saudi edu-cation minister. When I came down from my hotel room, the men in the lobby glared with such hostility that I thought they'd pelt me to death with their dates. My minder turned me back to the eleva-tor. "Go get your abaya!" he yelled. "They'll kill you!" (My Guard-ian Knew What Was Best for Me.) This was right around the time when fifteen Saudi schoolgirls had died in a fire because the *mu-tawa* wouldn't let them escape without their headscarves and abayas, a horrifying episode that shook the Kingdom. Confronted by carloads of screaming men whenever I wore my own clothes, I added more layers but still got into trouble. I was swathed in black with a headscarf at a mall next to the Al Faisaliah Hotel when four members of the *mutawa* bore down. They barked in Arabic that they could see my neck and the outline of my body, and they con-fiscated my passport. All this was happening against the backdrop of a storefront underwear display featuring a lacy red teddy. My companion, the suave Adel al-Jubeir, an adviser to King Abdullah and now the Saudi ambassador to Washington, managed to re-trieve the passport and obtain permission for me to leave the mall (and the country), but it took a disconcertingly long time.

With each incident, you feel more cowed and less eager to defy the dress-to-repress rules. For this trip, I had an abaya made so I wouldn't have to swelter inside the standard polyester ones in the baking heat. I didn't go for anything as gauzy as Dorothy Lamour's in *The Road to Morocco*. I wanted simple black linen. But the tailor tried too hard to give it a flattering shape, adding slits so high they could get my throat slit. When I wore it, my minders pestered me to put an abaya over my abaya. It reminded me of Martin Short's mischievous question about Hillary Clinton's nightwear: "Does she have a pantsuit on under her pantsuit?"

Still, this time around, I decided to look on the sunny side of repression. Feel guilty about not jogging? Don't even try! Tired of running off to every new exhibition? Lucky you—there aren't any art museums! Can't decide which sybaritic treatment to select at the hotel spa? Relax—the spa's just for men. And you never have to stress about a bad-hair day.

The two words you'll quickly learn are *haled* (permissible) and *haram* (forbidden)—the kosher and nonkosher of the Arab world. Since your old pastimes are now mostly *haram,* you'll have to pick up some new vices. Gorge on gamy camel bacon at Friday brunch. (Friday is the Muslim Sunday.) Develop a new obsession with tweezing and threading your eyebrows and blackening your Bedouin bedroom eyes—now literally the windows to the soul. Enjoy a country that is the last refuge of indoor smoking. I went to the cigar bar at the fancy Globe restaurant in Riyadh and enjoyed a "Churchill's Cabinet" stogie for 180 riyals ($50), with its "lovely notes of leather and cream, hints of coffee, citrus, and spice." To go along with beluga caviar and Maine-lobster snacks there was an elaborate wine presentation, with the waiter showing off the label of a nonalcoholic Zinfandel before nestling it in a silver ice bucket. "It's from California," he said proudly. I fell into tippling in the morning, starting the day with Saudi champagne, a saccharine apple juice concoction.

You might also want to emulate the spoiled Saudi set and just loll about until the sun sets, watching *The Bold and the Beautiful* or Glenn Beck on satellite TV. (There are no public movie theaters.) The Saudis have a homegrown version of the *Today* show in English, with their own Meredith Vieira in headscarf, promoting buttocks exercises and colon cleansing, and a hefty Martha Stewart doppelgänger in a babushka, baking dried-apricot sandwiches in flower shapes. It's all very cozy, even if the crawl underneath is crawling with less-than-flattering stories about Israel's treatment of the Palestinians. One night, deciding to take a risk, I smuggled a young Saudi man up to my hotel room to translate some of the scary-looking rants on TV by guys in *thobes* and kaffiyehs. Were they trashing the Great Satan? He told me that the serious-looking bearded guy talking a mile a minute was merely chatting about soccer, and another scowling fellow with intense brown eyes was just praying. Likely story.

Once out of your room, you can stroll through the malls with your girlfriends for some Bluetooth flirting, where Rashid and Khalid detect your cell phone network as you walk by and send text messages that range from chatty to creepy. One of my young married minders said he regularly gets hassled by the *mutawa* when he's out flirting with female friends: "They say, 'Can I ask who you are with?' and I tell them, 'Oh, she's my sister.' And they say, 'Your sister? Do you laugh like that with your sister?'" There's no date night in Saudi Arabia. The romance strictures here—a few virginal meetings, a peek under the veil, a marriage contract, an all-female wedding reception, and a check of the bloody sheets—make *The Rules* look like the Kama Sutra. In Jidda, there's a Chinese restaurant called Toki, where unmarried girls can show themselves off in front of likely prospects on a fifty-eight-meter catwalk. The prospects are not young men, however, but their mothers, who traditionally made the match with help from the *khatabah,* or yenta, who was sometimes sent over to surreptitiously look under the hood and kick the tires of the bride-to-be. She would give the girl a hug to check the firmness of her breasts and then drop something on the floor to watch the girl pick it up. When the young lady would bend over and her abaya lifted ever so slightly, the *khatabah* could see her ankles and infer the shape of the legs and derrière.

"The Time of Ignorance"

Back in the 1940s, when the oil began gushing, Saudi Arabia was the sort of place where the country's first king, Abdul Aziz ibn Saud, traveled in a Ford convertible with his falcons and shot gazelles from the car. The king knew the name of every visitor to Riyadh. Travelers could not move around the Kingdom without the king's express consent, and he personally tracked each one's odyssey. Some Saudis, who had rarely seen airplanes, assumed they were cars that simply drove off into the sky. Prince Sultan bin Salman is a natural choice for tourism czar, given that he was the first Muslim in space. In 1985 he went up as part of an international crew on the *Discovery* shuttle. Trying to find Mecca from space—imagine gravity-free kneeling—was nothing compared with persuading other royals (thanks to polygamy, there are now thousands of them) to consider the desirability of making Saudi Arabia tourist-ready. For one thing, Saudis don't have that fondness for their own history that the British and Italians do. Many pious Muslims look askance at civilizations that predate Islam ("the time of ignorance," as they call it), and they have reservations about archaeological digs that may turn up Christian sites. Archaeology was not fully recognized until the last few years as a field of study in Saudi universities. In other countries, many of the famed tourist sites are what you might call "big broken things"—Machu Picchu, the Colosseum. Saudis don't go for broken, or even slightly worn. You will never see a Melrose Avenue–style vintage store; it would be considered shameful to buy or sell old clothes. It's all about the new and shiny.

Prince Sultan was traveling through Tuscany a few years back, snapping pictures of big broken things and talking to preservation experts, when it hit him: maybe there was a way to get Saudis to appreciate their own ancient heritage. He gathered forty or so mayors and governors who liked nothing better than to tear down their cultural heritage, and showed them that they could develop historic sites where local crafts and fresh produce are sold in a "joyous" setting. The cultural education did not begin well. The prince had wanted the officials to see Siena. "And I get a phone call at four A.M. that woke me, and the pilot was calling. He said, 'I'm in Vienna.'" Eventually, the Saudi mayors and governors began to acquire a taste for old stuff. They've done five more trips, and one to Seville was coming up, though maybe they'd end up in Savile Row. (Saudis certainly know the way.)

Prince Sultan is now training native Saudis—who have always left the heavy lifting as waiters, maids, and drivers to a servant class of Filipinos, Bangladeshis, Indonesians, Pakistanis, and Indians—to work as tour guides, tour operators, and hotel operators. He hopes that Saudis will get better at sightseeing as they travel elsewhere. "Saudis are not trained as good tourists," he told me over tea one night. "They didn't know how to respect the sites, not throw Kleenex at places."

With Prince Sultan's assistance we flew to an attraction we'd never heard of before: the spectacular Madain Saleh, sister city to

Jordan's renowned Petra, three hundred miles to the northwest. After flying across the desert for hours, you suddenly come upon strange and wonderful classical structures. Today they're in the middle of nowhere. Eons ago, at the time of ancient Rome, they stood athwart the Incense Route, controlled by the Nabataean kingdom. An airport is only just being built, so we bumped down in our puddle jumper on what was essentially a cleared track. Our guide barely spoke English, but he was giddy with pleasure at finally having someone to show around. There are more than a hundred sumptuous sandstone tombs here, many of them cavernous, sculpted into solid rock between the first century B.C. and the first century A.D. Only in recent years have the Saudis come to appreciate Madain Saleh's value, registering it as a UNESCO World Heritage Site in 2008.

They're also restoring the old train station in Madain Saleh to its former glory, with a shiny black engine from the Hejaz railway, like the one Peter O'Toole blew up in *Lawrence of Arabia*. Don't bother asking about T. E. Lawrence here—he's remembered for selling the Saudis out. (Saudis love the movie, though, and spout lines from it like "Thy mother mated with a scorpion.") The guides in Saudi Arabia have a hard time staying on message, veering wistfully toward memories of time spent in the United States, studying in Palo Alto, San Diego, or Boulder. They still obsess about their college sports teams—staying up until all hours to watch games via satellite. At the Masmak Fortress, in Riyadh—the scene of a critical battle for Abdul Aziz ibn Saud—the guide soon lost interest in leading us among displays labeled "Some Old Guns" and "Cover for the Udder of the She-Camel" and began to wax nostalgic about a married woman named Liz in Grand Rapids.

In Abha, a cool, green, mountainous area to the south, near Yemen, we had our sole encounter with an actual Saudi tourist. He was checking out the Hanging Village, where some people of yore had settled on the side of a sheer cliff to get away from the Ottomans. Supplies were lowered down by rope. The Saudi was a paunchy man from Riyadh named Fahad, who liked to be called Jack. Jack, wearing a stained tracksuit, volunteered that he had once lived in Fort Worth. "I enjoy it," he said, taking a drag on his cigarette and giving Ashley and me an appreciative look, "when I see these girls with the smell of the United States."

Peeping Abdul

The charm of Riyadh is that it has no charm. The only visual icon, the one captured in snow globes at souvenir shops, is the city's tallest building, Kingdom Centre, the home of the Four Seasons Hotel and the Kingdom Centre mall. It is owned by Prince al-Waleed bin Talal, the billionaire nephew of King Abdullah who has been called "the Arabian Warren Buffett" by *Time* magazine. (Rudy Giuliani turned down a $10 million donation to New York from al-Waleed after 9/11 when al-Waleed suggested that U.S. policies contributed to the attacks.) The skyscraper features a V-shaped hole at the top, and Saudis tastelessly joke that it's "the Hijacker Training Academy."

A Jordanian staffer at the Riyadh Four Seasons complained to me that the only things Saudis do are "shop and eat, shop and eat." Or subject you to "ordeal by tea," as I've heard it called. At the ubiquitous malls, women covered in black robes and gloves, with only their eyes showing, shop for La Perla lingerie, Versace gowns, Dior handbags, and Bulgari jewelry. Beauty is a drug for Saudi women, even though they're stuck at home most of the time — or maybe because of that. Saudi Arabia is more than three times the size of Texas and glitters with three times as many Swarovski crystals. "Bling H_2O" water is imported from Tennessee. The shopaholism pauses only at prayer time, when metal grates come down over the stores. Men, who carry more of the burden of the five-times-a-day obligation, head off to the prayer rooms. The women wander zombie-like among the shuttered shop fronts. The atmosphere is watchful. Once, when Ashley tried to snap some pictures of Saudi women shopping at a lingerie store, a female security guard came running up to confiscate the camera. "Just walk away," a Western woman advised us. "She's a woman — she has no power over you." At last: a fringe benefit of misogyny.

The Kingdom Centre mall has a ladies' floor on top shielded by high, wavy frosted glass, so that men — with all the maturity of Catholic schoolboys in stairwells — can't peer up from below. Signs on the ladies' floor tell women, once inside, to take off their head coverings: that way, a Peeping Abdul can't disguise himself in female garb and wander lustfully among them. On the ladies' floor, you're actually allowed to try on clothes. On floors where the sexes mingle, you often have to buy whatever you want in different sizes and take it all home to try on. The mere thought of a disrobed woman behind a dressing room door is apparently too much for men to handle. There's something profoundly poignant about seeing little girls running around the malls in normal clothes, playing with little boys in normal ways — you know what's in store for them in just a few years. When I reached puberty, my mother gave me a book called *On Becoming a Woman*. When these girls reach puberty, they'll have a black tarp thrown over their heads.

In recent years, Riyadh has gotten a dash of sophistication. "Oh, my!" says Princess Reema bint Bandar al-Saud, the lovely Riyadh businesswoman who is a daughter of Prince Bandar bin Sultan, the former longtime Saudi ambassador to the U.S. "There's a new restaurant almost every week, and I assure you, the way they look, the way the food is, is on a par with — I wouldn't say the top 10 restaurants in New York or London, but definitely 11 to 50." There's a two-week wait to get a table at B & F Burger Boutique, even though it's just high-end fast food served in a hip decor. The concrete walls and dim lights evoke SoHo, and gender segregation is more subtle. The women wear abayas with fashionable trim, and the guys trade their white *thobes* for blue jeans. The religious police showed up on opening night; they wanted the music eliminated and the women screened off by bigger partitions. The restaurant obliged only on the music.

Going from Riyadh to the Red Sea is like going from black-and-white Kansas to Technicolor Oz. The main port of entry for hajj pilgrims, Jidda is Saudi Arabia's business capital. "The bride of the Red Sea" is home to many female entrepreneurs, and residents say they are trying to tell the rest of the country to relax. Women leave their abayas open in front, or wear nighties or tight jeans underneath. But the enticing blue mosaic pool at the Jidda Hilton is still only for men. I watched a Saudi man swim while a woman in "full ninja," as American businessmen here call it, tiptoed around the edge, chatting with him.

When I asked the concierge about the hotel mosque, he said I couldn't go in unless I was a Muslim. Later, Prince Saud told me that I could simply have asked the emir of the region for permission. (Like the emir's listed?) Men in the Kingdom often reflexively say, "No, no, no"—"*La, la, la!*"—to women because it's the safer answer. But an essential point about Saudi Arabia is that everything operates on a sliding scale, depending on who you are, whom you know, whom you ask, whom you're with, and where you are. Drinking is not allowed, but many affluent Saudis keep fully stocked bars. "Take off your abaya when you drink your whiskey," instructed one Saudi mogul as his bartender handed us cocktails in his home. Some Saudi men glean the future from coffee grounds, and many Saudi women love horoscopes, but police here snatched a Lebanese TV host and clairvoyant from a pilgrimage and sentenced him to death by beheading for sorcery. (After international media pressure, the execution has for now been postponed.) Non-Muslims are not allowed to enter the holy cities of Mecca and Medina. But Leslie McLoughlin led a tour near Medina prior to 9/11, where he could view the city and the Prophet's Mosque from his hotel.

Saudi Arabia may now be in semi–Open Sesame mode (and it's funny to see how many people have named their camels "Barack"), but the holy sites won't be officially open to non-Muslims anytime soon. On the highway to Mecca, a "Christian bypass" tells the rest of us when to turn off the road: heathens exit here. Perhaps from a distance you'll one day be able to glimpse what is expected to be the second-tallest building in the world, now being constructed by the bin Laden family real estate company. It is a hotel complex that will be topped by a clock six times larger than London's Big Ben. (The Saudis harbor a hope that Mecca Time will dislodge Greenwich Mean Time from its current prominence.) For now, even planes must avoid violating the holy cities, keeping safely away from sacred airspace lest infidels spy from above. There has been talk of building an Islamic, Disneyland-style park on the road between Mecca and Jidda. The Saudis find monkeys and parrots far funnier than mice and ducks, so watch out, Mickey and Daffy. And Qatar recently pushed the Gulf states to create a common Gulf Cooperation Council tourist visa, in order to make the region more attractive to cruise ships.

Jidda has many charms. The median strip on the corniche has a magical open-air museum, with huge, whimsical sculptures by Miró, Henry Moore, and other artists who created works consistent with Islamic values—that is, no representations of the human form. The neon-lit boardwalk is lined with snack shacks, toy shops, and mini amusement parks. But it's missing the sexy, seedy elements that make shore vacations fun. Instead of teenagers necking or kids splashing in the water, there are men spreading out prayer rugs on the seawall.

Libertarian Zone

I had bought a Burqini on-line from an Australian company, figuring I'd need one to go swimming. A Burqini—a burka bikini—is a full-body suit that resembles Apolo Ohno's Olympic outfit or the getup Woody Allen wore to play a sperm in *Everything You Always Wanted to Know About Sex* . . . But as it turned out I didn't have to swaddle myself in one, because I discovered a place called Durat al-Arus.

Sarah Bennett, a stunning thirty-two-year-old, blue-eyed California Mormon who converted to Islam and blackened her blond hair, now works in Jidda for a conglomerate. She wears Chanel abayas. Bennett took us to Durat al-Arus, a marina and tourist village where wealthy Saudis and royals have homes and boats. The architecture is 1970s, the colors are *Miami Vice*, and the mood is downright hedonistic compared with that of the rest of the country. It's a rare libertarian zone. Women can drive and wear what they want, and men and women can mingle without fear. I quickly commandeered a BMW from a cute sheikh so I could tool around for a few minutes in a meaningless spurt of emancipation. Then the sheikh, who wore a Jack Sparrow bandana and called himself "the Pirate," took Sarah, Ashley, and me out on his yacht, with a motorboat trailing behind, for some snorkeling in the turquoise Red Sea. He was a Muslim and served us only soft drinks as we made our way to a desolate desert island. But other than that you could wear a real bikini and live the high life: listening to club music booming from an iPod, eating melting butter-pecan ice cream and fresh berries, sipping flutes of sparkling pomegranate juice. With a small shock, I was struck by the sensuality of the scene—it was hard to believe this was Saudi Arabia. My thoughts drifted to the silent movie *The Sheik*, and the moment when Rudolph Valentino drags Agnes Ayres onto his horse in the desert and says, "Lie still, you little fool."

And that, I guess, is why they have the *mutawa*.

PORTER FOX

The Last Stand of Free Town

FROM *The Believer*

THE CONCENTRIC BOULEVARDS and tidy row houses of downtown Copenhagen instill an overwhelming sense of order in Denmark's capital city. There are no beggars lurking in alleyways or vendors hawking trinkets on the sidewalk. At night, blaze-orange street cleaners buff cobblestones to a dull sheen while workers blast graffiti off walls with an environmentally friendly jet of pressurized ice crystals. The effect is so striking that on a spring morning with the sun reflecting off the spires of Tivoli Gardens, Copenhagen appears more like a fairytale kingdom than the largest metropolis in Scandinavia.

So it was with some surprise that Danes turned on their television sets on May 14, 2007, to see fires burning in their capital's streets and gangs of police officers beating their countrymen with billy clubs. The worst of the fighting flared up along Prinsessegade Road in the Christianshavn neighborhood. A column of black transport vans filed into the street as residents hurled Molotov cocktails, rocks, and fireworks at police. Officers retaliated with batons and tear gas, and by that afternoon, the seventeenth-century streets had disappeared under a thick cloud of smoke.

The site was an ironic flashpoint for violence. Prinsessegade Road marks the northern border of a pacifist commune that has existed in Christianshavn since 1971. That year, a group of squatters overtook an abandoned army base east of Prinsessegade, barricaded the roads, outlawed cars and guns, and created a self-ruling micro-nation in the heart of Copenhagen. They called the eighty-five-acre district Christiania Free Town, drew up a constitution,

printed their own currency, banished property ownership, legal-
ized marijuana, and essentially seceded from Denmark. The traditionally liberal Danish government allowed the settlement at first,
dubbing Christiania a "social experiment." Then it spent the next
three decades trying to reclaim the area. Thirty-nine years and a
dozen eviction notices later, the nine hundred residents of Free
Town represent one of the longest-lasting social experiments in
modern history.

At the turn of the millennium, Denmark, the first country in the
world to legalize pornography and gay marriage, suffered the same
wave of Bush-inspired conservatism that swept through much of
Europe. (The Danes sent a submarine to support Operation Iraqi
Freedom.) In 2001, the Folketing—Danish Parliament—landed
in the hands of a conservative coalition for only the second time in
eighty-five years. The coalition (headed by Prime Minister Anders
Fogh Rasmussen) and its austere policies on immigration were
viewed by voters as necessary correctives to a lenient program that
had led to an overburdened welfare system. On the heels of the
controversial Muhammad cartoon incident, Rasmussen's government gained public support on its promise to put the Dane back in
Danish.

The next item on the party's to-do list—an initiative that had
frustrated conservatives for more than three decades—was to
eradicate Christiania once and for all. It took just three years to
pass parliamentary law L205 and begin what conservatives called
the "normalization" of Free Town. L205 mandated that the Palaces
and Properties Agency demolish fifty homes in Christiania, con-
struct four hundred new condominiums, charge market rental
rates, and turn management of the district over to a private leas-
ing company. To Christianians, the scheme represented practically
everything they'd stood against, and most residents refused to
abide. Unlike previous governments, though, Rasmussen's didn't
back down. It reinforced its efforts with heavy police intervention
and a public relations smear campaign—including dramatic sting
operations and petty drug busts that yielded few results but made
the evening news—that turned many Danes against the once tolerated, even beloved commune.

During the police action in May 2007, the government's stated objective was to demolish a rundown squatters' shack known as the "Cigarkassen," or "Cigar Box"; by late afternoon, government workers had reduced it to rubble. But at Christiania's southwest entrance, the insurgency had begun. Pale, waifish Danes wearing hoodies and backpacks darted through Christiania's alleys and surrounding streets, hurling bottles and rocks at policemen. Near Christiania's infamous Pusher Street, a television camera caught an officer clubbing a young man in a yellow T-shirt to the ground.

More vans arrived and protesters set barricades of furniture, tires, and cars on fire. Police reinforcements were summoned from all over the city, and the sound of sirens filled the streets. Over the next few days, word spread throughout Europe that Christiania was under attack, and hundreds of supporters from inside and outside the country poured into Copenhagen. As officers dressed in bulky black riot gear flooded Christiania's gates, the government braced itself for what would be one of the most violent episodes in Copenhagen's recent history. And residents in Christiania dug in for what appeared to be Free Town's last stand.

The 1960s were fertile years for micro-nations—the liberalism of the time manifested itself in tiny islands of autonomy. Erwin Strauss's 1984 book, *How to Start Your Own Country*, attributes many of the era's breakaway provinces to the writings of Ayn Rand. In 1969, a group of Rand followers robbed a bar to fund the fictitious nation of Oceana. Oceanians didn't have an exact site for their country, but boot camps were established to train citizens to defend it. At one point the group even planned to steal a nuclear missile to stave off potential enemies.

Most "ephemeral states"—like American Michael J. Oliver's "Republic of Minerva," founded in 1972 on a pile of sand Oliver dumped on a pair of reefs north of Tonga—didn't fare as well as Christiania. (A Tongan chief ran Oliver off.) Neither did "Sealand," created in 1967 by Paddy Roy Bates on a six-thousand-square-foot World War II antiaircraft platform seven miles off the coast of Britain. Bates was ousted by his own "prime minister" in 1978 but won the platform back after a daring helicopter raid.

From its inception, however, Christiania was less the brainchild of a single person than a response to a collective yearning. In 1971, a group of locals broke down the wall to Copenhagen's abandoned, and increasingly derelict, Bådsmandsstrædes army base. One hundred and fifty squatters followed, making homes in whatever spaces they could find. Anarchy buzzed in the streets of Copenhagen. The May 1968 student uprisings in Paris and subsequent Danish student protests in the spring of 1970 had given young artists and students confidence and purpose. A squatter movement cropped up in Copenhagen in response to a growing housing crisis and displeasure with the Danish government. After the invaders took the Bådsmandsstrædes army base, the alternative Copenhagen weekly, *Hovedbladet,* ran the headline IMMIGRATE WITH BUS NO. 8—THE DIRECT ROUTE TO CHRISTIANIA, and hundreds more arrived at Christiania's gates.

Police attempted to rout the settlers but were overwhelmed by their numbers. Looking to avoid violent confrontation, Danish officials gave Christianians three years to try their "experiment." But the following year the officials went back on their word and ordered the area cleared. Supporters swarmed the grounds and the police were outnumbered once again. This time the government decided to let Christiania "stay until further notice."

All the while, Christianians expanded the infrastructure of their budding micro-nation. A housing office was established in the Rosenhuset building to process prospective tenants and manage maintenance for the area's 170 structures. Residents began weekly common meetings to decide community issues like garbage disposal, large-scale construction projects, tenant applications, water, electricity, and government relations. The community's first rules: no buying, selling, or trading of homes; no violence; no gang affiliations; no guns; no cars. A law prohibiting hard drugs (but not *all* drugs) was added after a run-in with heroin addicts in the late 1970s.

I'd heard about Christiania while researching "temporary autonomous zones" (or TAZs, as named by anarchist writer Hakim Bey), and flew to Copenhagen in early 2006 to see the community before the bulldozers arrived. Beneath the orange glow of a new condo complex across the street and Denmark's first snowfall of the year, Christiania appeared more like a village from a Hans Christian Andersen tale than a self-ruling suburb. Small cottages balanced on top of one-room guardhouses; hobbit-esque shacks sported dragon-shaped chimneys. I could see meadows and giant maples and rock-lined pathways.

The area was so expansive it took my Ghanaian taxi driver nine repetitions of the word "Christiania"—accentuated by jabbings of his index finger—to demark the borders of the neighborhood's northwestern wall. He was excited to be here. He did the things in Free Town that people do in anarchist communes—talk politics, buy hash, and hang with his buddies in the pub long after the bars of Copenhagen had closed. It's a "good place," he quipped as we approached the northwest gate. Then he glanced across the street at the condo complex and said, "It will soon look like that."

A foot of snow had piled up—a surprise storm for a city surrounded by water—by the time I rendezvoused with my host for the next ten days, an excitable fifty-three-year-old named Emmerik Warburg, who'd discovered Christiania thirty-two years before, as a young artist. He brushed the snow from his jacket and loaded my bag onto his bike, a local Christiania design with two wheels and a cargo box on the front.

Emmerik led me down Christiania's main drag, the Long Road, past an old officers' barracks that had been transformed into modish, bohemian apartments. He pointed out the "Raisin House," an afterschool children's center that used solar power and composting toilets. Beyond that was a hole-in-the-wall vegetarian restaurant and, to the right, the terminus of Pusher Street, where dealers once sold hash from elaborately designed stands before the police shut them down in 2004.

We turned right at a carousel-size Buddhist stupa with a string of prayer flags circling it and two burning candles inside, then passed through a brick archway that opened into a clutch of interconnected homes. The complex was called Mælkebøtten (Dandelion) for the flowers that covered its common meadow in the summer. The whole enclosure, including the apartment I was to stay in for the next week, used to be a grenade factory, Emmerik explained. "Don't worry," he said. "They've all been taken away."

The apartment's interior was surprisingly clean, with touches of classic Danish design. Almost all the building material in Christiania is recycled. The front hall light was fashioned from a paper cylinder wrapped around a low-wattage fluorescent bulb, with a circular CD case fit into the bottom as a dimmer. Another low-wattage bulb over the bed was entombed in a coffee can. The woodstove was also a local design—half a fifty-gallon drum laid on its side with the vent on top. But the gas heater worked best, Emmerik said, as he leapt out the window to turn on the tank.

Things had been a bit tense around the neighborhood, he went on as he scrambled back through the window. There was lots going on. Lots to do. New Year's Day had marked the first L205 deadline —meaning that on January 1, the government was supposed to start demolishing houses. A few days before the holiday, though, residents received a letter saying the deadline had been extended. Still, he said, they were divided as to what to do. Some wanted to cut a deal; others refused to acknowledge the government's claims. The division ran so deep, Emmerik said, that half the town had skipped the last general meeting.

Christiania had changed, he said. Back in the day, residents acted as one. There was no obstacle too large for them to tackle. They managed massive construction projects, like laying sewer lines by hand, and renovated thousands of square feet of rundown buildings, without a penny from the government. Now, he said, the government refused to acknowledge the collective and dealt with Christianians individually. And infighting was crippling Free Town's efforts to fight back.

It's somewhere between ironic and ordained that Christiania was established on the former site of much historic Danish military action. The city ramparts on the eastern border of the neighborhood, first built in 1617, were reinforced later that century after Sweden's siege of Copenhagen. The Bådsmandsstrædes base, while active, housed the Royal Artillery Regiment as well as ammunitions laboratories and depots.

The following day, Emmerik walked me through the base to show what Christiania's settlers had done with the place. Poison-gas-testing chambers in Mælkebøtten had been transformed into airy pieds-à-terre with flower boxes, pastel-trimmed dormers, and wind chimes. Nearby in the Fabriksområdet district, blacksmith Charlotte Steen had renovated a bomb factory—designed to have the roof blow off in an explosion—into a Usonian town house, complete with a ship's bow and oak rafters collected from old boat-houses in Holmen. One of the most stunning homes in Christiania was occupied by machinist Helge Pyramide. Over nine years, he constructed his twelve-sided house, "The Twelve-Edge," using roof-ing tiles from a sugar factory and volcanic ash for insulation.

"The government can't seem to figure out how to solve this Christiania problem," Emmerik exclaimed as we strolled past a girl brushing a pony in one of Christiania's eighteen stables. "We keep telling them, we already *have!* We've been doing it for almost forty years!"

The defining characteristic of Christiania's homes, Emmerik explained, comes from the fact that it's against the rules to sell or trade them. Real estate speculators—and the excessive appreciation of property values—ritually kill art communities in the world's greatest cities, he continued. In Christiania, when residents move, they simply pack up their belongings and leave. So house design is based solely on the owner's needs, not resale value or even building codes. The result is some of the most innovative and acclaimed architecture in Europe. Several books have been published on Christiania's eclectic aesthetic. Well-known architects, like Merete Ahnfeldt-Mollerup from Denmark's Royal Academy, regard the district as a kind of "adaptive reuse" laboratory.

Christiania has come up with several social innovations as well, Emmerik said. After the ban on hard drugs in 1979, the community initiated a drug rehabilitation program that cured 80 percent of participants. (Five percent was considered successful in Copenhagen at the time.) Collective property management gave the poor and handicapped a higher standard of living while simultaneously creating a nurturing environment for artists. Every year the community feeds thousands of homeless and poor people on Christmas Eve at a massive banquet thrown in the Gray Hall. Businesses like Christiania Bikes (the maker of Emmerik's ride) have received government awards for entrepreneurialism and ship their products all over the world.

Emmerik explained the financial workings of Free Town as we strolled past the community kindergarten, designed to integrate children into society by using neighbors' yards as a playground. (In the 1970s, students were fed macrobiotic food, toy weapons were banned, and children held their own meetings.) All of Christiania's tenants pay a $380-a-month "use fee," regardless of the size of their home, and businesses pay according to their potential for profit. The cash is then put in a pot and divided between public programs like the building office (for structural repairs), children's facilities, the post office, a weekly newspaper, recycling, public toilets, water, and electricity. Christiania then pays the gov-

ernment a group value-added tax and additional funds for public
services like water and electricity. (Since the 1990s, the government has commended Christianians as "model citizens" for never
missing a payment.)

Leftover New Year's Eve fireworks boomed overhead as we
walked along the ramparts in Free Town's eastern quarter. A spotted mutt the size of a greyhound trotted by, and Emmerik boasted
that because Christiania's dogs go leashless, they are more docile. Gingerbread shacks with rainbows and Shivas painted on their
walls practically abutted the water. The front window on one was
broken, and the owner had left a note that read, "If you are going
to steal, then at least do it from people who can afford insurance."
Across a small bridge leading to the other side of the moat, Emmerik pointed to another sign. This one announced a meeting to
refuse the municipal government's demand that everyone declare
an individual address. (Christiania still uses a common mailbox:
DK-1440, Copenhagen.)

We ended the tour near an afterschool center. There was a small
beach and a canoe on the shore. Emmerik said the community
built the center to keep kids out of trouble after school. Then he
pointed to a mock real estate sign posted on the side of a hill that
read, THE FREE STATE CHRISTIANIA IS NOT AND WILL
NEVER BE FOR SALE.

The edict echoed a well-known quote from Ahnfeldt-Mollerup
regarding the government's desire to shut Christiania down. It was
not so much anarchy the government wanted to control, she wrote,
as it was proprietorship of a successful venture:

> Each and every little village in every corner of [Denmark] now has a
> small shop where one can purchase the style that already can be found
> at Christiania. So one can wonder about the anger and aversion many of
> the conservatives feel about this quarter's culture, one can wonder why
> Christiania should be replaced by conventional housing at just this point
> when the quarter's maladjusted style has become so mainstream. Per-
> haps the point is actually that it should not be torn down, but instead
> that bourgeois Denmark wants to buy Christiania and is displeased
> about it not being for sale.

By 9 A.M. on May 16, 2007, the fires around Christiania had died
out. Workers cleared barricades while commuters pedaled along

Prinsessegade Road to the Knippelsbro bridge. The air still smelled like burning rubber, but on Pusher Street, hash dealers were already out, covertly peddling sticks of Afghan crème.

The Copenhagen daily newspaper, *Politiken,* condemned the police raid as needless provocation. The Palaces and Properties Agency asserted that the Cigar Box had to be demolished under the auspices of L205. By midday, Christianians had rebuilt the structure. That afternoon, they held a housewarming party hosted by one of Denmark's best-known DJs.

The standoff continued through the summer, and Christiania's lawyer, Knud Foldschack, threatened to file seven hundred property rights lawsuits if the government continued to pursue L205.

Deadlock had long been Christiania's best defense. By the time lawsuits were decided, often a new government—looking to avoid controversy—had taken over the Folketing and buried the case. Foldschack estimated that his seven hundred cases would take a year to settle once filed, at which point the political landscape could change dramatically. The wait, he said, would be worth it. "You can only destroy a situation, a possibility, like Christiania, once," he said. "You can never restore it."

But Rasmussen called for and won—albeit by a slimmer margin —a surprise early election in the fall of 2007 and secured a second term. In Christiania, optimism dimmed. Ten to twenty police patrols a week randomly searched homes and hassled residents. (A year before, Amnesty International had called for an "independent mechanism for the investigation of human rights violations by the police" in Christiania.) Half the community wanted to fight the government; the other half wanted to take the government's offer to lease their homes at below-market rates. In the summer of 2008, Foldschack registered the lawsuits, and the fate of Christiania returned to the courts.

Many demonized Rasmussen's government for wanting to gain access to one of the last, and most valuable, undeveloped building sites in the city. But residents like Richardt Lionheart said that even before government intervention Christiania was evolving into the sort of free-market community it had been founded in opposition to.

During my visit in 2006, Lionheart spoke of the darker currents beneath Christiania's bohemian surface, and we continued the conversation via e-mail until last winter. He first came to the neighborhood in January 1972, to put certain sociological and political beliefs into practice. A week after arriving, he moved into the "Blue House" with two women. The threesome took over the second floor, which had been a changing room for soldiers. They removed rows of steel lockers and set up a telephone and hot water heater. They laid hardwood floors, decorated the place, and hosted meetings and parties. His greatest hardship in those days proved to be his relationships; eventually he moved out. When he returned two years later, he fixed up his own place and has lived there ever since.

Lionheart's first skepticism about Free Town came in 1984, when he was living in Colombia on a psychology research grant. That winter he received a letter from his brother, Eric, who'd been diagnosed with cancer and had fallen behind on his rent in Christiania. The district Eric lived in threatened to kick him out if he didn't pay. Richardt flew home and settled the debt, but, he said, things haven't been the same since.

A few years later, Richardt's neighbor died and his widow—a Swede who was new to Christiania—moved into her husband's house. But residents of the district told her she was not welcome. Richardt stepped in and, in keeping with Christiania rules, called a meeting to resolve the matter. Three days before the meeting, a posse broke into the woman's house, piled her belongings in the street, and reclaimed the home for someone of their choosing.

"Anarchy is a beautiful thing if people have very fucking high morals," he said. "If they don't, then it's lynch mobs. This was a lynch mob, I'd say. And the same with consensus democracy. You have to have very high morals to make it function. You have to have a very high level of energy as well."

There were other stories of arbitrary law and violence in Free Town. Since the beginning, the community used thugs to enforce rules and chase unwanted residents out of the neighborhood. In the housing pool, preferential treatment was sometimes given to applicants who had friends on the inside. In 2005, residents offered a troop of gay actors a home, then kicked them out after determining that they didn't comply with the "Christiania lifestyle." In 2004, a television journalist was violently threatened when he tried to erect a small house in Christiania, against neighborhood rules. The following spring, the drug scene on Pusher Street made headlines when six masked men fired automatic weapons into a crowd to avenge one of their members who'd been thrown out of Christiania. Several people were injured, and a twenty-six-year-old man was killed. In April of 2009, a twenty-two-year-old man's jaw was blown off and four others were injured when an unknown perpetrator lobbed a grenade into a crowd outside Café Nemoland.

The government blew many of the stories out of proportion in its campaign to close Christiania, but some of its base assertions were grounded in disquieting facts. While Christianians refused to recognize the government's authority, two thirds of the community received welfare and used city and state services like hospitals, schools, and roads. More than one hundred residents owned cars, and, because they couldn't park in Free Town, they clogged the streets of Christianshavn with them.

One point almost everyone, including most Christianians, agreed on was the fact that Free Town's drug trade had become its Achilles' heel. On one hand, the $174-million-a-year business filled area shops, cafés, and restaurants and made the neighborhood the second-most-popular tourist stop in Denmark, after Tivoli. On the other, it brought violence and a power imbalance that diminished Christiania's community mentality.

One night during my stay, I visited a former hash dealer some friends had introduced me to. "Andy" unlocked six deadbolts on two doors to let me into his apartment. He lived in Frederick's Arc, the largest timber-frame structure in Denmark and site of the 1979 heroin blockade. He'd put on weight since he stopped dealing and now went to the gym every day and played with the Christiania soccer club. His biceps and neck were well defined. He had a buzz cut and shifty blue eyes, seemingly aware of every movement in the room at all times.

Andy's apartment was outfitted with nearly everything a twenty-something bachelor could want—and, seemingly, everything Christiania historically opposed. The living room was appointed with a leather wraparound couch and a pool-table-size wide-screen TV. The kitchen was equipped with a multitude of fancy stainless-steel appliances and granite counters. The hardwood floors were sparkling new.

After starting as a runner on Pusher Street in the late nineties, when he was fifteen, Andy eventually set up his own stand in 2001. Individual busts were frequent leading up to the 2004 raid, he said, but the risk was worth it. When he was twenty years old, he was clearing $1,000 to $2,000 a day. He took extravagant snowboarding trips to Switzerland and spent $12,000 once on a two-week bender in Miami. He didn't work on Christiania's public projects or attend meetings. In a socialist country where income tax ranges from 43 to 63 percent, Andy was an instant member of Copenhagen's nouveau riche.

Since he quit pushing, Andy had been trying to reinvent himself. He pointed out a painting he'd been working on that seemed like an interesting abstract until he explained that it was a depiction of an enraged dragon breathing fire. I asked about an assortment of electronic equipment in the corner, and he said he was also learning how to DJ. When I inquired what he thought of L205, he answered that he hoped it would pass over, that things would stay the way they were. "I do what the lawyers tell me," he said. "I just give them money and trust they will do the right thing."

I went the following night to see Pusher Street for myself. The alley was empty, apart from three eidolic shapes crowded around a fire smoldering in a fifty-gallon drum. I approached a middle-aged woman reclining on a pile of wood chips and asked if she was selling. She nodded and asked how much I wanted. I told her I had one hundred kroner. She pulled a black stick the size of a small pencil from her pocket, and I handed her the money.

I went into Woodstock—Christiania's first bar, which opened in April 1974—and was hit by a wall of blue smoke and blaring country music. The bartender was either very drunk or very strange and laughed every time I counted out on my fingers how many beers I wanted, which was one. I found a seat at a long pine picnic table in the back and rolled a joint. As I tapped the butt on the table, a woman at the other end spilled her hash on the floor and yelled at me. She circled the table, alternately pointing and screaming for the next five minutes. When I finished rolling, she slammed her fist on the table and yelled, "Remember that?!"

I smoked the joint quickly and left. The clouds had receded for the first time since I arrived and there were a few stars overhead. I walked down Long Road, past the Raisin House and the stupa. The candles under the Buddha had been replaced and were burning, and a few lights were on in the surrounding homes. Less than a half mile from downtown Copenhagen, I couldn't hear any traffic or any noise at all. I thought of Emmerik and the original vision of Christiania and knew for certain that it was long gone. But walking into Mælkebøtten with blue moonlight reflecting off the courtyard, I still had to wonder whether that meant this place shouldn't exist.

French philosopher Michel Foucault said that there are no such things as utopias. A true utopia, he said in his 1967 lecture "Of Other Spaces," is a figment of our imagination. It is merely a concept of society in its perfected state. What people refer to as utopias, he said, are in fact heterotopias, "simultaneously mythic and real contestation[s] of the space in which we live."

"There are also, probably in every culture, in every civilization," he said,

> real places—places that do exist and that are formed in the very founding of society—which are something like counter-sites, a kind of effectively enacted Utopia in which the real sites, all the other real sites that can be found within the culture, are simultaneously represented, contested, and inverted. Places of this kind are outside of all places, even though it may be possible to indicate their location in reality.

Heterotopias come in many forms. From sacred grounds of ancient cultures to military schools in the twentieth century to cemeteries today, they reflect a certain aspect of the society they reside in. They also typically occupy a certain era, Foucault said, when "men arrive at a sort of absolute break with their traditional time."

In May 2009, it seemed Christiania's era was drawing to a close. The Eastern High Court ruled in favor of the Palaces and Properties Agency in the cases Foldschack had filed. Christianians decided to appeal to the supreme court. The court said it would announce a decision in January 2011, and the waiting game was back on.

Four months later, Christiania celebrated its thirty-eighth birthday with a day of parades, free food, and DJs. Supporters showed up in Native American garb and tie-dyed T-shirts. The mood was upbeat, but in photos and videos of the scene it looked more like a historical reenactment of the 1970s—complete with dozens of tourists watching from a safe distance—than a celebration of a thriving community. "As time goes by, I guess people are getting more realistic and are less positive to the communistic ideas," Lionheart wrote. "There's nobody today who defends communism. There's nobody who talks in the local paper at all. It's like everybody here just wants to have the right opinion instead of having their own opinion."

The comment reminded me of an experience I had just before I left Free Town in 2006 that seemed to speak to both the neighborhood's resilient spirit and its conflicted identity. I'd spent the evening alone in the Moonfisher Café, contemplating the many faces of Christiania. Two ceiling fans pushed thick tobacco and hash smoke around the coffee shop. I bought an espresso and set it on a homemade steel table. A few drunks laughed loudly in the corner. Pool balls clicked in the back room. A lookout announced that a police patrol was approaching, and smokers quickly shuffled hash and rolling papers into their pockets. The cops arrived, young-looking Danes with blue eyes, blond hair, and padded riot gear. When they left ten minutes later, a woman at the bar yelled, "We got you!" and bowed in mock reverence. A few seconds after that, a massive bottle rocket exploded beside the patrol.

In the bar, joints came out again and conversations continued with hardly a pause. I left and ran into a young girl and boy outside the entrance, cherub-faced Danes no more than six or seven years old. They'd rebuilt a snow barricade meant to slow police patrols. I smiled and waved. After ten days in Christiania, I was starting to feel like a local myself. They stared back, and the girl told me it would cost one hundred kroner to pass.

"I don't have one hundred kroner," I said, grinning.

"Eighty," she answered.

"Twenty?" I asked.

"Sixty"

"Thirty?"

The girl scratched her head, glanced at the boy. I gave her a pleading look and she said, "One hundred." I laughed and flipped her a twenty-kroner piece. She and the boy inspected it as I scaled the wall. When I got one leg over the top, they pelted me with two snowballs, square in the back.

KEITH GESSEN

Stuck

FROM *The New Yorker*

MOSCOW'S TERRIBLE TRAFFIC has been infamous for a while now, but in the past year it has come to feel like an existential threat. The first snowfall of last winter, in early December, paralyzed the city. Andrey Kolesnikov, the Kremlin correspondent for *Kommersant* and probably the best-known print journalist in the country, was unable to reach the airport in time to leave with Prime Minister Vladimir Putin for Nizhny Tagil. Instead of detailing Putin's manly adventures in the metallurgical capital of the Urals, Kolesnikov's column the next day described his own epic, failed journey to the airport. The traffic analysis center at Yandex, the country's leading on-line search engine, reported a record-breaking worst-possible rating of 10 for six straight hours. That night, a popular anti-Kremlin blogger, making his way along the river in the center of town, encountered an ambulance driver standing outside his vehicle throwing snowballs lazily off the embankment; he'd been in traffic so long, he explained, that his patient was now dead.

Mayor Yuri Luzhkov, who takes everything that happens in the city very personally, perhaps because over the years he and his wife have come personally to own a good chunk of the city, reacted decisively: he blamed the meteorologists. They had underestimated the snowfall. If they didn't start forecasting better, there would be trouble. In the following months, though, snow wreaked havoc on the city whenever it fell. In three separate instances, drivers of snow-clearing vehicles were shot at when they collided with other vehicles; one of the drivers, shot by an off-duty police officer, died.

Even without snow, the movement of cars through the circular maze of Moscow was incredibly frustrating. During rush hour on an overcast, slippery day in late February, the luxury Mercedes of a vice president of Lukoil, the country's largest oil company, collided at high speed with a small Citroën. The occupants of the Mercedes escaped with superficial injuries; the Citroën crumpled like a paper bag, and the driver and her daughter-in-law—both doctors—were killed.

The accident exploded into scandal. The police claimed that the Citroën was at fault, but automobile activists quickly found witnesses who said that the Mercedes had crossed over into the central emergency lane reserved for ambulances and police cars, and then into oncoming traffic. Especially infuriating was the Mercedes itself, a black S500 with a siren: for years, these besirened black Mercedeses had been running red lights, using the emergency lane, and otherwise tyrannizing other drivers. Some of them technically had the right to do all this, since they belonged to one of the federal security agencies in Moscow, or to Duma deputies, or to Putin; but a large number simply belonged to wealthy and well-connected individuals. Now they were killing people. Within days of the accident, the young rapper Noize MC recorded a furious song, "Mercedes S666," in which he ventriloquized the innocuous-looking Lukoil vice president as Satan: "All those satanic costumes, that's just tomfoolery. / Dressing up like that they'll never look like me . . . I'm working here on a whole other level. / I've got a suitcase full of cash to get me out of trouble." The song's chorus expressed the class conflict at the heart of the matter: "Get out of my way, filthy peasants. / There's a patrician on the road."

On a Monday morning a month later, two young women from the Caucasus set off bombs during rush hour in the center of the city. The first blew herself up at Lubyanka, the metro station just beneath the headquarters of the Federal Security Service, and the other did so at a nearby stop, forty minutes later. Emergency services reacted rapidly, and since there could be no question of ambulances making it through traffic from the site of the bombings to the hospital, the badly wounded were helicoptered out. Given the forty-minute gap between the explosions, however, the press began to wonder why the metro hadn't been evacuated directly after the first bomb. The response from a metro spokesman was immediate.

"You have no idea what would have happened if we'd closed down an entire branch of the system," he said. The city was so crowded, its functioning so tenuous, that it was better to risk another explosion than close off an artery. "The city is on the brink of transportational collapse," Mikhail Blinkin, a traffic expert, told me. "Moscow will simply cease to function as a city. You and I will be living in different cities. Some people will live in one neighborhood, and others will live in a different neighborhood, and that will be fine, except they won't be able to get from one neighborhood to the other."

I first noticed the extent of the Moscow traffic problem in the spring of 2007, while drinking a coffee at the Coffee Bean, on Sretenka, just up the street from the Lubyanka and around the corner from the Lukoil headquarters. It used to be that you couldn't get a coffee in Moscow for love or money, so I didn't mind that it wasn't good coffee and that it cost four dollars. That is to say, I minded, but what could I do? So there I sat, sipping my four-dollar coffee and looking out the window, when suddenly my sister appeared in front of the coffee shop and stopped, trapped in traffic. She had recently bought a navy-blue Honda Element, which looks like a motorized version of Fred Flintstone's car, with the driver sitting curiously upright. Farther ahead, Sretenka intersected the giant Garden Ring Road, which runs around the Kremlin at a radius of about a mile and a half and marks the border of the historic city center. For much of its length, it is twelve lanes wide; at certain points, it's eighteen. Still, it is often clogged. At the Sretenka–Garden Ring intersection, a police officer hand-operates the light to try to ease traffic, to no avail. So there was my sister, just twenty feet away from me, sitting down as I was, almost as if she were at another table. The moment extended in time; I sipped my coffee. When, eventually, the light changed and my sister moved forward a few car lengths, it was as if she had merely moved to another table. If the coffee were cheaper, I would have brought her one.

Several generations, even several centuries, had brought the city to this point. Its early rulers built Moscow as a concentric series of walled forts, with the Kremlin at the center. After the government abandoned Moscow in favor of St. Petersburg, in the early eighteenth century, the old capital developed haphazardly, like an enormous bazaar. In the post-revolutionary age, when the Bolsheviks moved the government back to Moscow to get farther away from the Germans, various fantasies emerged to reverse all this: avant-gardists imagined a socialist Moscow of clean right angles; others proposed simply abandoning the city. Many believed that the Kremlin, a church-laden symbol of medieval tyranny at the heart of the city, should be de-emphasized, or worse. By the time the Soviets were ready to do anything about it, Joseph Stalin was in charge, and under him the medieval character of Moscow was not fundamentally altered. Instead, the Stalinists built gigantic avenues that ran in all directions from the Kremlin like rays from the sun. There were few cars around to fill these avenues, but they provided a fine, broad line of sight for Soviet leaders during military parades.

Then came capitalism. The registration laws that had made it almost impossible to move to Moscow during Soviet times ceased to be enforced, and meanwhile chaos, deindustrialization, and ethnic violence roamed the peripheries of the empire. Very soon it became clear that what Moscow had lost in political authority it had gained, and then some, in economic authority. By the end of the 1990s, there were more people in Moscow from all over the former Soviet Union than there had been when the Soviet Union was a single state. People from rural Russia, the Central Asian states, and Ukraine came to escape poverty; people from the Caucasus came to escape the war.

All of them wanted cars. The city's plan with regard to this was not to have a plan at all. Planning was for socialists; under capitalism, the market would figure things out. In the post-Soviet years, Moscow filled up, first with kiosks, and flimsy freestanding grocery stores, and little old ladies selling socks. Eventually, these were replaced by office buildings and megastores and even luxury condominiums; the spaces once reserved for new roads or metro stations were given over to construction. Blinkin recalls a commission that he received from the Soviet government, only months before its collapse, to project the rate of automobile growth over the next twenty-five years. "We knew the trajectory of automobilization in many countries of the world, and so we predicted exactly what happened," he says. What happened was that the number of cars in Moscow went from 60 per thousand residents in 1991 to 350 in

2009. "And we were very proud of ourselves for being so smart. Then, a while later, I met some guys who sold foreign cars, who'd done a marketing prognosis, and without any of our international analogues or models they just thought, Well, restrictions are down, you can buy foreign cars as well as Russian ones, and they predicted the same rate of growth as we had! These car dealers predicted it." Blinkin was dismissive of the car dealers, but in the early 1990s they included some of the most brilliant minds in the country. The first great post-Soviet fortune, after all, was made not from oil or gas or nickel: that came later. It was made when Boris Berezovsky, a mathematician and game theorist, started selling cars.

Last spring, Mayor Luzhkov fired the head of the city's transportation department. Weeks earlier, the deposed chief had, like the three men who preceded him over the previous seven years, been harshly criticized for his failure to solve the traffic crisis. There are many problems that Luzhkov pretends not to know about, but traffic is not among them. In fact, it sometimes seems as if the mayor thinks of nothing else. Whenever he goes abroad, he returns with a magical fix for the problem; whenever he has money to spare, he builds roads and digs tunnels. He has waged a relentless war against traffic lights—"He has a childlike notion that if he could just get rid of all the traffic lights everything would be fine," Blinkin says—and on one central stretch running from the Kremlin almost all the way, but not quite, to Sheremetyevo Airport, outside town, he has just about eliminated them. He has turned numerous two-way streets into one-way streets and even proposed that the monstrous Garden Ring become one-way. Nothing helps. Muscovites continue to buy (and steal, and salvage, and order on eBay in North America, and ship to Finland) more cars than Luzhkov can build roads to drive them on.

The wise move would have been to invest in public transportation, to build up the city's justly famous but sparse metro network and bring back the trams that killed the literary editor at the start of "The Master and Margarita"; instead, Luzhkov has been cool toward the metro and actively hostile to the trams. Public transportation is for losers. Instead, he spent billions to widen the Moscow Ring Road (a beltway around the city) and complete the construction of the fabled Third Ring Road, a freeway between the Garden

Ring and the Moscow Ring, of which Muscovites had been talking since the 1960s. According to the traffic analysis center at Yandex, the Third Ring is now the most clogged artery in the city. Luzhkov is unbowed: he has begun work on a Fourth Ring!

"No city has ever constructed itself out of congestion," the transportation expert Vukan Vuchic, of the University of Pennsylvania, told me. "It's impossible." Vuchic visited Moscow in October and was depressed by what he saw, though also in a way impressed. "There are streets in the center that are four, five lanes wide in each direction," he said. "You'd think it'd be impossible for them to be congested, but they are congested."

In the past few years, visitors have often come to Russia to try to help. Last fall, I had lunch with Kiichiro Hatoyama, a traffic expert from Japan. As I learned later, Hatoyama is the son of Yukio Hatoyama, until recently the prime minister of Japan, but he was in Moscow in his capacity as a traffic engineer, to teach at Moscow State University. We ate at the Starlite Diner, a 1990s pro-American relic tucked into a small park, just off the Garden Ring. I wanted to know how a city with such vast avenues could have such awful traffic. Hatoyama raised three fingers.

"There are three main factors that determine a city's traffic," he said.

Finger 1: "Driver behavior." Do drivers care that if they enter an intersection before a light turns red there's a chance they'll get stuck and create gridlock? Russian drivers do not. Impatient, angry, they will seize whatever inch of road is offered them. Russian drivers are jerks. Hatoyama put this differently. "Russian drivers lack foresight," he said.

Finger 2: The traffic system itself, that is to say the organization of the roads. Moscow's radial character puts it at a slight disadvantage compared with cities laid out on a grid, like New York, but the disadvantage need not be decisive: Tokyo is also a radial city. Hatoyama's main criticism of Moscow is the lack of left-turn possibilities.

Finger 3: The social system, which is always reflected on the roads. One night last summer, I was out late and took a cab home. The streets at that hour were empty. As the cabdriver and I made our way past Pushkin Square, we noticed a policeman sprinting ahead of us and then mounting a traffic booth at the corner. The light turned red. He emerged from the booth and sprinted to a booth at the next corner. "Someone's coming," my driver announced. We sat before the red light for several minutes. Everything was quiet. Then a motorcade of black Mercedeses and SUVs appeared from the direction of the Kremlin, whizzed past us, and disappeared into the night. Ten seconds passed, and the light turned green. "It is a feudal structure," Hatoyama said of the privileges accorded Russia's elite in the traffic system. "It causes many problems." He had put down his three fingers and returned to his sandwich.

"Is there any other place that has that?" I asked. "Different rules for different drivers?"

Hatoyama chewed his sandwich slowly. When he answered, finally, with a single word, there was a certain satisfaction in his tone. "China," he said.

A few years ago, Moscow tried to institute paid parking in the city center. It was odd, after all, that one of the most expensive cities in the world should let you park for free. The authorities deployed men in orange vests to accept payment for parking on the street. Very quickly, fake parking men appeared, also in orange vests, and then the press reported that the real parking men were delivering only a portion of the parking revenues to the city. In the end, Mayor Luzhkov gave in to public pressure and canceled paid parking on the city's streets.

Moscow is now a riot of parking. Cars park in crosswalks, on traffic islands, in many of the quiet courtyards of the city center, in historic squares. Vuchic, of the University of Pennsylvania, compares it to Austria in the 1970s. "You would go to Salzburg to look at the Mozart statue," he said. "But you couldn't see it, because Salzburg was a big parking lot." The Austrians have since taken care of the problem, with zoning, signage, enforcement. In Moscow, things are getting worse. Throughout the city are signs indicating no-parking zones, but the rules are only occasionally enforced, and the fines are paltry. As a result, the Moscow pedestrian spends a lot of time scrambling over cars, or around them, sometimes being forced out into the street, even, because the cars have climbed onto the sidewalk.

Blinkin sees the parking troubles as a symbol of the city's general lack of a legal and planning culture. "Try that in Munich or Bos-

ton!" he says of parking on the sidewalk. For Blinkin, the author of
a legendary paper titled "The Etiology and Pathogenesis of Moscow Traffic," there are profound social and structural issues pre-
venting Moscow cars from moving. The broad avenues, for example, are good only for military parades. In New York, by contrast,
there is an elegant two-tiered road system: street tier, on which pedestrians are primary and cars secondary, and freeway tier (the
FDR Drive, the Brooklyn-Queens Expressway), where cars rule and
there are no pedestrians at all. According to Blinkin, there isn't a
single proper freeway in Moscow. Even the outermost ring, which
should serve as a beltway for cars trying to bypass the city entirely,
has, since its expansion a decade ago, sprouted dozens of shopping centers, each with several exits and entrances onto the highway. The proposed Fourth Ring is not going to solve any of this.
"You can't just keep sending people in circles!" Blinkin exclaims.
"They need to get off eventually, and then what?" The deeper
problem — or, rather, the only way that the many deep problems
can begin to be solved — is political: Luzhkov, who has been the
ruler of Moscow for nearly twenty years now, needs to go.

Blinkin is a slim, energetic man in his early sixties with a bristly
gray mustache. He was trained in the prestigious math department
of Moscow State University, but then, after underperforming on
the final exam on the history of the Communist Party, could find
work only at a research institute on traffic. "At first, I was disappointed," he told me. "But then I read some more and realized,
Some very smart, respectable people have worked on this stuff."
He spent nearly twenty years at two Soviet research institutes devoted to "urban planning," and in 1990 started a private think tank
on traffic. Blinkin loves driving, and, when we first got in touch,
owned a silver 1999 E-series Mercedes. But I could never get him
to take me for a drive in it. "I'm taking the metro today," he'd say
when I called. "You'd have to be an idiot to drive in these conditions."

In the past few years, as he has spoken out more and more,
Blinkin has come to resemble a classic dissident — the Sakharov of
traffic. Yet in a country where opposition figures are systematically
shut out of the media, Blinkin has more exposure than he can handle. "During the past week, I've been on TV four times," he told
me when we first met, "and I've lost count of how many print interviews." In the current political climate, traffic is a problem every-

one is willing to discuss: the Kremlin-controlled media because it makes Luzhkov look bad; Luzhkov because he's obsessed with it. Vuchic, who was born in Belgrade, was amused to note that he'd been interviewed by the old Party mouthpiece *Izvestia*. "Never in my life did I think I'd be printed in *Izvestia!*" he said.

Like other major cities, Moscow has a traffic center, with banks of large monitors showing many of the city's intersections. Several dozen traffic officers keep an eye on the situation, calling their men in the traffic booths to let them know what they should do. I got a short tour of the facility earlier this year, and it was impressive. The huge monitors; the policemen in uniform before them; the traffic moving, or sitting still, as the policemen watched—it gave a measure of the megalopolis, made it seem a manageable thing. But this was in some sense an illusion: although the police can watch, they are helpless. My guide pointed out the monitor banks for the poorer southern and eastern areas of the city, which are said to have the heaviest traffic. "Are those the worst parts?" I asked him.

He considered this, not wanting, perhaps, to offend the southern and eastern routes. "It's *all* the worst part," he said at last.

The police's main competitor in the realm of traffic information is Yandex, which began monitoring traffic on its website in 2006 and in 2008 set up a separate "analytical center," Yandex Probki (*probka* means traffic jam). Yandex Probki issues periodic white papers on the state of traffic, and maintains a blog with interesting traffic highlights, but its main task is to keep perpetually updated a now iconic three-color street map of the city, showing real-time traffic flow on a number of routes. Above the map is a rating of the overall traffic at that moment, from 1 ("The streets are clear") to 9 ("The city has stopped") and 10 ("You're better off on the metro"). Probki now has around half a million daily visitors in Moscow, putting it neck and neck with News and Images, with Weather just around the bend.

When I visited this past winter, Yandex occupied a low-slung modern office building behind the Kursk train station. Though in the center of town, it was too far to walk from the metro, and a white Yandex shuttle took me there. The tricolor Yandex Probki map played on a large plasma screen above the receptionist. Upstairs, one small room was given over to three men who represented the old guard of traffic-watching: as if in a miniature version of the traffic police center, they sat before computer monitors and kept track of nearly a hundred camera feeds from the streets of the city, swiveling the cameras where necessary to keep up with events, and checked what they saw against the big map. But the center has more sophisticated tools at its disposal. As Maria Laufer, the head of Yandex Maps, explained, setting up cameras all over the megalopolis would be prohibitively expensive. Other cities use sensors embedded in the pavement to measure traffic flow; in Moscow these have a hard time surviving both the weather and the road repairs the weather necessitates. So Yandex, Laufer said, came up with "something like communism—in the good sense of the word." Her colleague Leonid Mednikov updated the formulation: "It's a Wiki." At first, drivers had sent information by phone or by text. As more and more drivers started using GPS-enabled smartphones, Yandex asked them to download Yandex software onto their devices, so that information about their movements could be sent automatically to the Yandex servers. As the program grows, it is able to give an increasingly accurate and encompassing picture of the traffic situation at any given moment. While I was touring the office, it began to snow. Some time later, Mednikov entered the conference room, carrying his laptop before him like a lantern. "It's at 10!" he announced of the traffic index. "It went from 5 to 10 in an hour and a half!" And so it was that the Yandex shuttle, making its way back to the metro with me as its only passenger, got stuck in traffic as it approached the Garden Ring.

In more poetic moments, Blinkin will invoke Julio Cortázar's "Highway of the South," a 1964 story about people stuck in a massive traffic jam on their way back into Paris after the weekend, stuck in it for so long that they begin to live in it. ("At first the girl in the Dauphine had insisted on keeping track of time," the story begins, "though for the engineer in the Peugeot 404 it no longer held any importance.") Hearing this, I recalled Vladimir Sorokin's novella "The Queue," from the era of the Brezhnev stagnation, which is also about a line—a line of people waiting to buy something (it's never clear what, and they themselves do not know), the line so long, so complex, that they, too, begin to live in it.

We've been here before. The cars standing in endless lines on the crowded Moscow streets: they resemble nothing so much as the people who used to wait in endless lines outside the Moscow stores for Polish coats, Czech shoes, and, famously, toilet paper. Now, more comfortably, they wait for the light. They are willing to endure all manner of humiliation to keep driving. Recently, my friend Lyonya, a corporate lawyer, was stopped by the police and accused of drunk driving, even though he hadn't had a drop of alcohol in fifteen years. Another time, Lyonya found his car trapped in a courtyard where he'd parked, because its residents had put up a gate while he was gone; unable to find anyone to ask about it, Lyonya finally dismantled the gate with some tools he always keeps in his car.

Yet he continues to drive, and, driving with him in his long black Mercedes CL ("Comfort Leicht"), you can see why. The car is so intelligent, so solicitous, that it will not let you slam the doors entirely closed, for fear that you'll hurt your fingers. It waits a little, letting you get to safety, and only then does it shut the door. You get a different perspective on things from Lyonya's Mercedes. Outside, the city is filthy, muddy, filled with exhaust; the Mercedes rides smoothly, swaddling you in leather. The city is violent and chaotic and antidemocratic; in the Mercedes, you can listen to the liberals arguing, subtly, intelligently, on the last redoubt of independent Russian mass media, Ekho Moskvy. In Moscow, there are far worse places to be trapped.

Over the past few years, Moscow drivers have become one of the city's most active social groups, organizing to eliminate the corrupt meter maids and lobbying for more roads. After the death of the two doctors in the collision with the Lukoil Mercedes, a group of drivers began attaching blue sandbox buckets to the roofs of their cars, in imitation of sirens, as a protest against the abuse of the siren by the city's bankers and oil executives. It's been one of the most successful civic actions in years. And it makes sense: "car owner" is the one social category that has actually been created in the past twenty years, as opposed to all the social categories that have been destroyed. Perhaps this is the emergence, finally, of a propertied, stakeholding—and frustrated, selfish, neurotic—middle class.

On the morning of the subway bombings in Moscow, the city was thrown into disarray; only the emergency services managed to get anywhere. Photographs of the subway platform taken just minutes after the explosion showed medics among the debris, crouching over the wounded. When Blinkin, writing on an anti-Kremlin website, praised the emergency response, the commenters turned on him. "I was also impressed by the speed," one said, raising the old oppositionist dogma about a Kremlin conspiracy. "It seems they knew in advance what was going to happen, and where."

I asked my friends at Yandex what the traffic was like that day. They answered in a detailed e-mail. "After the first explosion, at Lubyanka (7:56), traffic jams began to form gradually at the adjacent streets," they wrote. "After the second explosion (8:36), congestion continued to increase and remained at a high level until 11 o'clock. By contrast, on a regular weekday congestion reaches its peak at 9 A.M. and then begins to drain off."

The next two days were more congested than usual, as many people who usually took the metro decided to drive to work instead. But Moscow could not function this way forever. "By Thursday," the Yandex analysts concluded, "the city had returned to normal."

It was true. Before long, the papers were reporting that the sons of two Moscow bureaucrats had been involved in an altercation. The son of a city prefect was stuck in traffic in his Lexus; the son of a municipal notary officer was riding his bicycle, weaving through the traffic, when he accidentally nicked the Lexus. The son of the prefect got out of his car and pushed the notary's son (a poli-sci student) to the ground. Humiliated, the notary's son went off and found a baseball bat somewhere—whether at home or at a sporting goods store the reports hadn't yet determined—and returned to find the prefect's son *still stuck in traffic.* He began smashing the windows of the Lexus with the baseball bat. When the prefect's son got out of the car again, the notary's son hit him, too, breaking his hand. Moscow's leading tabloid, *LifeNews,* posted a photograph of the prefect's son sporting a cast. A nice-looking young man, he was wearing a pink T-shirt that said *"Dolce & Gabbana."*

TOM IRELAND

Famous

FROM *The Missouri Review*

ON THE NIGHT of November 26, 2008, two men walked into
Chhatrapati Shivaji Terminus in Mumbai, India, and started shooting and throwing grenades into the crowds of travelers "indiscrimi-
nately," as reported in the official Indian account of the attack. In a
railway station that accommodates 2 million passengers every day,
a place where one can hardly stand during peak hours without being swept into a river of people, they couldn't very well have missed.
In minutes the dead and dying lay throughout the concourse, their
limbs splayed in grotesque postures, and blood pooled on the station's concrete floor.

The younger of the two, twenty-one-year-old Mohammad Ajmal
Amir Kasab, a native of the Punjab region of Pakistan, became famous when pictures of him taken during and after the attack circulated in the media. Sebastian D'Souza, a photographer with the
Mumbai Mirror, was in the office that night when he heard gunfire
from the train station and ran across the street with a camera. He
ducked into a train standing at one of the platforms while the two
gunmen stalked the concourse, taking turns shooting and reload-
ing as they went.

"They were like angels of death," said D'Souza. "When they hit
someone they didn't even look back. They were so sure."

To get a better angle, D'Souza moved across the platform into
another waiting train and, trying to keep his hands from shaking,
took a few frames with a telephoto lens as the two men crossed his
line of vision. They probably saw him taking pictures, he said, but
"didn't seem to care," or else they saw him as an opportunity to
gain some cheap celebrity as young jihadists. People who never

would have paid any attention to them otherwise would come to know and say their names.

In D'Souza's photograph, Ajmal Kasab is seen in profile walking through the station, an AK-47 assault rifle held in his right hand, a duffel slung over his left shoulder—everything he needed to stay alive and keep on fighting "to the last breath," as he characterized his mission later under questioning. His commanders in Pakistan had ordered him and the other nine to kill as many people as they could before being killed themselves. Although escape routes had been entered into a GPS unit later recovered by police, escape was not an acceptable outcome according to the terms of his contract, and capture was unthinkable.

The young man in the photograph is more attractive than he has any right to be: the boyish bangs, the proud chin, the jaunty stride, the expression intensely alert but not discernibly fearful or malicious. His evident excitement might be that of an exchange student on his own in a foreign country for the first time—in fact it was the first time he had left his native country—carrying everything he needs for a year abroad (replace the Kalashnikov with a cricket bat and you get an entirely different picture). He wears running shoes, gray cargo pants, a dark blue Versace T-shirt. There's a waterproof watch on his left wrist, and on his right wrist, the hand holding the rifle, he wears a red and yellow *mauli*, the yarn bracelet offered at Hindu temples in exchange for alms, meant to keep the wearer safe from harm.

At least three other photographs of Kasab circulated in the media soon after the attacks, though none as widely as D'Souza's—two stills from closed-circuit television cameras and one of Kasab in the hospital after he was captured; he was the only one of the ten terrorists who survived battles with police and security forces. One of the television images, very unlike D'Souza's photo, is of a young man with an expression of exaggerated malice, as if meant to conform to a popular idea of how a terrorist might look in the act of killing—a comic-book villain.

Then there was the photo taken in the hospital, in which Kasab is lying down, looking up at the camera. His face is scabby and bloated. He's too tired to summon any large emotion at this point, and his face betrays only weak contempt for the person holding the camera. It's the face of a man who knows he's going to hang.

*

I didn't yet know the name Ajmal Kasab when, two nights after the massacre in the railway station, I arrived in Mumbai for a month's vacation on the west coast of India. Neither I nor my partner, Anne, had ever visited India before, and we were anxious about finding our way in an unfamiliar city, still under armed attack when we landed. Gunmen of unknown affiliation had gone on a rampage, shooting civilians in a railway station, a movie theater, a restaurant, a Jewish center, and two luxury hotels in the Mumbai tourist district, the part of town where we would be staying for a few days before taking a train from that station en route to the rest of our vacation. Before leaving home I'd seen Internet photos of Indian security forces huddled behind emergency vehicles near the Gateway of India on the Mumbai waterfront, the shattered window glass at the Leopold Café, the dead bodies in the railway station. But it would be another month, after we left India safely behind, before I saw pictures of the one surviving terrorist and learned his name.

By the time we woke in Mumbai on the morning of November 29, all of the terrorists except Ajmal Kasab had been killed. Police were in the process of "sanitising" the Taj Mahal Palace — presumably, removing the dead from the building. A television camera had recorded the body of one terrorist being dumped from a ground-floor window at the Taj, and in the ancient tradition of desecrating the body of one's enemy, local channels showed the charred corpse falling from the window again and again.

There wasn't much else to see on TV: the soot-stained hotel façade, where fires set by the gunmen had burned and been put out; past-tense video of commando forces known as the Black Cats roping down from a helicopter to the roof of Nariman House, the Jewish center where a Brooklyn rabbi and his wife had been tortured and executed. We went for breakfast at a dosa joint on the corner and agreed, at least for one day, to keep away from the Gateway of India and the crowds that were sure to gather at the Taj.

After breakfast we looked quickly at a map and walked south in the direction of the Prince of Wales Museum, but it was closed because of the emergency. With no other destination in mind, we kept walking south and in fifteen minutes found ourselves staring at the damaged Taj Mahal Palace along with thousands of Indians who lined the seawall and strolled among the parked emergency vehicles.

We were doing the one thing we had agreed not to do, but faced

with the spectacle, we found it impossible not to look. Tired fire-
fighters sat on top of their fire truck, smoking, drinking Cokes,
checking out the crowds of sightseers. Black Cats in their commando getups stared sleepily at us through the steel-grill windows
of buses. There was grief but also a spirit of subdued celebration
among many of the onlookers: our guys had killed all but one of
their guys, and he would die, too.

One group of angry men stood out from the rest, bearing signs
and flags and crying out together, presumably for vengeance. We
kept well away from them and, stepping over exhausted fire hoses
and tangled television cables, walked back to the hotel, stopping
on the way to look at kurtas in Fabindia, a clothing store popular
with tourists.

Three policemen were camped in the corridor outside our room
at the Residency Hotel the next morning when I went out to get a
paper. The Residency was at the low end of hotels in the tourist
district, hardly the sort of place to be targeted by terrorists. Nevertheless, we had been placed under armed protection. Squeezed
together at the head of the stairwell, the three men stood up
quickly and wished me good morning. For a moment I thought
they were going to salute.

We walked north that day, a route that took us past Chhatrapati
Shivaji Terminus, and stepped inside to look at the scene of the
massacre. Most people who live in Mumbai still call it VT, for Victoria Terminus, but during the 1990s, under pressure from a radical
Hindu group, Shiv Sena, the station was renamed after Chhatrapati Shivaji Maharaj, the Marathi hero who established an independent state in western India in the seventeenth century. Shivaji is
famous in India for the same kind of bold guerrilla tactics that allowed the Mumbai terrorists to enter Indian territorial waters and
Mumbai harbor without being apprehended. A devout Hindu (his
war cry was "Hail, Lord Shiva!"), he was succeeded by Mohandas
Gandhi in his advocacy of an independent, secular Indian state in
which Hindus and Muslims could live peaceably together.

We'd first seen the station from the taxi the night we arrived
in Mumbai—the monstrous Victorian Gothic stone façade, like
something conceived in special effects, absurdly bathed in amber
floodlight at two in the morning. Outside it was extravagant and

dingy, the bas-reliefs of dignitaries and wildlife, British lion and Indian tiger, colonized with mold. Inside it was merely dingy. Even on a Sunday the place was mobbed. Railway police and a few National Security Guards were scattered near the entrances, but nobody was checking luggage. Nobody asked to see my passport.

Victoria has been compared to St. Pancras Station in London, the nineteenth-century "cathedral" of railway stations, which predated it by twenty years: a European building in every respect except the ground it was built on. Its choice as one of the targets of the attacks must have been determined by more than the most practical consideration — its density of human life. A monument both to India's colonial subjugation and to its independence, Victoria celebrates the country's initiation into the echelon of progressive, industrialized nations and the birth of its middle class. By including it in the list of targets, those who planned the VT attack evidently meant to add ideological insult to physical injury.

It wouldn't have done to stand there very long among the hurrying passengers and look up into the station's cathedral heights, as I would have liked. It would have been even less appropriate to look down and search for traces of blood on the floor, although it did occur to me to do just that.

There was a good deal of confusion surrounding Kasab's "identity," as his captors put it, immediately after the attacks. Lashkar-e-Taiba, the Pakistani group that has been accused of planning and carrying out the operation, gave its recruits false names while they were in training and changed those names on a regular basis. The ten eventually chosen for the assault trained for months, first together, finally in pairs, but they didn't learn each other's real names until after they had boarded the boat in Karachi on their way to Mumbai to carry out their mission.

Kasab means "butcher" in Urdu. The name of one's profession or caste is commonly used as a surname in India (Gandhi, for example, means "grocer"), and Kasab's captors may have taken his caste name for his family name. It was reported that he spoke English, then not, then that in addition to his native Punjabi he knew a few words of a Hindi dialect. In the absence of any more reliable information, his interrogators may have decided that "Butcher" was an appropriate label.

Whatever his name, Kasab was evidently nobody, one of thousands of poorly educated, unemployed young men who are continually being recruited by militant groups like Lashkar. In the days immediately following the attacks, there was speculation that he and the others represented a new class of terrorists—young, educated, middle-class Muslims acting out of political or religious conviction, angered by the persecution of Muslim populations in India, Kashmir, Palestine, Iraq, Afghanistan, Chechnya, Indonesia, and elsewhere. Such speculation was based largely on how the terrorists were dressed and on statements by eyewitnesses that they seemed well-off. But Kasab's confession to Indian police indicated that his family was poor, that he had gone to a Pakistani government primary school for only four years before dropping out to find work, and that he was largely ignorant of political causes or religious beliefs. Asked to define jihad during questioning, he said, "It means killing and being killed and becoming famous."

Kasab's native village, Faridkot, didn't have much to offer. His father sold *dahi wada* (fried dal paste with yogurt) from a street cart. The family often went hungry. Ajmal lived with his brother, Afzal, in Lahore and occasionally found work as a laborer. Between jobs he went home. Tired of dressing like a villager, on one such visit he argued with his father, who refused when Ajmal asked him for money to buy clothes.

Back in Lahore, he stayed at a home for runaways until going to work for a "decorator" for 120 rupees (about $2.50) a day in the town of Jhelum, a job he hated. Later he was raised to 200 rupees, but it wasn't enough to live on, so he teamed up with an older boy, Muzaffar Khan, and started robbing houses. Hoping to make better money, the two moved to Rawalpindi, rented an apartment, and began casing the city's wealthy houses.

In the version of his story that Kasab told police right after he was arrested, he and Khan decided that to succeed as professional thieves, they had to have guns. While searching for them in the bazaar during the festival of Bakrid (from the Urdu *bakr,* "goat"), the Festival of Sacrifice, they found a Lashkar-e-Taiba field office and made inquiries. Realizing that even if they managed to buy some guns, they wouldn't know how to use them, they followed directions to another Lashkar office. When the man who answered the door asked what they wanted, they said, "Jihad."

Traditional Muslims butcher a goat during Bakrid to commemorate Ibrahim's faithful offering of Ismail, his only son, as a blood sacrifice to God and God's compassionate answer, a butchered goat in Ismail's place. At the time he signed up with Lashkar, Kasab was more interested in advancing his career as a petty thief than in sacrificing himself to a cause that he wouldn't have adopted on principle. In so doing he joined the ranks of young men worldwide who, without anything resembling a livelihood, leave their village to find work in the city. Unemployed, faced with a choice between becoming a thief or a soldier, he chose what must have seemed the easier way and joined the mercenaries. At least he had enough to eat in his new job, decent clothes to wear, the identity that goes along with having an institutional sponsor, and, best of all, the opportunity to play with guns.

For six and a half months he was sent to one camp after another and put through a series of courses, first in physical exercise and weaponry—AK-47, SKS, Uzi, pistol, revolver, hand grenades, rocket launchers, mortars, bombs—later in swimming, marine navigation, the rudiments of urban warfare, and the workings of Indian security forces. Kasab did well and earned the approval of his handlers, who noted that he was a good shot. He and Ismail Khan were eventually assigned to the "VTS team"—Victoria Terminus station—and isolated from the other four teams in the final weeks of training.

They studied a map of Mumbai on Google Earth, learned how to get from Azad Maidan on the city waterfront to Victoria Terminus, and watched a video of commuters during rush hour at the station, morning and night, when the number of people in the station would be highest. After killing as many as possible, they were supposed to kidnap some others, take them to the roof of a nearby building, contact the local media by cell phone, and make demands in exchange for their release.

A little more than halfway through this period of training, Kasab was permitted to visit his parents for a month in Faridkot before the final and most intense stage of preparation for the attack on Mumbai—the first and only time he went home after the falling-out with his father. He still had no idea what he was being trained for, exactly, and even if he had been inclined to betray Lashkar, he probably couldn't have told his family where and when the attack was going to take place. They must have been curious to know what he'd been doing, why he seemed so fit and well fed, who his friends were, where he'd come by the new shoes he was wearing. One can only guess the extent to which he was able to confide in them before leaving home for good.

The official Indian dossier on the attacks is a brief constabulary account of the terrorists' journey from Pakistan by sea; their hijacking of an Indian fishing vessel; the murder of its crew and, later, after he had piloted them to their destination, its captain; their landing in an inflatable dinghy; and the various assignments undertaken by the five pairs of terrorists. Appended to the dossier is a list of foreigners killed in the attacks (the names of Indian citizens who died are not given) and a list of supplies the terrorists left behind on the hijacked boat, with photographs, presented as evidence that the men were in fact Pakistani nationals: "Made in Pakistan milk powder packets (Nestlé) . . . Shaving cream—Touchme, Made in Pakistan . . . Pakistan made pickle." Nothing about the pickle conclusively identified it as Pakistani, but the weight of the other evidence was strongly against it.

Ajmal Kasab and Ismail Khan took a taxi from the waterfront to Chhatrapati Shivaji Terminus. The dossier briefly tells how, when "challenged" by police in the station during their shooting spree, the two retreated to the vicinity of Cama Hospital, planning to gather hostages and herd them into some sort of stronghold. At this point their plan jumped the tracks. Confronted by police near the hospital, they shot and killed three officers, took their car, and drove toward the waterfront. There they hijacked another car and drove west along Marine Drive until they were stopped at a police barricade near Chowpatti Beach.

According to some accounts, Kasab sustained a minor wound during the showdown on Marine Drive, in which Tukaram Ombale, a junior police officer armed only with a *lathi* (metal-tipped cane), managed to grab Kasab's weapon long enough for others to subdue him. Ombale died later of bullet wounds. Civilian onlookers beat Kasab unconscious before he was taken to a hospital where, exhausted and dehydrated, he asked for a saline injection—possibly a first-aid technique he'd learned during his training.

At first he told his captors that he didn't want to die. Then he begged them to kill him, if not for his own sake—to escape the ordeals of imprisonment, trial, and execution that certainly awaited him—then for the sake of his family in Pakistan. His actions would not go down well with Lashkar-e-Taiba. Besides his failure to carry out his orders and die fighting, he gave detailed information, including names, to Indian authorities, and at one point, demonstrating how unmotivated he was by anything like conscientious belief, he offered to do for India what he'd done for Lashkar. What the photographer D'Souza had observed in the train station the night of the attack—that the two killers seemed "so sure" of themselves—had disguised Kasab's fundamental neediness, ignorance, confusion, and fear.

Anne and I took a taxi to Chowpatti on our third day in Mumbai, weeks before I learned of the gun battle that had taken place there, ending in Khan's death and Kasab's arrest. Chowpatti Beach was mostly empty that morning, at least by Indian standards. Girls in saris stood knee-deep in the water, wringing out their skirts. A boy was trying to fly a kite in a fitful breeze. Somebody had drawn a heart with a love message in the sand.

We crossed a footbridge over Marine Drive, the street where Khan and Kasab had run into the police barricade, and asked directions to Mohandas Gandhi's former residence in Mumbai, now a museum called Mani Bhavan. A simple two-story wood-frame building on a shady street, it might be put on exhibit in a museum of museums. The books in the downstairs library, cloistered in their glass-doored cabinets, seemed too precious to read, and a churchlike hush pervaded the place. The brittle, water-stained photographs; the caption informing us that Gandhi rode a bicycle to the temple, shaved without a mirror, and scavenged in the street; the sophisticated naiveté of his letter to Hitler, calling him "friend" (he addressed Roosevelt the same way) and urging him to please reconsider the destruction of Europe; Gandhi's sandals, drinking cup, spindle, and fountain pen enshrined in a case on the wall— all possessed an eerie, sanctimonious aura. An Indian man later told us that every city in India has its own collection of the Mahatma's domestic tools, just as in every religion the bones of saints proliferate over time.

Upstairs we looked at miniature three-dimensional tableaux of significant events in Gandhi's life, among them a doll-sized Gandhi and his followers gathering salt on the shore of the Arabian Sea in 1933 to protest the British salt tax, the original target of his *satya-graha* (truth-force) campaign. The "force" of that philosophy helped free India from foreign domination, but it didn't prevent the violence that took place before and after Partition. Both Gandhi, the martial pacifist, and Chhatrapati Shivaji, the martial conqueror, are loved, praised, and extravagantly idealized throughout India, though these days the Gandhian philosophy tends to be seen as a venerable but irrelevant remnant of the past, worthy in principle but not in practice, and it's the man of violent means whose name is more commonly invoked by public institutions like Chhatrapati Shivaji Terminus.

Famous Gandhi quotations had been framed and hung throughout the house. "The cry of blood for blood is barbarous," he said during the riots of 1946–47, when Hindus and Muslims slaughtered each other en masse leading up to and following the creation of a separate Muslim state, Pakistan. We'd heard that cry at the demonstration outside the Taj Mahal Palace the day we arrived in Mumbai, and while those who cried for blood cried the loudest, other Indians, among them the novelist Amitav Ghosh, were calling for restraint. What the terrorists mainly hoped to achieve by the attacks, he pointed out in the *Hindustan Times,* was the panic-stricken response of the Indian government—the sort of response that the government of the United States had been gulled into after 9/11.

The upstairs room that Gandhi stayed in at Mani Bhavan is much as it was when he stayed in Mumbai. Central to its few deliberately simple furnishings is a spinning wheel, the symbol of Indian independence. That work as hard and monotonous as spinning came to represent freedom from oppression remains one of the compelling paradoxes of the Gandhi legend. It wasn't machinery itself he objected to, he said, but the "craze" for it. Another Gandhian precept, the idea that one can gain real power through nonviolent means, seems equally dated in an age of terrorism.

I started following Ajmal Kasab's story after returning from India, on the basis of what others wrote about him and his translated statements, first to the police, later to the trial judge. The cunning, spectacular nature of the attacks guaranteed wide and detailed news coverage—a side effect of terrorism that its architects depend on to advertise their cause. These days such attacks are more like publicity stunts than acts of war, and it may have been the lure of publicity, as much as needing a job or righteous hatred of the infidels, that convinced Kasab to enlist. To someone faced with the prospect of becoming a beggar or a thief, the alternative of worldly fame and a glorious martyrdom might look like a much better deal.

Back home I studied the photo of the trigger-happy kid from provincial Pakistan striding through the railway station and wondered what need was great enough, or what principle important enough, to make him want to kill innocent people. For all the effort and expense devoted on the official level to protecting us from terrorists in recent years, relatively little has gone toward understanding what motivates them. It's not just that we can't know but that we don't want to know. To do so is to risk seeing ourselves less than favorably, for example, as monopolists of wealth, the people living in the big house behind a locked gate in Rawalpindi that Kasab and Muzaffar Khan dreamed of pillaging: another class of untouchables at the opposite end of the social scale.

Months after his arrest, a video of Kasab's interrogation in the hospital was published on the Internet with a captioned translation. There's a bandage on his neck, and he's obviously in pain. When they asked him why he'd done it, he said that his father had first encouraged him to seek work with the mujahideen: "[My father] said, 'These people make loads of money, and so will you. You don't have to do anything difficult. We'll have money; we won't be poor anymore. Your brothers and sisters can get married. Look at these guys living the good life. You can be like them.'"

Asked how much money they'd given him and if it had been placed in an account, he said, "There's no account. They gave it to my dad." Some terrorist organizations are known to pay the families of volunteers for suicide missions or those, like Mumbai, in which the recruits are sworn to die fighting. But in Kasab's case, it's not clear who paid what to whom. Shortly after he was imprisoned, before Pakistani officials cut his family off from further contacts with the press, a reporter tracked down Ajmal's father in Faridkot and asked him if he had received or been promised money in exchange for his son's participation. He replied, "I don't sell my children."

Kasab first appeared before a judge without leaving his cell, on closed-circuit TV, to minimize the chances of a Jack Ruby–style execution. A "bomb-proof, chemical-proof" corridor was built especially for him so that he can walk safely between his cell and the judge's chamber. When not in court, he speaks to no one and has nothing to do in his fetid cell but read the Koran, a book that it had never occurred to him to read before becoming a terrorist. At the start of the legal proceedings he asked for a Pakistani lawyer and was denied. His first lawyer was attacked in her home by rock-throwing Hindu activists. When she was replaced because of a conflict of interest (she was also representing the family of one of the people killed in the attacks), the court assigned Abbas Kasmi as Kasab's defense lawyer.

Kasmi doesn't go anywhere without bodyguards. The social club he belonged to has blackballed him. He believes in the righteousness of the Indian judicial system, saying, "We want to prove to the world that we are a civilized nation and we give a fair trial even to a so-called terrorist." When he complained that Kasab's cell had "no fresh air or ray of light" and relayed his client's request for some perfume to mask the stink, the press made a deafening mockery of it.

Kasab's initial confession to police, in the hospital, was ruled inadmissible during the trial because it had been given under duress. His lawyer entered a plea of innocent for him, and India was preparing itself for months of contentious legal proceedings when Kasab surprised everyone, his lawyer included, by standing up and saying in Hindi that he was not, in fact, innocent. He just wanted to be sentenced and have the trial end. The last I heard, he wasn't so sure.

Fourteen months after the attacks, Indian and foreign news media continue to camp out at Arthur Road Jail, Mumbai's oldest and by every account its worst prison, where Kasab is being held in solitary confinement during his trial. For all the hatred directed at him by the Indian public—most of whom want to see him executed as quickly as possible both for the sake of justice and to keep from wasting any more of the taxpayers' money—he's also become an object of widespread fascination. The media still hang on his every word, and in his new career as a spokesperson for terrorism he has come as close to living "the good life" as he ever will.

Thus far Ajmal Kasab has accomplished two of the three goals he named in his schoolboy definition of jihad: he killed, and he became famous. He has yet to achieve the third goal — "being killed" — thereby completing, however inadequately, the terms of his contract with Lashkar. His imprisonment and trial have already cost the Indian people much greater effort and expense than the execution of an ordinary murderer, but it might be worth all the trouble. The trial of one man accused of "making war on India" is a far cry from what the designers of those attacks may have hoped for: another round of warfare between India and Pakistan. It has diverted national attention from Pakistan to a single, powerless Pakistani citizen, who has achieved greater fame as the surrogate object of national vengeance than he ever hoped for.

"I do not want punishment from God," he told the judge. As if he had any choice in the matter. "Whatever I have done in this world I should get punished for it by this world itself."

The guilty man betrays his innocence.

VERLYN KLINKENBORG

The Vanishing Point

FROM *The New York Times Magazine*

AUSTRALIANS CALL THE NORTHERNMOST CHUNK of their continent the "Top End," a breezy moniker, as though Australia were a boiled egg sitting upright in an eggcup waiting to be cracked open with a silver spoon. Just how much Top End there is is open to debate, the kind that gets worried out with maps drawn in the dust. While I was there last September, I saw dust maps that gave the Top End most of Australia north of the Tropic of Capricorn — about a third of the continent. Others included only Cape York and the rather windswept-looking peninsula that includes the roistering town of Darwin, the capital city of the Northern Territory.

The Top End I visited was vastly narrower — the river flats and hill country just inland from Van Diemen Gulf. But it was still an imponderable slice of terrain, long ridges of sandstone giving way to the floodplains that edge Kakadu National Park, a UNESCO World Heritage site and the largest park in Australia — bigger than Connecticut and Delaware combined. To Australians, Kakadu and the country around it feels like an ancestral reservoir, a cultural repository with Aboriginal roots and an oasis of native biodiversity. Here, the sandstone endures, the monsoon floods come and go, and then the fires follow — erratic and regenerative in the early part of the dry season, unforgiving in the later part. But this oasis is going dry almost unnoticed.

This is a landscape that seems to ask, "Why have you come here?" There's no hostility in the question, only the indifference native to a continent of punitive, natural harshness. Every traveler will have a different answer. Mine was mud, and also, more broadly, the difference between nature as a norm and nature as merely what is, whether it should be or not. Here, the grandeur of nature is well disguised by the impenetrable thicket of life itself.

For weeks after visiting Australia, I found myself thinking about mud: the living mud on the banks of Sampan Creek, which insinuates itself into Van Diemen Gulf, not far from Bamurru Plains, a safari-style eco-lodge that opened here a few years ago. When the wicked tide falls on the creek's lower reaches, it leaves behind long, sloping shelves of ooze. In December, the monsoon comes, and when it does, Sampan Creek and all its fellow creeks and rivers break their bounds and spread their mud — an originating mud — out over the coastal plains. It daubs the fur of Agile wallabies grazing on the floodplains. The water buffalo seem compounded of it. The magpie geese glory in it by the tens of thousands. I saw a similar mud in the billabongs at Kakadu and beneath the freshwater mangroves at Wongalara, a former cattle station southeast of Kakadu that has been converted into a nature sanctuary by the Australian Wildlife Conservancy.

On Sampan Creek, canoe-length saltwater crocodiles come creasing down the banks, slicking their tiled bellies across the mud. They slip into the silted current, eyes like dark and watchful bubbles. You may be on dry ground, termite plinths all around you, the astringent scent of crushed tea tree leaves in the air, but a part of your mind will still be thinking of those estuarine eyes not quite looking at you, yet not quite minding their own business either.

One afternoon, I saw four young Australian men fishing in a Kakadu billabong. They were standing in a small pram with plenty of beer. Meanwhile, around the corner, a line of crocodiles waited their turn at the carcass of a water buffalo, which lay half in the water, its central cavity opened, its wet, white ribs showing. The crocodile at work seemed almost drugged by the turbid scent of decomposition. At long intervals, it drove itself up onto the ribcage, rolling sideways, then using its weight to tear free a mass of rotting flesh. It showed a white stump where its left foot had been, lost in some recent crocodilian controversy — the very antithesis of Captain Hook.

Throughout the Top End, I sensed an incoherence, an unresolved moral burden in the landscape. Take Kakadu National Park. It is a very recent creation, first proposed in the mid-1960s but not confirmed until more than a decade later. It is mostly escarpment country, gouged wilderness, a landscape of rock and time. And yet in some sense Australia has not yet decided what Kakadu should be —a reminder of just how new the conservation ethic is here and how hard it is to create coherent preservation schemes in a place where time collides the way it does down under. In some ways, Kakadu is an experiment in trying to resolve historical tensions rather than a place of natural conservation.

For one thing, Kakadu is one of the few truly national parks in the country—administered by federal, not state, authority, for the simple reason that it sits on Aboriginal land. One of the great sticking points in the park's recent history is whether Australians should pay an entrance fee. At present, the answer is best summed up by the empty site of the former east entrance station, expensively built and expensively bulldozed when fees were rescinded in 2004. The fees have just been reinstated.

Then, too, there is the critical shared management of Kakadu with its traditional owners, many of whom, mostly Aboriginal Bininj/Mungguy, still live within the park. They're conservators of the land and their traditions within it, visible in its rock art and its sacred sites, but the Aborigines hunt and fish throughout the park practically at will. They also harbor nonnative animals like buffalo and, notoriously, a herd of shorthorn cattle visible in the grasslands around Yellow Water, for reasons that are both spiritual and carnivorous.

The park's Aboriginal heritage is also overlaid with the more recent history of white holdings within its boundaries. The strangest and most significant is the Ranger uranium mine, which is still being worked within the park's borders. And then there is Jabiru—a town established to service the Ranger mine. The streets are quiet, utterly domestic in feel. Apart from the vegetation, and the flying foxes hanging dormant in a tree at midday above the elementary school, Jabiru could be a suburb of Dallas.

Like much of Australia, the Top End demonstrates that nature favors invasive species over native ones, at least in the short term. They proliferate. They burgeon. But what matters isn't only what invasive species do to the balance of life in the wild. What matters too is what they do to our minds, since that's where the difference between native and invasive is finally assessed.

In their proper element, for instance, cane toads are no more loathsome than any other toad, though they are poisonous. On the floodplains east of Darwin, they will be clustering near the oil lamps by night, bobbing for insects and getting underfoot. Or they'll be lying tire-flattened on the Arnhem Highway (the east-west road between Darwin and Kakadu) or splayed out, on their backs in a dusty paddock somewhere, their digestible meaty bits eaten away by the few birds that have already somehow learned how to eat them without fatality. For cane toads are relatively new to Australia, which is not their proper element.

Cane toads explain the wistfulness you hear among some Australians when they talk about their roadkill. "You used to see a lot of pythons dead on the highway," said Sab Lord, a legendary bush guide, as we drove one day across the Top End toward Darwin. The toads have spread outward across the country from Queensland cane fields, where they were introduced to help control beetles, and they have decimated the reptiles and birds that have eaten them. As a result, the roadkill census—which is how most people see most wildlife—reveals fewer and fewer native reptiles and more and more cane toads, which hark back to the Americas. The first cane toad arrived in Darwin only recently, and believe me, it was not welcomed.

I didn't fly halfway round the world from New York to see cane toads. But then that's the point of flying halfway round the world —to see what you didn't expect to see.

I didn't expect to see swamp buffalo in the Top End, either, and yet there they were, some domesticated and bucolic, some feral and simply rancid with anger, but all descended from the few Indonesian buffalo brought by the British to the Cobourg Peninsula in the 1820s. In the 1980s and 1990s, the government tried to shoot out the buffalo, to control disease. But the buffalo are making their way back, crossing out of the Aboriginal reserves, where they were never shot out, into Kakadu and the floodplains north of it. There, on places like Swim Creek Station, where Bamurru Plains is sited, the buffalo are a cash crop, gathered by airboats and helicopters in February during the monsoon and shipped back to Southeast Asia for human consumption.

One night, I walked back to my tent-cabin from the lodge at Bamurru Plains through the corkscrew pandanus palms. The full moon was high, cane toads were clustering in the dim glow, and the wallabies were moving through camp nearly silently. The water buffalo out on the floodplain had receded from view—drifting at sunset for the night into the woods, just up the trail from me. From outside, the inward-sloping walls of the tent-cabin looked opaque. But when I stepped inside and doused the lights, the sheer canvas seemed to vanish, and I was left with only the faintest scrim between me and the outer world, which lay in silhouette under the moon.

Out there was a realm of exceeding flatness, where salt water and fresh water are fighting over the land. Each has its season. Fresh water has the monsoon, when rain drowns the country. Across the Top End, Aussies lead visitors to high spots, extend their arms, and say, like so many Noahs, "All this will be under water during the wet"—the local name for the monsoon. Salt water owns the rest of the year, and it's always seeking to work its way inland, always trying to claim another portion of solid earth. As the planet warms and the oceans rise, this coastal fringe will be one of the drowned lands.

But for now there's still a temporary truce between salt water and fresh. One sign of it is the chenier just beyond the lodge at Bamurru Plains. A chenier—the name is Louisiana French—is a historic, hard-packed ridge of sand and shell rubble laid down by the sea. At Bamurru, it looks like a slightly raised roadbed, a foot-high levee. During the wet, water fills the floodplains and advances right up to the chenier, where the guides park their airboats. You'd be tempted to say that the coastline, some three miles to the north, had wandered inland. But the floodwater is fresh—runoff from the rugged sandstone escarpment farther inland, which sheds water like oilskin. And in this harsh but delicate landscape, where the overriding ecological concern is the balance between salt water and fresh water, the buffalo trails act as unwanted capillaries, breaking through the all but indiscernible high ground and allowing salt water to infiltrate the swamps.

I'd spent the morning on an airboat with a Scottish guide named Kat, flat-bottoming our way into the paperbark swamps. It wasn't merely the mud that seemed primeval. It was also the abundance

of life—the jabirus stalking the open shallows and the
chatter of magpie geese. Ducks rose in whistling clouds, and from
the tops of the paperbarks, sea eagles watched us, drifting among
the shadows. So did the crocodiles disguised as floating swamp
scum.

This was nearly the end of the dry season, and the shrinking
floodwaters had concentrated the flocks and extended the grassland, where buffalo and horses grazed in the distance. And because
large mammals are endemic in the American imagination of nature—in my imagination, that is—it was hard to perceive them as
historically "unnatural." There they were, after all, their presence
as undeniable as that of the wallabies and striated herons.

But the horses are wild, the feral relics of white men who came
to this district for the buffalo shooting in the late nineteenth century. The horses—"brumbies," in Australian—stand hock-deep in
water and develop swamp cancer: tumorlike, pustulant growths on
their legs and bellies and noses. This is the northern edge of a
continent-wide herd of feral horses and donkeys—about 300,000
horses and more than 5 million donkeys nationwide.

At Wongalara we flew low over the brush, stirring a small herd of
horses and donkeys. They loped ahead of our helicopter, casting
scornful glances in our direction. The true work of restoration
can't begin until these animals are gone.

At Wongalara, too, I watched a pitfall trap being set for small,
nocturnal marsupials—which is mostly what the Top End has for
native mammals. The trap is a long wall of toughened rubber belt-
ing. Mammals run into the wall and scurry down its length, only
to fall into a plastic bucket set into the ground. In the morning,
they're weighed, counted, and released. But scientists are finding
almost nothing in the traps anymore. The marsupials are ideal prey
for feral cats, millions of them, which are also devastating small
reptiles and ground-nesting birds. There are now indications of a
full-blown population crash.

Wherever I went, I felt I was looking at a hidden landscape. What
I needed most were guides to what could not be seen, to what was
invisible. I don't mean the Aboriginal spirits inscribed in the rock
of Kakadu itself. I mean the species that had gone or were going
missing. As the days passed, I found myself becoming more and
more a tourist of the vanished and the vanishing.

Saltwater crocodiles have rebounded since hunting was banned in 1971, and they now pervade nearly every body of water in the Top End. But for many other species, time in the Top End is now over. What makes it all the harder is this: the species becoming invisible through extinction were largely invisible to begin with.

Perhaps it would be easier just to take the Top End at face value: the uranium mine, the cankered horses, the missing mammals, the plague of toads. Perhaps it would be easier just to give in to the "naturalness"—to stand, as I did, one day, on a sandstone ridge with Sab Lord and look out over a beautiful grassland enclosed by rugged hills. Out on the plain, a herd of horses grazed beside a copse that might almost have been aspen. It looked more than natural. It looked like a pictorial vision of natural completeness, or would have if we'd been in New Mexico. But as we walked down the hill, Sab and I saw a small monitor—a type of native lizard—peering out of the stony shade. "That's the first one of those I've seen this year," Sab said, and there we were, back in the extinction we had never left.

ARIEL LEVY

Reservations

FROM *The New Yorker*

DO YOU LIKE SAND, quaintness, twenty-eight-dollar salads, parties under white tents, investment bankers, hip-hop stars, Barbara Walters, locally grown produce, DJ Samantha Ronson, and lovely tablescapes? Then Southampton is the place for you: a land of natural splendor and immodest indulgence. A Victorian cottage on Hill Street—nowhere near the beach—rents for $100,000 a summer. (The website advertising it says that it's "perfect for your staff or overflow guests.") A spacious place with a water view will set you back about $500,000. The real cost, though, isn't money; it's time. To get to the Hamptons, just east of Manhattan, you must sit on the Long Island Expressway—the biggest parking lot in the world, as they say—for hour upon hour of overheated immobility.

And it's only going to get worse, because the Shinnecock Indian Nation, based on a reservation just minutes from the center of Southampton, intends to open a casino—or several—on Long Island. A set of architect's renderings, picturing a great room with burgundy banquettes and rows of shining slot machines, is already hanging on the walls of a trailer that the three tribal trustees use as an office. The Shinnecocks want a "high-class Monte Carlo–type" operation, a member of the tribe's Gaming Authority said, somewhere "near our homelands in Southampton," and perhaps another, less posh facility in Nassau County. "If the Mashantuckets can have the highest-grossing casino in the world in the woods of Connecticut," a former Shinnecock trustee named Fred Bess told me, referring to the Mashantucket Pequots' Foxwoods resort, "just think what we could do twenty miles out of Manhattan."

The Shinnecocks have said that they will build roads to funnel casino traffic away from the LIE, but there are many people in the Hamptons—people who don't have the money to commute from Manhattan by helicopter but who are still rich enough to be accustomed to getting what they want—who are aghast at the prospect of more cars on the road, not to mention the unquaintness of a casino marring their manicured pastoral. Such people "do not want their idyllic environment hurt by the added traffic, congestion, and noise of a gaming facility," Senator Charles Schumer wrote to the Bureau of Indian Affairs several years ago. The state senator Kenneth LaValle said that the tribe was "blatantly threatening the quality of life on the East End."

But the Shinnecocks might be forgiven for considering their own quality of life, which is markedly different from that in the rest of the Hamptons. The median household income on the reservation, according to the 2000 census, is $14,055 a year. Only about six hundred people live on the Shinnecocks' eight hundred acres, which have the feel of a scruffy summer camp. During the day, you can hear the zoom of boys speeding along the bumpy roads into the forest on four-wheel ATVs. At night, jacked-up cars with hip-hop on the stereo cruise toward Cuffee's Beach, where kids go to hang out and hook up and get high. The land is green and wild, and most of the houses have an unfinished wall covered in white Tyvek house wrap or a roof draped in blue tarp. Because the land is held in trust by the tribe, it is impossible to get a mortgage on the reservation, where banks cannot foreclose, so young couples often add a room onto a family home, and houses grow into haphazard hugeness.

People still hunt in the forest and send their kids down to the water to collect buckets of clams, activities that the Shinnecocks view as part of their ancestral tradition. The tribe is indigenous to the spot. Since there is no evidence to suggest a large-scale migration onto or off Long Island, historians believe that the native people that Europeans encountered when they arrived, in the 1600s, were the direct descendants of the aboriginal inhabitants of the land, ten thousand years ago.

In the mid-seventeenth century, though, the Shinnecock population dwindled, when new diseases came ashore with the colonists. It became necessary to intermarry, and the Shinnecocks often married African Americans. Today, most Shinnecocks look black but feel Indian—an identity quite distinct from both the crisp Yankee austerity of Old Southampton and the flamboyance of its more recent summer immigrants. The reservation is an insular place, and nearly everyone there is related. If a member of the tribe was in the hospital, Marguerite Smith, a tribal attorney, told me, "two hundred of us might show up and claim we are immediate family."

The question of whether to open a casino—which many Shinnecocks see as inconsistent with their traditional way of life—has created the kind of disagreement you might expect from people living in what is essentially an endless family reunion. In 1996, at a tribal meeting in the cinder-block Shinnecock Community Center, a discussion about the possibility of building a casino exploded into a brawl. By the time it was over, people were throwing chairs at one another and one trustee's brother had bitten a woman's finger to the bone.

"You just look at this place," Mike Smith, who has been the pastor of the Shinnecock Presbyterian Church for twenty-five years, said, one afternoon a few months ago. He was walking near his house, on Little Beach Road, which he shares with his wife, three grown children, and three grandchildren. "You go down to Cuffee's Beach, the DuPonts and the Vanderbilts and the Rockefellers are right there." Looking out on Shinnecock Bay, one sees the sandy spit of Meadow Lane, studded with grand old estates, just across the water. The Shinnecocks' parcel of forest and beachfront would be worth billions of dollars if it were ever for sale. "It makes no sense, no logical sense, for us to still be here in light of that," Smith said. "But here we sit."

Aside from three-card monte and Wall Street, Manhattan doesn't have much in the way of gambling. New Yorkers travel south to Atlantic City, or up to Connecticut, to gamble. Long Islanders take a high-speed ferry to New London or Bridgeport, near the Pequots' and the Mohegans' casinos, the two largest in North America.

This maritime movement of business from the East End of Long Island to Connecticut follows a pattern established centuries ago. The currency that sustained the fur trade between European settlers and native people was wampum—beads made from the purple interior of clamshells. The Shinnecocks produced wampum

from shells found on the banks of Long Island Sound and brought
it by canoe to Connecticut, where the Pequots, a more powerful
tribe, controlled the local economy. Only when the Pequots were
routed by the Europeans, in the Pequot War of 1637, did they begin trading with the settlers directly. A Shinnecock casino would, in
a sense, renew that direct exchange.

The Foxwoods and Mohegan Sun casinos are enormously successful, and their earnings have transformed the Indian nations
that operate them. Before the Mohegans started their business,
they were a scattered group of mostly impoverished individuals.
Now they are a model of organized prosperity. If you could use a
scholarship, health care, child care, or retirement benefits, it is far
better these days to be Mohegan than it is to be American.

Since the inception of the United States, Indian governments
have been recognized as sovereign entities, exempt from taxation.
But the Indian Gaming Regulatory Act of 1988 requires tribes
to negotiate compacts with states in which they operate casinos,
and those compacts almost always include a revenue-sharing agreement. Last year, the slot machines at Foxwoods and Mohegan Sun
were the Connecticut government's biggest private source of reve-
nue, yielding $362 million. Foxwoods has eleven thousand employ-
ees, making it one of the largest employers in the state.

Once a tribe is federally recognized, it is eligible to open a casino, and the promise of wealth attracts financial backers to pay for
the necessary builders, lawyers, and lobbyists. The Shinnecocks
have been pursuing recognition since 1978—nine years before
the Supreme Court ruled, in *California v. Cabazon Band of Mission
Indians*, that states have no authority to regulate gambling on reservations. In support of their claim, they have submitted more
than forty thousand pages of documentation substantiating their
history and lineage. Meanwhile, tribes across the country have
bloomed into thriving mini-nations, while the Shinnecocks, as
Lancelot Gumbs, a senior trustee, said, have remained "stuck in
the Stone Age."

This summer, after thirty-two years, the Bureau of Indian Affairs
declared that the Shinnecocks had met the seven criteria for federal acknowledgment, and that their petition had been provision-
ally approved; after a thirty-day waiting period, they would finally
have tribal status. One of the trustees, Gordell Wright, described a
celebratory mood: "We're going to be doing a lot of singing and

eating." But, a few days before the waiting period ended, a group calling itself the Connecticut Coalition for Gaming Jobs filed an objection with the Interior Board of Indian Appeals, arguing that "a new casino in Southern New York will mean job losses and higher taxes for Connecticut." The group's spokesman refused to disclose anything about its membership or its financing.

The Shinnecocks were shocked, but their financiers of the past seven years, Marian Ilitch and Michael Malik, were not. The two have started casinos with, among others, the Little River Band of Ottawas and the Los Coyotes Band of Cahuillas and Cupeños. "Every time we do this, some bogus front appears to delay the process," their spokesman, Tom Shields, told me. Both the Mohegans and the Pequots have denied any affiliation with the Connecticut Coalition for Gaming Jobs, but, Shields said, "it's obvious who benefits by having the Shinnecocks delayed."

Ilitch and Malik, for their part, have reportedly paid lobbyists more than $1 million to meet on the Shinnecocks' behalf with Governor David Paterson, Senator Kirsten Gillibrand, and Senator Charles Schumer's chief of staff; they paid another million to the Washington lobbying firm Wheat Government Relations. But their investment is negligible compared with the potential payoff. Ilitch owns a casino in Detroit that grosses $400 million a year. "In the twenty-two years we've been involved with Indian gaming, so far, knock on wood, we've not had anybody fail in the process," Malik said.

The Shinnecock reservation is bordered on the north by Montauk Highway, a two-lane strip that stretches west from the more glamorous parts of Southampton. During the past three decades, since the Shinnecocks began selling tax-free cigarettes, it has become crowded with businesses — Eagle Feather, Rain Drops, True Native — that have turned the edge of the reservation into a kind of theme park of Indianness and smoking. The largest of them, the Shinnecock Indian Outpost, has two totem poles in the parking area, and sells cigarettes, moccasins, and lobster rolls. There are also Navajo blankets, toy tomahawks made in Korea, and many varieties of dream catchers. Gumbs built the store on his mother's land allotment, and is regarded as one of the most successful entrepreneurs in the tribe.

On the day I visited him, Gumbs was wearing a button-down shirt with eagle feathers embroidered on the breast pocket, a gold neck-lace with a bear-claw charm, a big, gold-toned watch, and an asser-tive cologne. He is fifty years old, with a long black braid down his back, and he speaks at an unusual volume. In the deli section of his store, Gumbs told me that he grew up "on the powwow trail," visit-ing other reservations throughout the East for festivals and cere-monies. "I saw true governments in action," he said. "Whether it was education, whether it was health care—all of these things that we're talking about now—other tribes were doing that back then. And it always baffled me as to why we felt like we were there, when we were light-years behind." Gumbs has long been the tribe's most vocal advocate of gaming. "I guess that was the motivating fac-tor, and just listening to the other men in the community saying, 'Damn, we don't have nothing!'"

Gumbs led me out of the store so that we could talk in private. We passed a series of burgundy cottages where children were play-ing with a baby raccoon in the yard, and walked toward a two-story building with a wooden Indian standing guard out front. Inside was a room the size of a high school gym, where Gumbs's yellow Hummer was parked next to a forty-five-foot RV. There was a bar in one corner, and the walls were decorated with Mylar tassels. High overhead was Gumbs's DJ booth, where he spins records when he rents out his cavernous bachelor pad for parties.

"Even though our children went to the public school, the major-ity of them were behind all of the ethnic groups. We're behind even the Latinos now!" Gumbs said. "You have these two tribes that spring up miraculously out of thin air right around us and create two of the largest casinos in the world." He did not believe that the Mohegans had anything to do with the Connecticut Coalition's ef-forts to sabotage the Shinnecocks, but he wasn't convinced about the Pequots. Gumbs said that if he found out that any Indian na-tion was involved, he would consider it an act of war. "We will go after them just like they came after us," he said. I asked him if he meant by creating competition. "There's a lot of other ways," he said, ominously, "but I'm not going to get into that."

Gumbs has been elected trustee eight times, and in that capacity has taken requests from dozens of prospective investors. In 2003, he helped make a deal with a man named Ivy Ong to develop a casino and resort hotel. The trustees chose Ong from many suitors, Gumbs said, because "being Chinese, he had a great appreciation and understanding of cultural values and cultural issues." (Gumbs is a firm believer in ethnic profiling. A few days after our meeting, I received an e-mail from him asking why I didn't have children: "Is it as I've been told a Jewish woman's lack of interest in sex?") Though the Shinnecocks lacked federal recognition, they planned to build a 65,000-square-foot facility in Hampton Bays, on an idyllic eighty-acre parcel of beachfront woodland that the tribe holds. Ong intended to run a bus directly there from Chinatown in New York City.

When this plan became public, it revived a dispute that has persisted for almost four hundred years. The Town of Southampton, the oldest English settlement in New York, was established when colonists purchased eight square miles of land from the Shinnecocks in 1640. In exchange, the Shinnecocks received corn from the settlers' first harvest, cloth coats, and a promise that particular areas would be reserved for their use; it was also agreed that the English would "defend us the sayed Indians from the unjust violence of whatever Indians shall illegally assaile us." This arrangement held until 1703, when the tribe sold its remaining land, for the price of twenty pounds, plus a thousand-year lease on a parcel that included 3,600 acres known as the Shinnecock Hills. The two groups cohabited fairly happily for the next 150 years, though the settlers complained that their livestock kept falling into holes that the Shinnecocks dug to store food through the winter.

In the middle of the nineteenth century, wealthy New Yorkers began to transform the area from farmland into a seaside resort. In 1859, a consortium of investors petitioned the state to break the Shinnecocks' lease, and an agreement was sent to Albany, signed by twenty-one members of the tribe. According to the Shinnecocks, the document was forged; some of the signatories appeared twice, and others were tribe members who had died. Days later, the tribe sent another petition to Albany in protest. The state legislature approved the transaction anyway, and the Shinnecocks were reduced to their current land base. They became the servant class of Southampton, cleaning homes, cooking, and caddying at the Shinnecock Hills Golf Club.

Over the years, the tribe has tried by various legal means to reclaim the land, whose value has been assessed at $1.7 billion. Marguerite Smith, the first member of the tribe to become an attorney, told me, "I went to law school with the message from the elders 'You have to do something for your tribe.' When I finished, they said, 'You go and get those hills.'" But Gumbs and others on the reservation have argued that the land, most of which is now privately owned, will never be reclaimed through the courts. The tribe will have to buy it back, and the casino will provide the means. "We lost our land through white man's greed, and we're going to get it back through white man's greed," Fred Bess said.

At the time of the Hampton Bays development, Gumbs and the two other Shinnecock trustees took out a series of full-page ads in the local papers, trying to drum up enthusiasm for a casino. They hired a public relations firm and started a website. ("FAQ: Traffic is a big problem in our region. Won't this add more traffic congestion? A: Any Indian gaming facility would be part of the traffic solution, not part of the problem.") On March 5, 2003, they held a press conference in the woods, alongside a phalanx of bulldozers. "This is about the preservation of our people," a trustee named Charles Smith announced. Then the Shinnecocks held a "turtle walk," a procession through the forest to relocate box turtles so that they wouldn't be crushed. The machines rumbled after them.

When they were finished, a five-acre chunk had been denuded, and many people in Southampton—and on the reservation— were horrified. "That was ridiculous—you don't make a political statement with a bulldozer," Pastor Mike Smith told me. "You don't go desecrating one of the most pristine pieces of property on the East End of the island out of pure greed, which is all that was, because then you lose all credibility and integrity about being, quote unquote, stewards of the land." Several environmental groups sprang up to oppose the project, and Patrick Heaney, the town supervisor at the time, accused the tribe of trying to "absolutely destroy the community character not only of Hampton Bays but of all of Southampton."

Gumbs was irate. "Nobody asked us anything as to whether we wanted the big mansions around us, whether we wanted these big roads, the traffic!" he told me. "Now, all of a sudden, when we want to do something that's economically viable for our community to help sustain the people, you're saying no?"

The town and, eventually, the state sued for an injunction and forced the tribe to cease construction. Ivy Ong vanished, leaving the Shinnecocks in debt—as, it turned out, was his habit. Not long after the Hampton Bays debacle, the Seminole tribe submitted a statement to the BIA, claiming that its partnership with Ong had cost nearly $20 million in fines and lost income. Ong was sentenced to more than three years in federal prison.

But in Gumbs's view Ong was never the antagonist; his neighbors were. "The elders thought, Well, we have a good relationship with the town and they're our friends," Gumbs said. "I said, 'You don't understand! This is the new Southampton. You've got new money, new people. They don't give two craps about the Shinnecock Indian Nation.'" He added, "The old Southampton, yes, there was probably a lot of mutual respect and understanding there —even though we were the housemaids and the dishwashers and the lawn-cutters. Of course you're going to have a nice relationship if you're the servants. Yes, suh, mastuh." In any case, Southampton's opposition to a casino in Hampton Bays galvanized the Shinnecocks, which some members of the tribe think was Gumbs's intention all along.

The acquisitive ethos of the Hamptons, where even the purchase of a copper faucet is an opportunity for self-expression, does not extend to the reservation. The Shinnecocks' professed values are communal and anti-materialist, and "for the benefit of the tribe" is a kind of mantra. The Shinnecocks could sell even a small piece of their reservation for millions of dollars, but to do so would be unthinkable. Every decision the tribe makes is meant to be in the service of the collective and the land.

"We don't separate ourselves from our surroundings," the trustee Gordell Wright told me. "That's a connection that native people have to the land itself. It's just, like, you." Wright, who is thirty-eight, was brought up in New York City and in Germany and did not move to the reservation until he was an adult, yet his passion for the place is his primary qualification for leadership. The trusteeships are volunteer positions; Wright is currently unemployed, having left his job as a deliveryman for Home Depot.

The Shinnecocks' group-mindedness has been reinforced by the process of applying for federal recognition, which entails an exhaustive inquiry into who belongs to the tribe. The BIA requires proof that every person listed as a tribe member is the direct descendant of someone who lived on the reservation in 1865. According to the tribe's own policy, babies born to Shinnecock mothers are automatically included on the tribal roll. But if a baby's parents are unmarried and only the father is Shinnecock, the child is ineligible for enrollment. "There's a saying," Fred Bess told me. "Mama's baby, Papa's maybe."

The question of legitimacy has been particularly vexed, because most members of the tribe do not look the way American Indians are expected to look. "That's what this whole federal-recognition process has been about," Roberta O. Hunter, a Shinnecock lawyer, told me. "Are you who you say you are? Are you really authentic?" Hunter majored in anthropology at Bennington, and she said that in the twenties scholars got "interested in the 'red man' and the 'vanishing race,' and everybody raced out West." The academics, she suggested, were in pursuit of motion picture Indians. "Those stereotypes of who's an Indian and who isn't an Indian, those were based on all those groups west of the Mississippi. I don't look anything like that," Hunter, who has dark skin and kinky hair, said.

Anxiety about being perceived as insufficiently Indian was one of the reasons why it took the Shinnecocks so long to gain federal recognition. The BIA's history of the tribe's efforts at recognition is shot through with allusions to its ambivalence. "I don't think the Shinnecocks are much interested in petitioning," the executive director of the Indian Rights Association wrote to the Office of Federal Acknowledgment in 1984. "I think they believe they've managed all right so far, and they're not anxious to diddle around with a system that is working." Some tribe members were fearful of submitting to the process. "You had people who were older that were just, like, 'Be quiet. Don't make any waves,'" Hunter told me. "There was a voice that said, If you step up, you're going to get knocked down, because you know they just think we're a bunch of niggers."

Long Island's Native Americans have been marrying African Americans since the seventeenth century, when the Dutch started bringing slaves into New York. John Strong, the premier historian of Native Americans on Long Island, told me, "Slave status was defined by law in terms of the woman—a child becomes the property of the mother's owner. If you're a slave and you want to make sure your children are free, you marry an Indian woman."

But if slave status was defined by maternity, racial status was defined by color. "If the father was black and the mother was Indian, or vice versa, and the child comes forward with a claim to Native American identity, the white arbiters say, 'Oh, no, you can't jump up a notch in the hierarchy—you're black,'" Strong said. "When I came here, in '65, you'd go in any of the local bars and they would talk about the Shinnecocks as 'monigs': more nigger than Indian." It's a slur that you still sometimes hear in the Hamptons.

Hunter and Lance Gumbs represent a generation of Shinnecocks who came of age in the sixties. College-educated and influenced by the era's movements for social justice, they started to question what the tribe was entitled to. "I really had such a vision about being able to come back to this community," Hunter told me. "I said, How perfect is this? Because you've got a landmass, which is what so many other groups"—the Black Panthers, lesbian separatists, certain passionate vegetarians—"wanted: a place to really infuse with whatever those cultural values were."

But Hunter feels that that kind of idealism has not prevailed. She calls Gumbs a "real exploiter," and says that the procession of cigarette shops on Montauk Highway is the result of unregulated greed. "Nicotine, the most addictive substance that we've got going on—this is what we want to hold up as our sovereign right?" she said. Though she has no objection to the idea of a casino, she feels that the way Gumbs and others have pursued their objective has been unethical. "What I am always focused on is process," she told me. "Are you having full participation of our membership? Do you have accountability and transparency? No."

Every major decision that the Shinnecocks make is put to a vote before the entire tribe. But elections can be compromised. For many years, the annual votes for tribal trustees were public, and, many Shinnecocks told me, there was retribution for the wrong vote and bribery for the right one. "All of this to me is so connected to why things are still so screwy here, and you can have someone get elected like Lance Gumbs," Hunter said. In 1992, Hunter was elected to the Southampton Town Board, and is the only nonwhite person to hold elected office in the town. She has also run for the office of tribal trustee three times, but no woman has ever been elected.

Gumbs believes that he is putting his tribe first, too. He thinks that the profits from the casino should be used to develop infrastructure and improve education; his priority, he told me, is avoiding the creation of a welfare state. "You cannot take vast sums of money and put it in somebody's hands who's never had money and expect them to know what to do with it," he said.

Some tribes pay out casino profits in per capita disbursements, which can be substantial; the Chumash Indians of California, for example, reportedly received $428,969 apiece in 2005. As the prospect of a casino has become increasingly bright on the Shinnecock reservation, an unusual number of people have been contacting the enrollment office. "Everyone is coming out of the woodwork," Winonah Warren, the seventy-one-year-old president of the board of directors at the Shinnecock museum, told me. "Oh, everybody wants to be Shinnecock now."

One night in August, Pastor Mike Smith sat shirtless in denim cutoffs in a sweat lodge in the woods behind a cousin's house. Twenty people, most of whom were drumming and chanting with ferocious abandon, were packed in tight around a pit of red-hot rocks under a frame of branches draped with heavy blankets. Though Pastor Mike, as everyone calls him, is a Christian, he comes to these traditional ceremonies once a month. He does not join in the chanting or the drumming, just the sweating and, silently, the praying. He prays that he will stay sober, as he has for the past twenty-four years. He prays that the young people in his tribe will resist the drugs being sold down at Cuffee's Beach. And he prays for the men selling the drugs, who, after all, are Shinnecock, too.

Pastor Mike is against gaming. "We're already dealing with alcohol and drugs, and we're dealing with it over pennies," he said, when the ceremony was finished. "Can you imagine what would happen with the influx of cash?" Organization and discipline, he believes, are what's missing from his community, not money. "If you look at Mashantucket, if you look at Mohegan, if you look at anyplace that has a casino, the only thing you hear about is the glorification of the wealth," he said. "They don't talk about the social upheaval that comes as a consequence."

Pastor Mike is a traditionalist. When the women of Shinnecock gained the right to vote in tribal elections, in 1992, he was one of only four men to vote against it. Smith, who is sixty-one, is nostalgic for the reservation that he grew up on. He remembers "sleeping out in the woods as kids," and a sense of absolute freedom, safety, and belonging. "Look out there," he said, motioning toward the green expanse in the moonlight. "What more do you need?"

But Gumbs is not alone in thinking that the tribe has more to lose by remaining poor than it does by risking radical transformation. Robin Weeks, who for many years sat with Hunter, Gumbs, and Bess on the Shinnecock Economic Development Committee, has been a strong proponent of gaming. He grew up with his mother, who is blind, and five siblings, in a house on the reservation that had no running water. "We had an old potbelly stove with coal and wood and whatever else we could burn—newspapers, old clothing," he told me. "Sometimes it would get so cold in the house the water would freeze and we'd have to put it on the stove to heat it up so we could wash for school." Weeks was born in 1955. "I tell people, 'You can see all of these things—the pump, the outhouse—in old movies. This is what I grew up in.'"

Weeks is now a senior admissions adviser at Stony Brook University. While completing a graduate degree in education, at Hofstra, he studied abroad, and the experience was transformative: "I got to travel all over Europe, and it just opened up the world to me. I could always see it from a distance in terms of looking across the water at all the millionaires in their mansions—I always saw a glimpse of it, but I was never a part of it. I wanted to bring this back to my community; there's more to life than we saw growing up, than struggle and sadness and violence." Weeks attended public schools in Southampton—as most Shinnecocks have since their one-room schoolhouse closed, in 1951—and he worked as a janitor at lunchtime and after school. "I saw that there was unfairness," he said. "I saw that there was inequality. And, in fact, by the time I was fourteen I got involved in some very negative, destructive things. Looking back now, it seems like a rite of passage: the more you could drink and the more you could fight, the more of a man you were."

Today, the words "rez mob" are scratched into chairs and bathroom stalls at Southampton High School. In 2006, a group of college students who were home for the summer in Southampton were assaulted in one of their families' back yards. One of them told me, "A group of guys, thirty of them from the reservation, walked into the yard and started attacking everyone. They had a problem with some white kid who wasn't even there." Though the attackers wore bandanas over their faces, he recognized one of them as someone he had known since childhood. "The first thing I did was say, 'What's going on, man, what are you doing?' And he just started swinging at me."

In 2007, in the largest coordinated law enforcement effort in the history of Suffolk County, state troopers and DEA agents raided the reservation and arrested fourteen people for possessing guns and selling heroin, marijuana, and cocaine. One of the young men incarcerated after the raid was Awan Gumbs, Lance Gumbs's son, who had been conducting at least part of his business from his father's deli. This past August, a seventeen-month-old baby named Roy Jones was punched to death on the reservation, allegedly by his mother's boyfriend, who explained, "I was trying to make him act like a little boy instead of a little girl."

Pastor Mike thinks the problems persist because of "an attitude that because this is a reservation we're untouchable, so we can do whatever we damn well please and there are going to be no consequences." He tells his congregation, "Our problem isn't employment; it's employability." I asked him if he thought the Shinnecocks should have their own tribal police force once they've gained federal recognition, and he laughed. "Some folks would say fine, but, see, I know us," he said. "I know us. And I wouldn't trust nobody with a gun."

One day this fall, Lynn Malerba, the first female chief of the Mohegans, spent the morning meeting with Connecticut's gubernatorial candidates, and then visited her parents for coffee at the retirement home that her tribe built with casino profits. "There's a gym downstairs, and a Wii," Malerba said, walking through the bright entry hall. Malerba's mother showed me her apartment: the laundry room, the two bathrooms and bedrooms, and the view of a courtyard of well-tended rhododendrons and hostas. In the eighties, she was among a group of Mohegans who pooled their money to pay for the tribe's only telephone: "We hooked it up in the church closet!"

Malerba drove to the Mohegans' burial grounds, past dozens of kids holding tennis racquets and baseball bats, on their way to camp—which the tribe pays for, along with day care for the children of its members and employees. Nearby is a huge glass building, overlooking miles of countryside, that the Mohegans are erecting to house their government and cultural offices. At the tribal museum, a team is working on reconstructing the Mohegan language. The wealth generated by Mohegan Sun pays for the tribe's health care and college scholarships, too, and for assistance to first-time homeowners. Each tribe member also gets a cash payment; Malerba told me that the amount was "a private family matter."

Malerba said that she hoped the Shinnecocks succeeded in opening a casino, even if it hurt her business. "We're ten miles away from the Pequots, and we've been able to coexist," she said. "I could never take that philosophical stance, to fight another tribe. Wouldn't that be disingenuous to say that we as tribal nations are all one, and to then work aggressively against a tribe achieving economic independence as we have been able to do?"

The Mohegan nation is like a tiny Scandinavian country—a peaceable kingdom where the young are educated, the old are cared for, and everyone has help with medical care and housing. "Casinos are great in terms of an economic engine and if the revenues are provided for good purposes," Malerba said. She sounded just one cautionary note. "Whether tribes have a business or not, you always have to be really careful about how you choose your leaders," she said.

This fall, a judge dismissed the Connecticut Coalition's petition, and the Shinnecocks became the five-hundred-and-sixty-fifth federally recognized tribe. Gumbs e-mailed me, "This Nation of people will always remember October 1st, 2010, as our independence day," and signed off with a celebratory "Ah! Ho!" The tribe can begin construction on a casino as soon as it negotiates a compact with the state. Until then, the annual powwow remains the Shinnecocks' only source of tribal income.

At one difficult point in the nineties, the powwow was rained out two years in a row, and all services had to be suspended owing to lack of funds. But this year the weather was crisp and bright, and there was a line of cars along Montauk Highway waiting to turn onto the reservation. On the powwow grounds, a cleared field behind the Community Center, thousands of people shopped for wampum jewelry and stood in line for succotash and fry bread while they waited to watch the traditional dancers and drummers. Pastor Mike sold soda with the medicine man, a friend of his.

Pastor Mike introduced me to his aunt, who wore a deer-hide dress and a necklace of shells. She told me that in the early fifties the Great Cove Realty Company tried to build a subdivision on a strip of the reservation. Great Cove got as far as pouring foundations before the trustees, including her husband, persuaded the district attorney to intercede, and the developers were forced to abandon the project. The memory of it pleased her. "My husband worked in a restaurant kitchen, and one night the Great Cove guy came in drunk and said, 'I'm going to kill that savage!'" she recalled. "Those were the kinds of things that happened. It sounds strange, but we were poor but happy—all one big family, maybe four hundred of us." She wrinkled her nose. "Now they're out for money. Money is the root of all evil."

Lance Gumbs, Gordell Wright, and the third trustee, Randy King, wore eagle-feather headdresses, pelts, and beaded, purple-fringed tunics, as they led a procession of Indians from across the Northeast. A representative from the Mashantucket Pequots stood just behind Gumbs; war had apparently been averted. As people chanted and danced for hours, Harriett Crippen Gumbs, Lance's mother, sat selling silver jewelry and children's tomahawks, next to the snow cone stand. Despite the economic transformation that a casino would likely bring, she did not think federal recognition was going to change anything. "You've got to know the white man wants this reservation," Crippen Gumbs said, her white hair shooting out from under a baseball cap. "You know what their excuse would be now?" she asked, and leaned in close over her jewelry counter. "'You've intermarried too much. You're no longer Indian.' Well, who the hell are we?"

JESSICA McCAUGHEY

Aligning the Internal Compass

FROM *Colorado Review*

THE FIRST PAGE of the *Orienteering: Sport of a Lifetime* brochure reads: "With a map and compass in hand, you head into the woods. It is a beautiful day and you are about to start off on an adventure: Orienteering." At least I think that's what it says. I can hardly read the text, soggy from rain dripping from the looming trees surrounding us.

My father and I stand at the edge of the woods in a Maryland state park at noon on a Sunday, waiting to begin our day of orienteering in an effort to improve, or at least test, our sense of direction. We look awkwardly at the other people waiting, a couple dozen of them chatting as though they already know one another and wearing very serious athletic gear. Our own jeans will be wet and mud covered by the end of the day.

Perhaps irrationally, I sometimes become terrified by the idea that when the world ends and I have to flee my city, my GPS may not be charged. When my father bought it for me as a gift a few years back, I quickly became dependent on it in the same way I rely upon my eyeglasses or electricity. That little screen probably saves me about forty cumulative hours a year that would otherwise be spent driving around, lost.

My whole life, I've been going in circles. While the GPS seems like it's solving this problem, I'm pretty sure it's setting me up for a fall. I've heard several friends with an impeccable sense of direction say they can no longer tell north from south because they've become too dependent on the TomTom or the Garmin stuck to their dashboard. If these people, previously capable of taking on the role of navigator on road trips, can't figure out which direction to flee from the burning city when the time comes, I have to wonder what will become of me.

For years I have been under the impression that I was a lost cause, spatially. I can't read maps. I don't know which direction is which (although in the past couple of years I've started, in a sad, proud way, noting east or west when the sun is low, clearly on its way up or down). I can drive the same route a dozen times before I know which turn is mine. This makes me feel pathetic and, again, a little bit scared about how incapable I am.

As any self-help book will tell you, the first step is to understand your handicaps. I've found that this is true whether I'm reading to improve my relationship, reduce my carbohydrate intake, or assert myself in the workplace. I worry that sense of direction is different, though—maybe because there's less out there to understand. It's an elusive skill. Scientists all over the world are interested in it, but very few have come up with anything definitive to explain it, much less to help us learn our way out. *It's about gravitational pull,* some say. Or, *It's all about cell orientation in the brain.* These statements mean nothing to me, which is all right, because they're still up for debate in the scientific community. For all of the research that's been done, sense of direction is still a pretty abstract concept. What most scientists do agree on is this: on a super-simplified level, the brain needs three types of information to help us find our way. First, it needs to know where we are currently. Second, it needs to know the direction we're heading. And third, the brain needs to calibrate our "current movement state" in relation to our goal destination. (This is the exact same process that a GPS follows, incidentally, if we're breaking things down to a fifth-grade level.) Essentially, the process continually asks, "Are we going the right way?" A brain (or an impressive, expensive piece of electronic equipment) with all of these bits of information can provide an answer.

Terminology is important when discussing anything complicated, but when it comes to sense of direction, we tend to use terms interchangeably, but incorrectly. Often sense of direction gets mixed up with *wayfinding,* which actually refers to finding one's way on the open ocean, using a combination of the sun, stars, and ocean swells. *Navigation* is another term that does not, it turns out, mean the same thing as sense of direction. Although it's closer than wayfinding, navigation technically refers to finding one's way using electronic aids—like a GPS. *Pilotage* is used less often, but still seeps into articles and conversations. This term, which originated in the 1570s, actually means finding one's way with the use of recognizable landmarks—such as recalling a turn by the familiar coffee shop on the corner.

The terminology is disorienting, but the words matter less than the goal. I don't need to run my vessel back to shore. I'd just like to be able to get to my brother's condo without the directions I printed a year ago, secretly stored in the glove box and referenced every trip.

With this simple goal in mind, I began taking steps to improve my non-GPS-aided sense of direction. As I researched ways to improve, I came across several websites on orienteering, a "sport" in which participants race around in the wilderness with maps and compasses, trying to be the first to find a series of flag markers. This seemed less like a sport and more like hell, but it had the potential to be helpful.

Because my dad seems to know everything I don't, I called him to talk about it.

"Orienteering? Never heard of it," he told me.

I told him what I could from my cobbled reading and about my improvement goals. My dad is quick to tease me about my worthless sense of direction, although I've always suspected that his own is not too much better, that he is simply quieter about it.

"So, that's about it," I said. "All these nonprofit orienteering clubs host events in parks scattered all over the world. They're just open—anyone can come, and you pay something small, like ten or twelve dollars, to join for the day."

"Huh," he said. "I'm in. When are we going?"

I envisioned my father and myself, covered in dirt and bits of bark, lost in the woods with flags tucked into our belts. The image was only slightly less terrifying than imagining myself alone in the same situation.

A few weeks later, armed with a map of the park, directions from the Quantico Orienteering Club's website, *and* a GPS, we set off.

Here's the truth: on the way to the park, we got lost. We each tried to blow it off, claiming poor mapmaking and a lack of updates for the GPS software, but we knew it said something more about us.

As my father drove in circles, I read out loud from the "Beginner's Instruction" I'd printed from the website.

"*The goal is to find numbered 'controls,' in numerical order, in the fastest time possible . . . go over your clue sheet for a description of features, list of control codes . . . a triangle is the start (and usually the finish too) and circles highlight features.* Are you getting any of this?" I asked.

"No," he answered, his eyes on the wet road.

I continued: "*White equals normal forest, which is different from USGS maps . . .* What are they even talking about?"

"I have no idea," he said.

Although research doesn't point to sense of direction as a hereditary skill, anecdotal evidence seems to. Little definitive work (the word *definitive* being key here) has been done on the "born with" versus "acquired" nature of directional sense. What has been determined is that how a person *perceives* his or her directional capabilities is usually pretty accurate. Those who think they have a good sense of direction are usually right, and those who know they can't find their way back from the bathroom without a scale map know their limits as well. When people are asked to rate their directional sense and then find their way, the correlation is more or less dead-on in terms of who gets lost.

What this means practically is this: You've gone astray on a road trip with two people. One claims to have a good sense of direction and one claims to lack it. However, they both think they know the way. One says left and one says right. Open the car door and push the one with no sense of direction out onto the road.

Most people admit to realizing their poor sense of direction when they began driving. For years I tried to convince myself that my constant confusion was chance, but eventually, I had to give up the lie. Just after graduating from college, one Sunday afternoon I found myself performing a "practice" drive on Interstate 95 in northern Virginia the day before a job interview. I lived an hour and a half from the location (I planned to move if offered the job). I-95 is known to be one of those highways that are somehow packed at all hours, every day, and I didn't trust myself to find the office under pressure, despite the fact that it was just off the highway. So, instead, I spent Sunday plotting out my course, sitting in traffic, and searching the empty building for the entrance. The day was exhausting, but worth it as I pictured myself lost without the dry run, calling my interviewers, and sobbing on the side of the road, which I suspected was less acceptable than the similar calls I often make to my father. I got the job and consulted my written directions every day for months as I commuted.

After finally finding the park, we stand at its edge. I hear movement in the leaves, and both my father and I look up from the map to see a dozen deer. They seem to see us as well, but they don't take off the way deer usually do on the side of the road. Instead, they run gracefully, slowly—jog, really.

I tell my dad that I have never been so close to so many deer. They were only twenty yards away. Or maybe a hundred yards. Or a hundred feet? Two hundred?

The ability to estimate distances is closely tied to sense of direction. Is that building fifty feet away or three hundred yards? No idea? Me neither. This is a telltale sign of a poor sense of direction. Other questions to help determine one's directional abilities include *Can you read a map? Do you like looking at maps? Can you use a map without turning it to orient your actual placement?* Umm, no, no, and no. *Do you recall the locations of things, like, say, the salad dressing aisle at the grocery store?* Absolutely not. *Can you automatically reverse directions? Do you easily find your way around unfamiliar buildings?* No and no.

A lot of these indicators refer to "mental rotation" skills, also known as the ability to conjure up a "cognitive map." The idea of a cognitive or mental map, introduced by psychologist Edward C. Tolman of UC Berkeley in 1948, is one of the only ways we can measure sense of direction, or at least our ability to store and retrieve information about our environment. Essentially, a cognitive map is an imagined setting. If you close your eyes and picture your childhood bus stop, or the layout of your house, you're creating a cognitive map. Some people suggest that those of us with a poor sense of direction either don't make such maps, make only limited versions of them, or can make them but can't reclaim information from them.

Most commonly, however, mental rotation skills determine whether or not you have to turn the map to figure out which direction is which. If you use mental rotation, and use it well, you don't need to turn the map; the manual rotators inside your brain do it for you. Mental rotation skills also allow us to imagine what something looks like from the side, or upside down, whether it's a painting or the layout of a neighborhood. Many people have adequate mental rotation skills for a certain period, but lose them when things get complicated. For example, I may be able to keep track of the direction of the highway for a couple of turns after the exit, but after a few more, I lose my bearings completely.

On orienteering day, there is a lot of map turning.

We leave the deer and walk down a short path, following the triangle-shaped, orange ORIENTEERING! signs. We find the registration table and get in line. We avoid eye contact with our fellow orienteerers and instead make jokes about their tight pants. Every few minutes someone takes off running from the front of the line —it is a timed sport—and darts suddenly into the woods while holding up a map in one hand and a compass in the other. We both laugh hysterically every time this happens.

When we reach the table, we're given a small, plastic "e-card." A man behind the table instructs us to insert it into the electronic punch unit by each flag, or checkpoint, along the orienteering route to confirm that we successfully found it. We're then told three times: *You must punch the e-card at the end so we know you've made it out of the woods.* The orange e-card slides onto my middle finger, and I slip the attached wristlet over my hand, imagining the search party that will surely be sent out for us.

"There are a lot of people with foreign accents," my dad says. I turn to him, ready to reprimand him for what I think might be an inappropriate comment when I realize that there really *are* a lot of different accents. It makes sense. Orienteering originated in Sweden in the early 1900s but wasn't introduced to the United States until the middle of the century. Local clubs here branch out from the U.S. Orienteering Federation (USOF), but apparently the group isn't much for marketing, as the "Sport of a Lifetime" never really caught on in this country the way it did in Europe and other areas of the world.

After waiting in another line for a few minutes, I trade the car keys for a compass, as collateral, and ask a man behind the table when the "orienteering orientation" I read about on the website will begin. I'm told that it isn't as formal as all that, but he'd be happy to give me a quick introduction. I wave my dad over and we all look at a map in a plastic covering. The man holds the compass against the map, showing us how to determine "north," both on the page and in the park. He then places his finger on one of the marked checkpoints and turns the compass, explaining that by determining the direction of the destination in relation to north by using the compass, we will know exactly where to trek.

I glance at my dad and he raises his eyebrows, lifting one corner of his mouth as if to say, "I hope *you're* getting this."

I picture us lost in the woods, trampled by deer, who probably despise orienteering day—all the spandex, all the e-card beeping. I imagine them discussing what in the hell it is all these assholes are doing out here in the rain anyway. *A compass?* I hear them say. *Ridiculous.*

Sense of direction in animals is both (a) easier to study than it is in humans, and (b) really, crazy impressive, comparatively. Case in point: one species of snail, when taken from its home in a cloth bag, is able to orient itself and find its way back for up to forty miles. Last week, I went to a new CVS approximately three miles from my house. I got lost on the way home.

Migratory birds are often noted as having the most impressive animal sense of direction, which makes sense. About 80 percent of North American birds migrate, some over oceans and across continents. One bird, called the red knot, travels eighteen thousand miles round trip each year from the tip of South America to the Arctic and back again.

For years, theories have been thrown around about sense of direction in migratory birds. The birds use landmarks, some people said, or they depend upon an amazing sense of smell. They use the stars, others suggested. It turns out they use an internal, magnetic compass, which is, in a sense, recalibrated every night based on the direction of the sun as it sets. In 2004 scientists tracked migratory songbirds—gray-cheeked thrushes—catching them just before their departure and placing them in an artificial magnetic field. When they were released, the birds flew through the night on the wrong path, and then stopped and corrected themselves by 90 degrees, back toward their desired destination, as soon as the sun rose.

At least we understand the need for the birds' sense of direction. They migrate. Fair enough. Some animal behavior related to directional sense, though, remains a mystery. Last year, after looking at photo after photo of cattle fields, a team of German and Czech researchers discovered that cows tend to align their bodies facing either directly north or directly south, regardless of where they are in the world. Why are they lined up this way? How do they know to do it? Although it's assumed that the positioning has to do with the magnetic fields of the earth, no one seems to be clear on the specifics. These invisible magnetic lines might be strong enough for the cows to sense them, but why is that beneficial to the animals? No one knows.

The magnetic field is oddly prevalent in all kinds of animal orientation. Termites line up along its cardinal axes—either north to south or east to west. If the nest is turned, they will reorient themselves to these directions. If a strong magnet is placed above the nest, it throws them off. Yellow eels also use the magnetic field. Honeybees do too. And salmon.

Homing pigeons are more of a mystery. It was long thought that they, too, relied solely upon the magnetic field to find their way. In studies that disrupt the field, the pigeons' path was thrown off. But, in 2004, after tracking pigeons with GPS satellites for ten years, researchers at Oxford University announced their—let's be honest, ludicrous—findings: rather than using the sun for directional bearings, it turns out that the pigeons use roads they've traveled in the past as a guide, turning at junctions and, sometimes, even going around traffic circles. Then, three years after this study, different scientists found that iron-containing structures within the birds' beaks apparently also aid in their sense of direction. They might even have the ability to use "atmospheric odors." Long story short: when it's time to flee, those pigeons are going to be safe in some faraway bunker long before I am. Apparently so will snails and termites.

"Okay," my dad says as we start walking. "The lake is over there, and according to the map, we're supposed to curve around to the left of it."

I raise the compass on the string around my neck. "Should we be using this?" I ask.

"It's up to you," he says. I look at the map and realize that we should be able to use the landmarks—the lake, the marked trails —instead. (Read: we should be able to cheat.) This is helpful, because neither of us, we agree, understands how to use the compass in relation to finding our way around this park.

Like calculating square footage or break dancing, using a compass is something I've repeatedly tried and failed at. I get the basic concept, but not the next steps: *The needle is pointing NW, so . . . ?* Other people apparently love these things, though. There's a surprisingly big market, it turns out, for compass-related gifts. One can purchase compass tie tacks, compass cufflinks, compass necklaces, pocket compasses. I adore the idea of a businessman standing in the woods, holding up his French-cuffed sleeve to see if he should head deeper into the trees or turn back. Two different people have given me compasses for my car. The thought is there, but they're practically worthless. I can't picture my destination on a map anyway, so I don't know which way I'm supposed to be going, even if I can determine north, south, east, or west.

My dad and I do not use the compass once the whole day.

Whether it's animals homing in on magnetic fields, or the orienteerers using their hand-held compasses, most scientists agree that magnetics plays a large part in one's sense of direction. In the late seventies, an experiment was done that proved magnetic fields contributed in some way to the "internal compass" of humans as well. Scientists loaded up a bus and blindfolded the passengers and announced that they were placing magnetic bars on everyone's heads, although in reality half were magnetic and half were brass. The bus drove around for a while, then the scientists asked everyone to identify their current compass direction. Overwhelmingly, those wearing magnets were less capable than the control (brass) group.

Magnetics plays a role, but it's not *all* magnetics. It's not *all* anything, in fact. Mysteries breed myth, and sense of direction is a big enough mystery that all the crazies come out with their suggestions. *Poor sense of direction stems from left-handedness,* some say. *Oh, it's tied to dyslexia,* others claim. *People with a poor sense of direction are simply inattentive.* Or, *They're stupid.* Some say, *Sense of direction is connected to geometry. Can't understand angles? You won't have any directional abilities.* Others argue, *People with no sense of direction are proba-*

bly mildly dyspraxic (a disorder related to difficulty carrying out a plan, physical or otherwise). Still others say that it stems from not spending enough time outside as a kid. Or that those involved in sports at a young age develop a better spatial ability and, therefore, a better sense of direction.

Then there is, of course, the gender theory.

"Men have a better sense of direction because of the whole 'hunter-gatherer' thing, I think," my uncle tells me when I bring it up. "We were supposed to go out and collect food and roam away from the cave to do it, whereas women were safest staying in one place, taking care of the babies."

This is a surprisingly popular theory, at least among people I know, which may say something about the people I know. It's a hot topic among scientists as well, although it rings distinctly true or false depending on whom you ask. While there are definite gender differences in the way people approach finding their way, no one seems to agree on whether the approaches taken by men or by women are more effective.

Men are more likely to use "survey strategies"—using north, south, east, and west descriptors—than women. Women are more likely than men to use route strategies, such as landmarks, or stating the approximate time it takes to travel between two locations. Neither strategy is proven to be markedly more effective than the other.

Women do, however, consistently rate their sense of direction as worse than men. We also know that among children, boys do have better mental rotation skills. In one study, girls and boys were each given a map and asked to "mentally" make their way across town without rotating it. Then they were asked to state whether they would be turning left or right at particular intersections. The boys, unfortunately, rocked this experiment compared to the girls. Some attribute higher testosterone levels during fetal development, suspecting that they may aid in developing the part of the brain responsible for mental rotation, but no one can really say how much this has to do with factors more associated with "nurture" than "nature."

Some research does suggest that this spatial ability carries over into adulthood, and other researchers adamantly dispute it. One study, conducted by what I'm guessing was a pretty unpopular researcher, suggests not only that women have a worse sense of direction than men, but that gay men have a worse sense than straight men. The study showed gay men, straight women, and lesbians navigating with the same weaknesses, which included a lack of ability to rely on local landmarks, increased time needed to analyze spatial information, and poor routing in general.

What researchers do agree on is markers: If I ask the average man how to get to the Thai restaurant near my house, he'd tell me to go eight hundred yards and then turn left, then wind down the road for another half of a mile. The average woman would tell me to turn left at the yellow house, and then go down until I see the coffee shop. When I see it, I'll know the restaurant is just a few minutes farther. In explaining a route, men will more often cite distances and cardinal directions like "north" or "west." Usually, women cite landmarks.

After a half hour or so of wandering and inserting our e-card at the first few checkpoints, my father and I round a corner and find ourselves walking alongside a father-son team in matching red windbreakers.

"It is your first time?" the father asks in a thick, charming eastern European accent.

"Can you tell?" my dad replies, smiling.

"It is for him as well," the man says, pointing to his little boy, who looks to be about nine.

As they walk ahead, I tell my father to stop watching them. The brochure clearly declares among the Golden Rules of Orienteering: "Do not follow other orienteers!"

While stalking other orienteers is considered cheating, it's a strategy I have mastered when it comes to finding my way outside of the woods. In addition to following others, I am big on repetition. The first few months of a new job has me whispering "Left, left, right" every time I exit the elevator and try to find my office. I also count the rows whenever I walk up the ramp of a dark movie theater toward the restroom: "one, two, three, four, and left." I repeat it the whole time I'm gone so that I can find my seat again— this after once accidentally sitting down next to a stranger during a particularly suspenseful scene of the film *Coyote Ugly*.

In using these strategies, I'm not trying to increase my actual abilities the way I am by orienteering. Instead, I'm simply trying to get where I need to be in whatever way I can—a common desire for those of us who tend to get lost at every turn. Other coping mechanisms I've heard: *I print directions to and from any new destination and keep them in a binder in my trunk.* Or, *I leave myself voicemail messages with landmarks.* And *I don't drive* or — the worst — *I never go anywhere alone.*

In my efforts to improve my directional ability, I came across a book called *Never Get Lost Again.* It's small, and the cover features a drawing of a blonde woman in cargo capri pants standing on a compass and holding a map. A friend saw me reading it and said, "She's not even looking at the map!" This should have been a red flag. The book provides absolutely no useful information. The author's suggestions include such gems as "Get clear, specific directions," "Learn to read a map," and "Ask for directions." Very helpful, indeed. *Oh, if only I'd known to get directions all these years.*

What is helpful, then, for improving non-GPS-aided sense of direction? Very, very little, it seems. The sun always seemed like a safe fallback, at least in terms of east and west. However, in fact, the sun doesn't rise and set exactly due east or due west. There's some seasonal variation, I learn, which is really just one more factor working against me.

The orienteering techniques were slightly more useful, though in more of an "I'm-lost-in-the-woods!" kind of way than a "How-do-I-get-to-Chipotle?" kind of way, which is closer to what I really need. One strategy I was particularly impressed with is called the "Shadow-Tip Method." You start by finding a long stick and planting it in a relatively clear spot of level ground where you can see the shadow. With a rock you mark the spot on the ground where the shadow stops. The direction of the shadow is west "everywhere on earth," several sources explain. Then you wait fifteen minutes, mark the shadow's new spot on the ground, and draw a straight line in the dirt from the first to the second. This marks the east-west line. You go from there.

This makes absolutely no sense. How can it always be west? you ask. It turns out, the shadow will move in the exact opposite direction as the sun, and the sun always moves west. So, the next time I'm lost in the woods with access to a watch and a piece of tree, and a better memory than I currently possess, I'm set.

Of eight orienteering courses, which increase in difficulty, we've chosen to do course number 1, which winds only along park trails.

It is, I suspect, the course most often utilized by elementary school children. Remarkably, my dad and I get really lost only once, between flags seven and eight, near the end.

As we've hiked I've tried to note about how long it takes us to walk to each flag, as compared to the distance shown on the map. The shorter distances end up being around ten minutes, and the longer ones are fifteen or twenty. The rain has picked up and we've both commented several times how much we're looking forward to lunch when I realize we've been walking for quite a long time on one of the shorter jaunts. As I stop and pull out the map, I ask, "Did you see which way that guy and his son went?"

"Isn't that against the rules?" my dad asks, stomping to get some mud off of his sneaker.

The orienteering map is one of the most intricate, least decipherable pieces of paper I've ever seen. The legend shows thirty-four different symbols and their corresponding objects or terrains, all included in an 8 ½ × 11 sheet. One can find anything from the symbol for "stony ground" or "impassable cliff" to "knoll/small knoll/dot knoll." Black boxes show buildings. A building up on our right seems to correspond with one of the boxes above the wide circle we've been hiking. I point this out and suggest that as we're halfway around the circle already, we should just keep walking and complete it, then go from there. My father thinks it's a different black box. In the end, neither of us is right, and it takes us another half hour to find the next flag.

The *Orienteering* brochure wants me to know that "getting lost should not be scary for many reasons" and that "wandering around will only worsen the degree of 'lost' that you are in." This information makes sense in theory, but in practice, who hasn't been *absolutely sure* they'd find their way after just one more turn or another few miles?

People getting lost is big business. In addition to GPSs made specifically for cars, we can now add the technology to our cell phones and even our stopwatches when we run. And outside of this technology, there are companies like Corbin Design, a firm based in Michigan focused on providing buildings and campuses with clear directional signage. Their slogan is "People get lost. We fix that." I don't think they do, though. Good signage is not unlike the GPS —helpful in the moment, but a Band-Aid for a larger problem.

Technology and design can help us find our way, but they don't improve our skills at all.

In my grandfather's pool when I was a kid, I'd lie on a squeaky, blue plastic raft and close my eyes. He would grab my hand and swim around the pool, tugging me along on the raft behind him, our wrinkled, chlorine-seeped fingers entwined. He'd tread water while spinning the raft slowly. Eventually, he would stop and ask me to guess where we were in the pool without opening my eyes. By the diving board? In the shaded corner? Dead center? This was not a large pool by any standards, but besides the occasional coming and going of the bright sun, I had no tracking device. Inevitably, I'd guess: "By the back, near the cabana!" or "In the shallow end by the steps!" My guess was invariably wrong. Then we would switch and he'd climb onto the raft. Before he was even settled, splashing cool water onto the almost-burning plastic, I was off, spinning him as fast as I could while pushing the raft to all four corners of the pool. When I was exhausted, I'd say, "Okay, what do you think?" He was right every time.

So why could he do it and I couldn't? Grekin, the author who offered the worst advice ever, uses the term "directionally challenged" when describing the people of the world who, like me, can't find their way back from CVS, or figure out which way is north or in which end of the pool they're floating. She also calls having a poor sense of direction "a real disability," though I suspect the American Disability Association would disagree. Sense of direction is a mystery in the same way as sense of time or sense of balance. You have it or you don't. Research is continually being done, but it's not easily understood.

Some people call sense of direction the "sixth sense." But this isn't quite right either, as not everyone is born with a sense of direction in the same way that most people are born with the other five. Sure, some folks can't hear or see, but both anecdotal and research-based evidence tells us that far, far more people are born each day without a sense of where they are in the world. And it seems to me that, for all of my attempts over the past thirty years, it's almost as impossible to improve one's sense of direction as it would be to regain lost hearing or sight. Loss or lack of such a true "sense" is surely a worse plight, but in some ways we can look at them similarly. There are things we can do to compensate, or work

around our deficiencies—Braille or sign language, for instance—
but for all of my trying, I'll never be able to *train myself* into having a strong, intuitive sense of direction. And if that's the case, then
is there anything wrong with cheating? In this way it seems that
the car compass or stacks of secret directions or counting rows in
a movie theater is almost *more* impressive than truly recognizing
whether I'm going north or south on an unmarked road. In working to understand and improve my sense of direction, I've realized
that I'm going to be memorizing, learning by rote, forever—and
that using a GPS isn't cheating but instead a work-around that
makes life easier, less frustrating. I wish finding my way came natu-
rally, but it never will. And if I'm going to be wandering through
life blindfolded with a magnetic bar strapped, figuratively, to my
head, I might as well be able to hear that little box bolted to my
dashboard as it tells me, "Left turn ahead."

Eventually, jeans soaked up to our knees and our stomachs growl-
ing, we buzz the final checkpoint, just twenty or a hundred yards
away from the registration stand. The event has taught me nothing
about finding my way, minus a few tricks with shadows and sticks.
I want to view the whole day as useless, a day in which I learned
only that those with strong directional skills like tight pants, but it's
just as much my fault. When I didn't understand the compass les-
son, I didn't ask for clarification. I just found another work-around
strategy and used the lake and the paths as landmarks, immediately abandoning the challenge of mental mapping—the reason
I'd come in the first place.

When we give back our compass, we're handed a printout of our
total time on the course, as well as the time it took us to travel between each station. This allows for "comparing times with your fellow orienteerers." I glance around at a couple of eight-year-olds
who beat us, and then at the athletes who found their way through
gullies and "impassable cliffs." My dad and I agree, without speaking, to skip this comparison step. We try to remember where we
parked the car, and then program the GPS with my address, less
sure of how to get home than snails in a cloth bag.

JUSTIN NOBEL

The Last Inuit of Quebec

FROM *The Smart Set*

THREE SUMMERS AGO, looking for adventure, I left New York City and drove to California for a newspaper job. One evening while jogging, I noticed a glowing rock high on a hill. A few weeks later, I pitched my tent beside it. After work, I'd trudge up my hill in the moonlight and sit for hours under the rock. On some nights, strange howls kept me awake. I wondered if there was a land where people still lived in skins, gathered around fire, and believed in magic and not God. Looking for that land, I quit the paper and traveled to Nunavik, an Inuit territory in Arctic Quebec.

On Canada Day, I landed in Kuujjuaq, a community of two thousand on the tree line. An icy wind spat cold rain. On the shores of the Koksoak River, families picnicked beside their SUVs and Canadian flags flapped in the drizzle. "Things are changing so fast," said Allen Gordon, the head of the Nunavik Tourism Association. I later learned that his wife was the first one in town to ship north a Hummer. We celebrated the holiday at the Ikkariqvik Bar, a cavernous dive without windows. There were darts and a disco ball. "If you're a woman, you'll win a sewing machine. If you're a man, you win nets. If you don't want either, you'll get four beers," shouted a lady selling raffle tickets. A teen dressed in black showed me a tiny silver pistol, and someone collapsed on the edge of the dance floor. "We are drunk because it's Canada Day," said a man at the bar. When the raffle lady stumbled back onstage, she was too drunk to announce who had won what.

Kuujjuaq is regarded as a *city*, severed from Inuit traditions. To find magic, I needed to go farther north, so I boarded a propeller plane for Ivujivik, a town of three hundred on the stormy coastline where Hudson Bay meets Hudson Strait. Trees disappeared then reappeared and then disappeared for good. This was tundra—a sopping, pitted landscape that shone brilliantly in the sun. Confused ribbons of water connected an endless splatter of lakes, some green, some yellow, some with red edges and bright blue centers. Ancient channels were etched in the stone. We unloaded and picked up passengers in Inukjuak and Puvirnituq. Over Hudson Bay, a passenger spotted a pair of belugas.

A drunk woman named Saira showed up at the airport in a Bronco packed with relatives and wanted me to live with her. We had met in Kuujjuaq at the home of a woman who peddled black-market booze. Saira was drunk on Smirnoff at the time, but had somehow remembered my travel plans. I ignored her. A construction worker dropped me at a drab house on the edge of town occupied by a security guard named Chico who I had been told would have a free room. A man with a beat-up face came to the door. "Why are you here?" he asked. I explained. "I can't wait to get the hell out," he said. "I hate this place."

I was in e-mail contact with a nurse who supposedly had a room, but that too evaporated—her boss was in town. Reluctantly, I sought out Saira. She opened the door with a grin. "I'm drunk," she said, "but it's okay." I joined her and a niece with whittled teeth at a table covered with empty Budweiser cans. The women looked at me and giggled harshly. They bantered in Inuktitut. Saira explained that she was getting evicted in a few days. "We will live in a tent in the back," she said, "and come in to take showers."

I stepped out to clear my head. A stiff wind whipped whitecaps from the cobalt strait. I headed for it, walking over dinosaur egg–like rocks littered with ammo boxes and potato chip bags. At the edge of a headland, long rolling swells beat the boulders and blasted spray skyward. Beyond, the sea swirled. I stood there for some time, thinking about good meals and the New York subway. The strong wind dragged tears across my cheeks. I later learned this was the site where hunters once came to woo belugas into the bay so others could harpoon them.

Ivujivik had one store, a cooperative, which serves as a bank, post office, hardware store, and grocer. There were no bars and no restaurants. There was a school, a health center, a municipal building, and a power plant that burned diesel fuel imported by a ship that comes twice a year. Homes were red, orange, blue, green, identical warehouse-like structures subsidized by the Quebec government. Each had a water tank and a sewage tank, and trucks circled daily, refilling and relieving. All roads ended a few miles outside town. I was there in late July, and for children, who represent nearly half the population, these were the dog days of summer.

Kids began the day in small groups that expanded as night neared. Afternoon activities included hide-and-seek, cavorting atop shipping containers, pouring buckets of water over slanted wooden planks, and watching a bulldozer demolish a building. By nightfall, which lasts from 9 P.M. until well past midnight, children can be roaming the streets in groups of ten to twenty. Often, they get rowdy. The summer I was in Ivujivik, youths regularly broke into the youth center to steal video games. In an adjacent community, a posse comprised of kids as young as twelve pummeled a man with a hockey stick and golf clubs.

Teens had rosier options. Some worked at the co-op or for the municipality, driving the water and sewage trucks. Some wandered like the younger ones, but with more gadgets. Several tore around on dirt bikes, and quite a few had iPods. Gangsta rap was very popular in the North, and there was even a local group—the North Coast Rappers, or NCR. One morning, I hung outside the co-op with a teen in black jeans named Lukasi, who said he would introduce me to a member. Sure enough, a thuggish youth emerged to meet us. He wore a baggy T-shirt with a picture of Tupac, his head in a bandana and bowed. Plastic diamonds protruded from the shirt, whose owner was also named Lukasi. He coolly lit a cigarette provided by the other Lukasi and discussed NCR, a three-man group that rapped over beats made by a computer synthesizer program. When I asked what they rapped about, Lukasi paused briefly, then said: "Bitches and ho's, mostly."

In August, I noticed a flier in the co-op about a bowhead whale hunt in the community of Kangiqsujuaq, several hundred miles down the coast. Bowheads can live for 150 years and weigh as much as five school buses. The Inuit of Nunavik had not landed one in more than a century, although locals had been pushing for a hunt since the mid-1980s. At that time, the Hudson Strait bowhead was designated as "endangered" and hunting was prohibited. The Inuit claimed that the whales were plentiful. In 2005, a study by Canada's Department of Fisheries and Oceans confirmed the Inuit's suspicions, and in 2008, the Inuit of Nunavik were granted permission to hunt one bowhead. Kangiqsujuaq was chosen as the hunt site for its proximity to known bowhead grounds and the hunting prowess of its inhabitants. I e-mailed an editor at the *Nunatsiaq News,* a paper delivered across the Arctic by propeller plane. She said they'd pay for a story and photos. I hitched a ride on a canoe headed south.

Kangiqsujuaq, a town of six hundred, was bursting at the seams. The Inuit were delirious over the chance to eat bowhead *maktak,* or whale skin. On a blustery day I joined a group of Inuit at a sort of tailgate for the bowhead hunt. We picnicked on a barren knoll outside town that overlooked a rocky cove with several fishing boats and a dozen or more canoes. Tinned anchovies, sandwich pickles, Ritz crackers, Spam, and a jar of Miracle Whip were spread over an impromptu plank table. A man with a buzz cut approached our group from the water's edge, his eyes hidden by tinted shades, and the women shrieked. In each hand he grasped a fat, glistening Arctic char. Two ladies with buns of gray hair tucked beneath colorful bandanas laid the fish on a dismantled cardboard box. We squatted in the dirt and went at them with pocketknives and curved blades called *ulus,* slurping flesh from the skin as if spooning grapefruit. The meat was bright orange and sticky. "Chew the bones," the fisherman, whose name was Tiivi Qumaaluk, said. "They're the best."

The Inuit reached what is now northern Quebec more than two thousand years ago. In winter they dwelt in igloos along the coast, skewering seals and walruses at breathing holes in the ice with ivory-tipped harpoons. In summer they tracked caribou into the interior, ambushing them at river crossings or chasing the animals toward hidden archers. Whales were corralled in shallow bays with kayaks made from sealskin stretched over bone. Polar bears were immobilized by dogs and then knifed. Still, famine was common. Elderly that slowed the group were left behind to die. Clans that settled near Kangiqsujuaq fared better than most. The large tides created caverns under the frozen sea that could be reached at low tide by chipping through the ice above. In times of hunger, hunters scavenged these caves for mussels and algae. "There are numerous indications that starvation and famines accompanied by infanticide and even cannibalism were not rare," writes Bernard Saladin D'Anglure, a twentieth-century anthropologist who spent time in Kangiqsujuaq.

By the late 1800s the Hudson Bay Company had built several trading posts in Nunavik, and in 1910 Révillon Frères, a French fur company, opened one in Kangiqsujuaq. Inuit hunters stopped traveling with game and began searching for fox, which they traded at posts for nets, guns, and metal needles. Inuit began camping around stores rather than by hunting spots. They developed tastes for foods they had never eaten — flour, biscuits, molasses, tea, coffee. From the posts also came disease and dependence. "About 15 families camped in the settlement," reads the 1928 log from a Hudson Bay store operator in the Central Arctic; "they have no inclination to hunt or exert themselves but are content to sit around in a state of destitution."

By the 1960s, the North had become such a black eye that the Canadian government took steps to recuperate the region. Teachers, health care workers, and police were sent north. Homes and hospitals were built. Dogs were corralled by the police and shot. Some Inuit youth were shipped to southern schools against their will. The government's aim was to quell poverty and spur development, which to them meant providing Inuit with Western educations and eliminating sick dogs. But to many Inuit, these actions appeared to be part of a much more sinister agenda, the annihilation of their culture.

In 1975, the Inuit and their native neighbors to the south, the Cree, protested the Quebec government's seizure of their land for a massive hydroelectric project and received a settlement of nearly a quarter of a billion dollars in what was called the James Bay and Northern Quebec Agreement. The Inuit's share went toward the creation of the Makivik Corporation, a development agency charged with promoting economic growth and fostering Inuit-run businesses. Makivik is presently invested in construction, shipping, fishing, tanning, and air travel. They recently started a cruise ship company.

*

Kangiqsujuaq was trying to get itself on the adventure travel map. Much of the town's funding comes from a nearby nickel mine. Recent tourist-oriented projects have included an elder home, a community pool, a new hotel with a $400 suite, and a visitor center for a remote provincial park that protects a 2-million-year-old meteor crater said to contain the purest water on earth.

When I entered the office of Lukasi Pilurtuut, who manages the Nunaturlik Landholding Corporation, which oversees development in Kangiqsujuaq, I found him alone at the end of a long table with his laptop, wearing a cap, jeans, and sneakers. Sunlight streamed through large windows, and the hilltops surrounding the town gleamed with freshly fallen summer snow. He was an ace student in high school but dropped out of a Montreal college after just three semesters, homesick. "It wasn't the problem of going to school," he said, "it was more the problem that I couldn't go hunting."

Dependence has made some people lazy, said Pilurtuut. The Canadian and Quebec governments subsidize housing and health care, and many Inuit also receive welfare checks. In 2007, high nickel prices helped the mine turn record profits, and each Inuit resident of Kangiqsujuaq received a check for $4,700. Some families got checks for $30,000. They bought ATVs, SUVs, dirt bikes, snowmobiles, motorized canoes, computers, and flat-screen TVs.

Tourism money will be different, Pilurtuut said. Rather than destroying tradition, it could bring it back. In fact, this was already happening. As we spoke the phone rang several times. "Yes!" he cried during one call, and then turned to me. "We have good news, four single kayaks coming in today." The Inuit invented the kayak, but no one in Nunavik remembered how to operate one. Kangiqsujuaq had to order kayaks from southern Quebec and hire an outside guide to train locals.

On a crisp summer evening, I raced into the strait to greet the bowhead hunters on a bright orange government speedboat. The sun sank through thin clouds and spilled across the horizon like paint. "This is so special for us," our navigator, a man named Tuumasi Pilurtuut, said to me, practically speechless with joy. "We're back with our ancestors."

The hunters fired flares to mark their position. A tremendous cheer went up as we arrived, and strips of *maktak* were passed aboard. "Better than beluga," Pilurtuut said between chews. Lines of turquoise fire billowed in the night sky—the northern lights, in their first appearance of the season.

The Nanuq, the boat to which the whale was secured, motored through the night and reached the cove near town where I had tailgated the week before shortly after dawn. The bowhead was moored to three orange buoys on the edge of the bay, where it bobbed, with a long knife called a *tuuq* stuck in its top, until early afternoon, when the tide lowered. Canoes ferried hungry onlookers to the site, and the slicing of *maktak* began. Naalak Nappaaluk, a revered elder and the only man alive who remembered stories about the bowhead hunts of yesteryear, sat on a rock with a pad of *maktak* nearby and tears in his eyes. Nappaaluk had a shot at a bowhead as a teen, but it escaped through a lead in the ice. "Today, I have seen people standing on the bowhead for the first time," he told me through a translator. "It's overwhelming." A bulldozer that had been intended to flip the whale had trouble making it to the site, and the majority of the meat rotted. When I returned three days later, the stench was so potent that men were vomiting uncontrollably.

One tradition that had survived intact was the caribou hunt. Nearly a million caribou dwell in Nunavik, and when a herd nears towns, offices empty. By mid-August the chatter around Kangiqsujuaq was that the animals were close. One morning at the grocery store I ran into Tiivi, the man who had caught the char at the tailgate party. He invited me to go hunting with him the following day.

Tiivi killed his first caribou at age nine while looking for bird eggs with his five-year-old brother. Unable to cut the carcass themselves, the boys rushed back to tell their mother. "She was so excited," Tiivi said, "she was like shouting of joy." In his teens he worked as a garbage man, and at twenty-one he took a job pulverizing rock at the nickel mine, earning a $2,500 paycheck twice a month.

Tiivi married a janitor from the mine and they moved in together, living in a town on the Hudson Strait called Salluit. The marriage was a nightmare. Fights were frequent; in one she bit him, leaving a knotty scar over his bicep. Another time she plunged a steak knife into his chest. He was medevaced to a hospital on the other side of Nunavik for a tetanus shot. "The next day I couldn't lift my arm because all the muscles were cut," he said. One night, while she was asleep, he snuck out with just the clothes on his back. While visiting cousins in Puvirnituk, he met a second cousin named Elisapie. "A lot of different girls tried to be with me but I refused them all because I saw Elisapie and I wanted only her," said Tiivi. "She was so fine looking." They recently married.

I met Tiivi at his home just after 9 A.M. He wore muck boots, grease-stained pants, and a hunting cap. He carried a rifle for caribou and a shotgun for geese. We were joined by his aunt, Qialak, and his brother, Jimmy, who trailed us on a second ATV. On a ridge patterned with jackknifed rocks Tiivi signaled a shiny outcrop where carvers come for soapstone. Cumulus clouds splotched the sky and sunbursts lit mats of lichen red and orange. "There might be some gold particles," Tiivi said, as we crossed a stream. "Our land is full of minerals."

With mud splattering from the tires, we descended a spongy slope then looped around a lake where the week before Jimmy and Qialak had strung nets. Tiivi and Qialak reeled them in, half a dozen flapping Arctic char. "So fresh the heart is still beating," Tiivi said. Qialak sliced open the bellies of the females and wailed — two had eggs. I held a sandwich baggie open while she scooped in the long slimy packets.

We sat at the water's edge and slurped the bright orange flesh from flaps of skin. The meat was sticky and chewy, like a fatty piece of steak. The fresh blood tasted sweet. We drank tea from a thermos and ate packaged biscuits. Tiivi smoked two cigarettes and then we left. A muddy track led above the lake to the next ridge. Arctic poppies bobbed in the breeze. Jimmy spotted snow geese.

"They're going to land because of the wind," said Tiivi. We abandoned the ATVs and crouched low. Jimmy and I followed Tiivi along a sliver of wet land behind a low rock ridge. We crawled close on our bellies. When the geese took flight the men bolted upright and fired. Two birds fell. One goose lay sprawled in the tundra with wings still beating. Its handsome white coat was ruined by a single red smear. Tiivi pinned its chest with his arms. The long neck slowly lifted and the head cocked sideways and gasped. "Now it's dying because I'm holding the lungs," he said.

With a soft thud the head dropped. "Hurray!" Tiivi said and peeled a Clementine. He tossed the squiggled rind aside and gave me half. Qialak looked at me beaming. "You're probably getting the experience of a lifetime."

On a ridge above a river, under a sunset the color of skinned knees, Qialak spotted a large buck. Tiivi slowly extended his arms above his head, bent his elbows out, and pointed his fingers skyward, imitating antlers. The buck stared at us intently then resumed foraging. A smaller buck beside him followed suit. We splashed across the river and sped, sheltered by the ridge, toward the buck. Its impressive rack was just visible above the hill's crest in the grainy light.

"Stay low," Tiivi said. He crept up the ridge, rested on a rock, and fired several shots. The buck rushed forward frantically then halted. It seemed not to know where to step next. Tiivi fired again and it swayed. Its massive head lowered to the ground, eyes still open. The body slumped. Labored, spastic breaths rose from the ground. The younger buck remained for a moment then darted.

Everyone produced knives; Tiivi held one in each hand. The buck lay on its side, its chest heaving. Tiivi approached from behind, and it kicked the air violently. He jabbed a knife into its neck, then jostled the blade back and forth. As darkness fell the three Inuit dismembered the carcass. Everything was taken but the head and intestines. Tiivi tied his parts in a bundle — heart, hindquarters, filet, stomach, ribs. Recrossing the river we washed our hands and drank cold river water from our palms. "I'm all clean," Tiivi said.

During my last week in Kangiqsujuaq, I met with Father Dion, a Catholic priest originally from Belgium who had been in Nunavik for nearly five decades. He was a tiny, puckered man whose congregation was dwindling, but he was a bull. He laughed loudly, spoke with a thick French accent, and commanded respect from everyone in town, young and old, Inuit and non-. His church was a pintsized building in the center of town, and he lived inside. When I knocked one drizzly day, he didn't hear me. I entered. He was on the couch, in leather sandals with socks and a sky-blue sweater, watching CNN.

He shook my hand with a strong grip and heated a cup of tea in an old microwave, then served it to me with the last two of a package of biscuits. He handed me a pair of ivory binoculars wider than they were long and suggested I view the Hudson Strait, which he had a clear shot of. When he was nineteen, the Germans invaded Belgium. Father Dion was in the seminary and went to war. When it ended he was given the choice of working in a hospital in his home country or being sent as a missionary to the Congo. He chose Congo, a dreadful two years. "It was hot," he said. "A lot of animals, a lot of sickness." Afterward, he requested to be sent to the Arctic, where Belgium had some missionaries stationed. He arrived in Nunavik in 1964, and spent his first nine years in a community of three hundred called Quaqtaq. He survived a famine and a fall through the ice on a snowmobile. "I have a very strong esteem for these people and how they survived in such harsh conditions," he said. "I appreciate them very, very much."

Father Dion addressed some misconceptions. The dogs were shot because they were starving and had been eating Inuit babies. The schooling the government imposed on the Inuit helped create a generation of bright leaders. A change he wasn't fond of concerned the church. Newer community members were now following the Pentecostal church, whose loud hectic services made some think the group was a revival of shamanism. Inuit once depended on shamans to bring good results in a hunt or lift them out of famine, but shamans could also bring death. "It was a kind of liberation when they disappeared," said Father Dion. Shamans were replaced by the Catholic Church.

I asked Father Dion if the Inuit would be better off as Nunavik modernized. He chewed his cheek and looked out the window at the gray town. The tide was going out, leaving black pools of water between the rocks. A septic truck passed. "When I arrived, this land was empty," he said. "Nothing. No houses, nothing. People were living in tents in the summer and igloos in the winter. Now, they have enough to eat, warm houses, transportation, communication. They don't fight for survival."

Just before I left, Tiivi began a job managing the new elder home. I stopped in to stay good-bye. A hefty woman in a pink nightgown was working on a puzzle of a snowy European forest. The place smelled of new furniture and cleaning agents. Tiivi led me into his office. The walls were bare, and he had taped a black trash bag over the window to keep the sun out. On his desk was a flat-screen computer; the screensaver was a shot of his son taken during the bowhead whale hunt. "So," said Tiivi, indicating his office items, "I have a good job."

Summer ended, and I returned to Kuujjuaq days before the first blizzard hit. In mid-September, I flew to Montreal and boarded a Greyhound bound for the border. My bus crossed into the U.S. at midnight and by dawn I was in New York City. The day was warm and breezy, the city still smelled of summer. I began an internship at *Audubon* magazine, but without enough money to get an apartment, I moved back in with my parents, in the suburbs. Unable to sleep in my teenage room, still lined with posters of conspiracy and aliens, I set up the tent in a wooded spot near where my childhood dog was buried.

I imagine that in a far-off land, harbored by the heartwood of a massive forest, there are a people who still remember how to do the things their ancestors did and there are still shamans and nobody has ever heard of God. I don't know how long that place will last or even if it deserves to, but surely it will soon enough be gone.

The leaves turned crisp yellows and oranges and fell to make large colored mats on the forest floor. Holes formed in the tent and spiders moved in. It got cold and I moved out. I had saved enough money from the internship for a cheap spot in Brooklyn.

TÉA OBREHT

Twilight of the Vampires

FROM *Harper's Magazine*

THREE DAYS BEFORE MY FLIGHT to Serbia, the Devil inter-
venes: my mother, who is supposed to meet me in Belgrade, falls
into a chasm on a Moscow sidewalk and shatters her ankle. That
she has gone through life without ever having broken a bone before makes her, according to her own mother, a casualty of my intentions. It is a bad sign. My grandmother, waiting for me in Belgrade, advises me to cancel my trip; her fears are reinforced the
following morning by a phone call from one of my Serbian contacts—a journalist who was supposed to meet with me has gotten
wind of my mother's accident and pulled out of her agreement to
help. "What now?" my grandmother asks, and fumes when she
hears that I am determined to press on.

It may seem strange that I have returned to the Balkans to hunt
for vampires when I get so many of them in my adoptive home-
land. Since immigrating to the States in 1997, I have formed an
uneasy acquaintance with the legion undead peopling the American imagination: Anne Rice's beautiful, tortured ghouls; *Buffy's*
ridge-faced villains and morally confused male leads; countless cin-
ematic and literary variations on Bram Stoker's nightwalker, from
Elizabeth Kostova's historical reinterpretation of Vlad Țepeș to
Francis Ford Coppola's shape-shifting, costume-changing warrior-
beast. But the power of the newest trend is incredible: vampires of
all shapes, sizes, convictions, and denominations are swelling the
national bestiary. My undergraduate students at Cornell deny reading Stephenie Meyer, but whenever I ask them to compose lists of
their favorite books, it seems like fully half include Darren Shan's

The Vampire's Assistant. My office window looks over the Commons and into the living room of a young woman from whose walls *Twilight*'s Robert Pattinson leers up, his smile signaling with indecently little ambiguity that it is sexytime.

Two days later, when I call to tell my grandmother I've missed my connecting flight in Paris, she answers the news with silence. This latest cosmic setback has turned her worst fears—heretofore an unpleasant possibility—into something inevitable. When I finally arrive in Belgrade, I discover that she has placed an open pair of scissors under my bed, blades turned doorward, to keep the Devil at bay.

Despite my immigrant's success in acclimating to many things American—I too now buy fruit based on its appearance—I have never been able to reconcile myself to the domestic breed of vampire. Where is the figure of terror, the taloned monster, the walking corpse, the possessed animal? How are they vampires at all when they are so busy righting humanity's wrongs and bewailing their ethical conundrums instead of mischieving and murdering like my grandmother seems to think they should?

Unlike his Western relation—that handsome, aristocratic, mirror-wary antihero—the Balkan vampire is typically confined to living and hunting among the laboring classes and is most accurately categorized as an evil spirit or demonically possessed corpse that frequents graveyards, crossroads, and other areas devoid of the protective powers of domestic spirits. Also a Western conceit is the vampire's pallor; whereas female vampires are beautiful and white-robed, most firsthand accounts indicate that male vampires are ruddy, corpulent peasants, whose affect—once unearthed—is that of a freshly gorged mosquito. In animal form, the vampire is not strictly limited to the bat but can appear to its victims as a cat, a dog, a rodent, or even a butterfly. These manifestations are not to be confused with vampires that were never human in the first place, which may even assume a vegetal guise (among numerous indignities through history, the Roma suffered the obscure nuisance of vampire watermelons). To further complicate matters, and despite recent trends that have marketed the werewolf as his archenemy, the Balkan vampire is often conflated with his lycanthropic cousin, since both share more or less the same agenda; in Croatia, both vampires and werewolves are known by the term *vukodlak*.

Vampir is probably the only Serbian word used the whole world over, and its significance in the lexicon of former Yugoslavian nations is evidenced by its derivatives, among them *vampirisati:* to engage in vampire-like behavior, an accusation directed at drunk husbands returning home at dawn, teenagers hovering over drug deals in doorways, or anyone caught stealing leftover cake from the fridge at 2 A.M. This is not to be confused with the more specialized *povampirisati se:* to turn oneself into or become a vampire, a process that is unnervingly easy, and that does not require a sanguinary exchange with another vampire. If a man's life ends abruptly, unexpectedly—if he is murdered or accidentally killed, if he commits suicide, if he falls victim to a sudden illness, if his last rites or burial are improperly conducted—he becomes more susceptible to the influences of demons that can possess and reanimate him. That is not to say that evil spirits in southern Europe have nothing better to do than float disembodied through fields, waiting for a cat to jump over a newly buried corpse so that they can dart into it. Whether a spirit will revisit the living is above all influenced by the dead man's own character and by how he was regarded in society: if a man is known to be a sinner, an alcoholic, unneighborly in any way; if his life is marked by conflict or degeneracy, then he is, in those villages where public perception and gossip are as good as truth, predisposed to vampirism.

Once risen, the vampire makes his way to the nearest village—this is sometimes his hometown, or the place of his death, and almost always a community sufficiently isolated so as to demand the combined effort of all residents in order to stake him. His mission is to visit sundry misfortunes upon the locals. This rarely involves the consumption of blood; he prefers to enter villagers' homes and asphyxiate them by sitting on their chests while they sleep. A less malevolent spirit will indulge in simple mischief—flinging dinnerware, inducing uncharacteristic behavior in domestic animals.

Whereas garlic, holy water, and crucifixes are commonly accepted apotropaics across the Balkans, scissors under the bed are also popular, as is the black-handled knife buried in the doorstep to cleave incoming evil in half. None of these methods cause the vampire's flesh to burst into flame; nor is there any indication that direct sunlight poses a lethal threat to vampires, although vampires do tend to be nocturnal and recoil from the crowing of roosters. Methods for destroying vampires are many—some, such as the boiling and disposal of vampire vegetables, are fairly simple, while others necessitate complex, clerically assisted rituals—but the most reliable weapon against vampires has always been *glogov kolac,* the blackthorn stake. The vigilant vampire hunter must find the vampire's grave, open it, and, having determined that the body shows the appropriate signs—the absence of rank odor and rigor mortis, a vibrant flush to the cheeks, the growth of "new" hair or fingernails, a quantity of fresh blood welling in the mouth—plunge the blackthorn stake through the heart, at which point the corpse lets out a blood-curdling shriek. Afterward, depending on the region, the head or limbs may be severed, the body turned over, the mouth filled with garlic. In some instances, the entire corpse is burned and the ashes scattered in the nearest body of water to carry whatever may be left of the spirit on its way.

The village of Kisiljevo lies some seventy-five kilometers east of Belgrade, where the Danube borders western Romania. Its name did not appear on any map of Serbia I had been able to find, nor does it hold an impressive position in the country's political or religious history; but three hundred years ago, its fields and streets were the stage for a vampire drama of unprecedented international significance. The attacks at Kisiljevo probably would not have warranted a mention had the village and its troubles not fallen under the watchful, disbelieving eye of Austria following the Peace of Požarevac in 1718. Austrian accounts of the case, detailed in the newspaper *Wienerisches Diarium,* tell the story of Petar Blagojević, a peasant who began appearing to Kisiljevans in their sleep ten weeks after his death in the summer of 1725. Those he visited—a total of nine villagers in seven days—reported that they awoke to find Blagojević strangling them, and later died of what witnesses called a twenty-four-hour illness. Blagojević's widow, who fled Kisiljevo in the aftermath of these tragedies, claimed to have encountered her dead husband in their home, where he demanded his shoes. In an attempt to regulate mounting hysteria in the region, Austrian authorities intervened, sending a delegation of priests to investigate.

We strike out for Kisiljevo in the early morning. At the wheel: Goran Vuković, our driver, who moonlights as a fountain builder. In the back seat: Maša Kovačević—seventh-year medical student at the University of Belgrade; lifelong friend and token skeptic—who has requested that we wrap her in a bloody shawl and turn her loose in the village to inspire the locals if things start off too slowly.

We take dusty one-lane roads through wheat fields and sprawling vineyards yellowing in the sun. Beside the chicken-wire fences and staved-in roofs of derelict farms, the vacation homes of Belgrade families are slowly coming together, their yards littered with bricks, coils of wire, chunks of Doric columns, marble lions, upended flowerpots. We almost miss the Kisiljevo turnoff, indicated by an unspectacular arrow affixed to a lamppost; I am a bit surprised, having expected to find the village name chiseled into a roadside boulder by a quivering hand, or a beflowered shrine of the Virgin to turn back evil spirits, or perhaps a little blood smeared across a sign as a warning to us. Instead, the road tapers past bright white houses and window boxes of red carnations brimming with such welcoming Riviera charm that I find myself wishing the town would invest in a fog machine.

The village square is empty except for three shirtless old men sitting on a low wall in the shade; but here, at last, we catch a hint of something otherworldly: opposite the community center—where the death certificates of recently deceased villagers hang in the window—stands a blood-red house. We sit in the car staring at it, the silence around us—which has, until this moment, felt disappointingly like the silence of a lazy day in the hot countryside rather than the silence of a haunted village—tightening. The paint looks newly applied, thick and shining, and to the left of the door, above a shuttered window in shivers of black, hangs an enormous, spread-winged bat, its profile sharp and maniacal. I am raising my camera to document it when Maša explains, "That's the Bacardi bat. This must be the bar."

We obtain the cell phone number of Mirko Bogičić, the town's headman, from the convenience store on the corner, and Mirko, without being forewarned of our arrival, drives down to accommodate our quest, abandoning preparations for the summer fair in nearby Požarevac. He is a potbellied, strong-jawed man, and he takes us to his house, where his wife serves us homemade *zova* juice, made from elderberries, in flowered cups. The walls are adorned with pictures of spaniels—Mirko, in addition to being a village headman and full-time farmer, is employed as a dog-show consultant.

He is also working on a book about Petar Blagojević. In 1725, at the height of Kisiljevan hysteria, when the Austrian officials supervised the exhumation of Petar Blagojević's body, it was acknowledged by everyone present that it was entirely un-decomposed. His hair, beard, and nails had continued to grow, and a new layer of skin was emerging from beneath the old one. "Mind you, this was forty days after the burial," says Mirko. "And when they ran the stake through his heart, fresh blood rushed from his ears and nostrils."

Mirko has clearly rehearsed this story; but he does not laugh it off, and the authenticity of the vampire is a point about which he is adamant: Petar Blagojević is the genuine article, the first vampire to be officially certified by the Austrian government. "Here, just across the Danube, is Transylvania and the Romanian Dracula," Mirko says, gesturing toward the river. "But we know him to be merely a legend. They made of him a profitable business."

Kisiljevo has had less success with the salability of its ghoul, but this has not kept the town off the radar of true vampire aficionados. The previous year, two German students came to interview Mirko; that same summer, a paranormal researcher came to sweep the graveyard above town with a detector that led him to an "enhanced energy field" around one of the oldest headstones. In fact, Mirko gets so many visitors asking the same questions that he has the whole itinerary preplanned: he gives me a photocopied page from the legendary Serbian almanac of all things supernatural, which I have been unable to find in Belgrade, and takes us to see Deda Vlastimir, who is said to have encountered an actual vampire.

"Not Petar Blagojević," Mirko says, assuring us that once disposed of, a Kisiljevan vampire stays dead.

Vlastimir Djordjević—affectionately known as Deda Vlastimir—is a ninety-two-year-old Kisiljevan with whiskered cheeks and kind, sleepy eyes, who greets us delightedly in the garden. While we arrange ourselves around the patio table, his white-haired daughter fusses over us, bringing our day's second round of homemade *zova* juice. A great-great-grandson hovers in the kitchen doorway in his pajamas.

"Hear, now, how it was," Deda Vlastimir says, obliging us with high Balkan oratory. "In this village much was said about these vampires, and every once in a while there was something to be seen as well. It is three hundred years since that vampire, that Petar Blagojević—and thus he is practically a legend—three hundred years since they found him fresh in his grave and he caused much grief here. And some people believe, and some people do not believe—but there was another vampire, this Baba Ruža, whom I myself met one night. I had been visiting a friend and was returning home when suddenly before me appeared a woman, a tiny little woman, whose face I did not see. She appeared before me, and I said, 'Who is this?' and she turned to me and vanished."

I am disappointed that he does not say anything about pursuing Baba Ruža with a blackthorn stake, so I ask: "Did you believe?"

"Well, hear me," he says. "I was afraid. My friend's father had to take me home. And there is something in that belief, because three days later, in the house in front of which I saw her"—he taps the table with his knuckles as he says this—"there was a murder. A father killed his son-in-law. Three days later. And right away around the village it was said that these vampires were responsible."

"Evil forces," Mirko cuts in, "evil spirits. Things like that never happen on their own, we must accept that." Deda Vlastimir agrees. "These beliefs," he tells us, "are not written down—but this makes them stronger."

A few months before my expedition, I finally got around to watching Djordje Kadijević's legendary 1973 film, *Leptirica*. The film is based on a short story by the celebrated Serbian writer Milovan Glišić, and, due to the communal nature and rarity of film premieres in the former Yugoslavia, immediately became, upon its airing on national television, a cultural touchstone of my mother's generation. The film was something she used to tell me about when late-night conversations turned toward the horrific and the bizarre—which, in my family, happened on a weekly basis. In some regards, *Leptirica* (The She-Butterfly) is a love story. Its plot follows Strahinja, a young shepherd from Zarožje, who, in an effort to prove himself a worthy husband for the beautiful Radojka, volunteers to spend the night in the village water mill, where the vampire Sava Savanović has supposedly been strangling millers. Accustomed as I am to American vampire films—especially those that combine love stories with Gary Oldman dropping from the ceiling dressed as an oversized green bat or Hugh Jackman shooting Dracula's snake-jawed brides out of the air with an improbable crossbow —I scoffed at my mother's warning. How scary could it really be, this Serbian throwback to the campy Hollywood monster flicks of the 1950s?

As it turns out, the success of *Leptirica*—shot on a shoestring with a cast of ten actors who, combined, have a total of some ninety lines—hinges on the power of suggestion, palpable even from behind the sofa cushions, where I spent the majority of the film's runtime. Whether with the steady pulse of the mill wheel at night or the simple but unforgettably odious black hand in the flour, *Leptirica* paralyzes by holding forth the possibility of a glimpse, never completely revealing what the victims face. In what it does reveal, however, the film overcomes its budgetary and technological limitations by leaving absolutely no room for romantic notions of redemption: Radojka, corrupted by the butterfly carrying Sava Savanović's spirit, changes before the viewer's eyes from a delicate-featured ingénue into a gasping, razor-toothed creature with a hairy face, something much closer to a werewolf than a vampire. The result is both tragic and obscene; the viewer feels tainted simply by having witnessed her ghastly transformation.

Whereas such imagery evokes the southern European vampire's status as an ineradicable spiritual plague, capable of wiping out entire villages, the Western tradition has always, and especially recently, treated vampirism as a source of provocatively desirable sexual power and physical prowess, a force that, with the correct application of human affection, can be overcome. The model for this elegant revenant was perfected on the shores of Lake Geneva in 1816, during the Year Without a Summer, when persistent rain drove Lord Byron and his guests indoors, forcing them to amuse themselves by composing ghost stories: Byron wrote the apocalyptic "Darkness"; Mary Shelley, *Frankenstein;* and John Polidori, "The Vampyre"—which blazed the trail for Bram Stoker's more enduring *Dracula* (1897).

In their brutally single-minded pursuit of sustenance and lack of remorse for their own monstrous compulsions, both Polidori's Lord Ruthven and Stoker's Count Dracula are faithful to their origins. But whereas the original vampire desires seclusion and anonymity to pursue his bloodlust, recast as a figure of nobility he ventures into society—suggesting loneliness, a desire to rejoin the living, a touch of self-reflection. Add to this various other liberties, and 150 years later vampires are sleeping in canopy beds, refrigerating sheep's blood, and breeding armies of little vampirelings to infiltrate the world's most exclusive guest lists.

As for old-school Sava Savanović, there is no desire for redemption, nor evidence of his having been slain; at the end of the film, his butterfly-guised spirit flutters away, presumably to generate more black-clawed bloodsuckers elsewhere. Moreover, research into his origins suggests that his water mill still exists. If Petar Blagojević, whose fate at the hands of all those stake-wielding Austrians was well documented, continues to haunt contemporary Kisiljevans beyond the grave—indeed, *beyond* beyond the grave— then surely, I reason, the presence of an undefeated vampire must be that much more palpable in the community he once terrorized.

Zarožje, like Kisiljevo, is of no particular importance to cartographers. But to properly explain the degree of its godforsakenness, I must fall back on an old Serbian idiom—*vukojebina,* which translates roughly as "wolf's fuck," suggesting a location so isolated that its inhabitants, lacking even sheep for sexual companionship, turn to comforts lupine.

Two and a half hours out of Belgrade, the road to Zarožje climbs into bright green hills dotted with farmhouses, their pastures ending in steeply sloping pine forests that gird the bare mountaintops. Just past the sign for a thirteenth-century monastery, a fogbank rolls onto us suddenly, clinging to the windows, smothering the sun as we slow to a crawl. From the back seat, Maša's voice is increasingly enthusiastic. *"Extra,"* she says, using an Englishism that's become Serbian slang for "awesome." *Ambiance* at last.

The absence of road signs makes us nervous, so we stop the next person we see, a rail-thin man who materializes out of the fog in the vanguard of a flock of sheep. I roll down the window and Goran shouts: "Pardon, good shepherd, but is this the way to Zarožje?"

The man leans on the car and swings his head inside. He is middle-aged, but his face is furrowed with the lines of outdoor labor, and he smells heavily of lanolin. His three remaining teeth are yellow. "Are you looking for that vampire?" he asks us. When we say nothing, he tells us those are stories, just stories, then points us forward into the mist. "That way."

Once we've left him behind, Maša offers that Sava Savanović may be the only reason anyone comes up here; the road has been empty for miles, and we are winding past houses where the dead are buried in front yards, their marble headstones wreathed in roses and fenced off with chicken wire. These houses seem deserted, but then we see a woman bent over a tub of laundry on a cottage porch. I roll down the window to ask for directions. "Pardon!" I call to her. "Is this the way to the water mill?" She looks up, then lifts the tub and moves indoors.

"Pardon!" we shout to one household after another, but everything about the locals' demeanor indicates that we will not be earning any invitations for *zova*, that we are on our own. Standing ankle-deep in the runoff from a sty teeming with massive pink hogs, we yell at a house whose TV we can hear through the screen door. "Pardon!" Maša and I shout in unison, but when a man comes out, belly bulging beneath a white undershirt, shuffling across the porch in oversized and uneven green socks, he only grumbles at us unintelligibly and turns his back.

At the next cluster of houses, the residents have recently slaughtered some goats. The skins are stretched out, drying on a line in the sun. Goran says, "Let's not ask these people," and guns the engine.

Then there appears from around the next bend a figure who looks like someone to whom you would surrender your last biscuit if you were a character in a Hans Christian Andersen tale: he has a feathered cap and a walking stick and a suspiciously cheerful air for a white-haired man crutching his way up a fifty-degree incline. "About seven more kilometers, and you'll reach the big church," he says. "Go past it, and then keep going until you get to the trail that leads to the river. You'll find a chapel, and then the water mill is two hundred meters away." At the church we find, side by side on the doorstep, a fifty-dinar bill and a severed squirrel's tail. Goran, who was born in a small village, can explain the money—if worshipers are moved by fear or despair while the church is closed, they sometimes leave offerings on the threshold. He has no theories about the tail.

Our tires, after braking on gravel for fifteen downhill kilometers, are beginning to smoke. We leave the car and follow the sound of the river that rises from the trees below us, down a slippery footpath through the undergrowth and into the field at the bottom of the valley. The chapel, a squat white hut with shuttered windows, sits at the field's edge, gray granite cliffs looming up behind it. On the other side of the river at the bottom of the slope, we find what we've been looking for.

Sava Savanović's water mill is a low wooden building that stands amid thickets of *kopriva* (nettles) with its back to the river, door yawning wide. We wade through the river and then the nettles, the leaves clinging to our pants, fluorescent grasshoppers diving into our faces. The lintel and sides of the water mill are covered in graffiti, evidence of decades of visitors who have beaten us to the vampire's lair. I am discouraged by the defacements: in Serbia, popular haunts tend to double as garbage heaps, and the more rancid the trash, the more legitimate and desirable the hangout.

But the interior of Sava's water mill is pristine. The river whispers along the walls, and picturesque cobwebs hang from the rafters, thick and shining in the light that filters through the cracks in the roof. The milling implements are laid out neatly by the rusted mill wheel, and in the corner sits a small, tidy mound of ashes and sticks. Goran notes that the sticks have been sharpened into points. Someone has been here, and recently.

On the highway at the top of the mountain, after our car has suffered the drive back up the gravel track, we come across a burnt-brown old man wearing a traditional *šajkača* cap and woolen vest, sitting at the roadside, keeping an eye on the flock grazing across the road.

We pull up to him: "Pardon. Do you know anything about the vampire?" He peers into the car and says: "You mean from the water mill?"

"Yes," we say.

"Have you been to the water mill?"

"Yes."

"That's my water mill!"

The man's name is Vladimir Jagodić, and his family has for many generations owned the land on which the water mill sits. Standing by the highway, his hands behind his back, he assures us that there's nothing to the stories about Sava Savanović. "There was a great famine in those days," he says. "And this man—a very clever man—would go into the water mill at night and throttle the millers a little and then steal their flour. You see?" His smile is full of satisfaction. "But nobody died, nobody was killed here. I had a grandmother of ninety years who would tell me these stories—but she knew, too, that nobody was killed."

He tells us that when he was a little boy his father would make him spend the night in the water mill to make him brave, and that in all the years he slept there, all the nights he walked home in the darkness, he has never once seen anything.

Then he says: "This isn't even the right water mill. There was a much, much older water mill not too far from here, a stone water mill, where those attacks happened. But there's nothing left of that one, only a ruin. So when they come to take pictures, they photograph mine." When we ask him why, in that event, his father forced him to spend the night in the wrong water mill, he changes the subject and tells us that these fears did not exist during the days of Tito.

There is, he insists, no vampire in Zarožje. For the potential victims of the vampire who does not exist, Zarožans have built a lonely little chapel in a field below a goat-horned granite peak, kept within running distance of a water mill barricaded by thorns in case the stakes inside it fail. Pay no mind, the locals tell us, to those stories about Sava Savanović. But we leave feeling that we just missed him.

The scholar Paul Barber offers a straightforward, anthropological explanation of vampirism, attributing the etiology of the Balkan vampire to ignorance regarding disease and the decay of bodies. He draws parallels between vampirism and medieval myths surrounding contagion. He reasons that peasants, evaluating the body of a suspected vampire in the grave, misinterpreted the effects of different soils and climates on decomposition rates; misunderstood the normal deterioration of skin and nails as new growth. The shriek of the vampire following a staking is easily understood if you know that the human body, after weeks in the grave, lets out a moan if the gases that have been building in the lungs are suddenly forced out.

This direct route from coffin to creature leaves out one element crucial to understanding the regional pervasion of vampirism: Balkan religion rests on tradition rather than belief, superstition rather than faith, and despite the propagation of Islam and two branches of Christianity, the influence of the occupying religions was never particularly deep; scratch the surface, and you find a reservoir of shared pagan influence, which all comes down to the same thing: faith in God, whether shrined by a cathedral, basilica, or mosque, takes a back seat to fear of the Devil. (My grandmother, a Bosnian Muslim, would rather protect me from him with an icon of Saint George than with nothing at all.)

This is not the Devil as Antichrist or distant source of temptation or maître d' of a posthumous fire pit. The Balkan Devil is a walking pestilence, an organic household entity, and his hands are on everything that is dear or fragile; so we spit on newborns and call them ugly; we avoid staking a claim to good health or publicly discussing the pleasures we most look forward to in our lives; we shroud even our suffering, for fear he will enhance it. He sits at the shoulders of all our most certain plans, ready to upend them, a full-time Olympian troublemaker. The saints protect us from him, but only if we embrace a prescribed etiquette of daily rituals and protective tchotchkes, and then only maybe. "God willing," we say, but God is just a buffer.

Indeed, God's absence from the mindset of Communist Yugoslavia seems to have been one of the key reasons why the reign of Josip Broz Tito, however corrupt and iron-fisted, has retained its widespread reputation as a golden age. It is no surprise, then, that when God made his trifurcating comeback following the dissolution of Tito's regime, the Devil—appearing, as always, in a hundred guises: some vampiric, some idolized, some despotic, and some more newsworthy than others—followed him back into the region's life, and remained there.

The resurgent vampires secured a particularly firm bite on Serbian political theater. In 1987, a pivotal moment for the Socialist Party's increasingly destabilizing post-Tito government came in its unexpectedly fierce denunciation of the editors of *Student* magazine at Belgrade University, who had mocked the national observance of the Marshal's birthday as "The Vampire's Ball." During the war years that soon followed, one of the more histrionic talking heads on national television repeatedly promised viewers that vampires would arise from their graves to vanquish enemies of the state (lest the undead minions fail to discriminate between friend and foe, the prognosticator went so far as to advise keeping on hand plenty of garlic). As for Slobodan Milošević—who had sat at the helm as Tito's age of gold fell apart; who died in 2006 while on trial in The Hague; and who is buried in the vampire-rich locale of Požarevac—in advance of the one-year anniversary of his death a media-savvy local artist, later claiming to have acted in an abundance of caution, hammered a four-foot blackthorn stake into his coffin.

For a week after Zarožje, Maša makes a show of piling garlic onto everything I eat, and then packs me off to Croatia. Her bloodletting, brain-sampling duties at the University of Belgrade preclude her from joining me, but Veljko, a painter who lives in the Dalmatian fishing village of Zaostrog, agrees to act as guide, provided his name is changed in order to prevent any supernatural retribution for his involvement.* He is a lanky, loose-limbed man with a ponytail of gray hair who has cultivated the art of living simply, and who fills me in on an important local *vukodlak* while his little car clings to the tight curves of the coastal highway that will lead us to Potomje, the beast's lair. Two hundred years ago, he tells me, a sailor from Zaostrog, having left the mainland to seek seasonal work at the vineyards across the bay, arrived in Potomje to find the villagers there in a state of great distress. For several months, the village had been marauded by a sinister *vukodlak*, who would knock on people's doors at night and strangle those who answered. It is unclear why the villagers did not think to stop answering their doors after dark. At any rate, the village priest said to the sailor, "Your house is next, beware tonight." So the brave sailor resolved to stay up, hiding behind the door, and when the *vukodlak* came knocking, the sailor chased him through the vineyards and across the fields, where he disappeared into a blackberry thicket. The sailor hurled his knife after the ghoul, and the following morning returned with a priest and some villagers to burn down the brambles. The fire revealed a stone mound, which the sailor struck with his knife, in turn revealing a tomb inside of which the *vukodlak* was sitting. He

---

* Several other names have been changed with this same precaution in mind.

looked up at his pursuers and said: "As I could not kill you, now you must kill me."

No two ways about how this story ends; however, before they killed the *vukodlak*, the villagers asked him whether he had accomplices. Unlike his Serbian counterparts, this Croatian vampire was not a solitary mischief-maker; nor was he particularly loyal to his fellow ghouls, because he divulged their hideouts without even leveraging the information to bargain for his un-life. The first of the two remaining *vukodlaks* is said to have been staked under a nonspecific oak tree on the island of Mljet; the other, also long forgotten, was dispatched in a potato field outside the fishing village of Trpanj.

Potomje's current village priest, whom we accost outside the church, knows nothing about the *vukodlak*. The oldest man in town —whom we ambush as he is walking home from church with an armful of decapitated flowers—will not give us his name, and also claims to know nothing of the *vukodlak;* but he, too, declares that nothing would have come of our line of questioning in Tito's day. And Barba Niko, at ninety-five an also-ran for oldest man, also professes ignorance of the village's vampire son; but, he says as his wife and daughter usher us in for lunch, he does know something, something that suggests the vampire's legend has survived only by undergoing an unusual transformation.

"For many years in this village," he tells us, "it's been said that there is a curse. Carry anything into or out of the stable between Christmas and New Year's, and vermin will come from the vineyards to pluck the eyes from your livestock." It happened to the two spinster sisters living across the road from him forty years ago, and it happened to Barba Niko himself. A neighbor once brought his family a gift of wheat, which they foolhardily stored in the stable on a day between Christmas and New Year's. "We had a beautiful lamb back then," he says, "just one, a lovely thing. The next morning, my mother called me into the stable to see it fallen dead, with both eyes plucked out.

"Nobody breaks the curse," he says.

The villagers all swear that the creature who gnaws on their livestock and keeps them out of their storehouses in early winter is unaffiliated with anything as laughable as a *vukodlak*, but this does not explain why the rodent with uncanny timing arises from the

very fields in which the *vukodlak* met his end, or why many blackberry patches outside Potomje bear signs of recent scorchings. The
fields are rife, too, with Iron Age Illyrian burial mounds, shining piles of white rock that dot the hills all the way to the mainland. These tombs are sacred, and even the Dalmatian people—
in whose homes, gardens, and church foundations you will find
enough Greek and Roman sarcophagary to rival the storerooms of
the Vatican—will not touch the ancient graves.

Veljko's father is Barba Nenad, a fisherman who, in addition to
having lived on the Adriatic for more than five decades, also raises
livestock and makes his own *rakija* and wine, the strongest in town.
Over lunch late that afternoon he is amused, but not surprised, by
my near misses in Kisiljevo, Zarožje, and Potomje, and is uncon-
vinced that the rest of my journey will result in the desired encounter. He tells me about the evening he heard the guitar in his room
play itself in the dead of night, how he sat up three times and three
times it stopped, only to start up again once he'd turned off the
light.

"Who knows what it would have meant to me if I hadn't sat up
and had a look at that guitar," he says. "Would you believe it? There
was a mouse inside."

In the tiny Croatian village of Otrić-Seoci lives Živko, a respected
headman renowned for his fluency in regional lore. His threshold
is the last stop on our vampire itinerary, his well of tales the final
reservoir from which, Veljko assures me, I will acquire the esoteric
knowledge I seek.

We call on Živko in the early evening, but he is not at home. His
house sits at the far end of the village, in the shade of an ancient
walnut tree, looking out over olive groves and vineyards. The spot
is so close to the Bosnian border that my mobile telephone lights
up every five minutes to alert me that my carrier and rates have
changed, as some distant cell tower struggles to make the distinc-
tion between Croatia and its eastern neighbor. The two women sitting on the veranda in black dresses and slippers tell us that Živko
has asked us to wait for him. As we linger through sundown, the
goats come back from pasture—first we hear their bells tinkling
on the hill above the house, and then they appear, shaggy and slit-

pupiled, clustering together on the trail. The herd dog on their heels, a sleek black mongrel whose paralyzing stare means business, considers me from a distance as he drives the goats down the slope and into the stables below. He calls the stragglers, and when an uncooperative, blaze-faced buck shows defiance by making a determined charge at me, the dog intercepts it, urging it through the gate.

One of the women, who has seen my awkward dive out of the path of the oncoming goat, laughs knowingly. "No goats in the Nativity," she says.

With the darkness comes Živko in his yellow van. He has been out buying a *rakija* still, he says, and I am unsettled by him from the beginning; perhaps it is his portly stature and red face, or the fact that he is not nearly as old as I expected, or the thick hoarseness of his voice, which betrays his having just eaten a large meal, or the moonlit circumstances of his arrival.

He tells us about what people believe, about ghosts in a neighboring home, about the spells necessary to cast an evil spirit out of the house. He tells us about a scorned woman who would come to his bedside to throttle him in his sleep, and how he would awake to find his house empty, a cat staring at him from the open doorway. Živko's brother, an elderly man who has caned his way out of the house and is offering us grape juice, chuckles at this, and says something about how Živko's amorous attentions turn women into cats. Undeterred, Živko describes his ability to commune with the dead, a gift with which he was born but discovered only as the result of his uncanny experiences with a children's game; about the communications he has made on behalf of friends, of family, of the loved ones who tend to be far more restless than those who are already gone.

He tells us about the *vile*, Croatian mountain sirens, jealous spirit-women whose whims range from seducing men to fomenting war to playing girlish tricks on the villagers. "You come into the stable in the morning," says Živko, "and the horse's mane and tail have been braided tight, like the braid of a girl." He has seen it himself: no human hands can untangle a braid a *vila* has made, and cutting the hair will kill the horse.

Night has fallen, and the generator across the street has gone quiet. The village is empty, and there is barely enough light for me

to see Živko's face. It takes me a while to realize it, but his arrival by
night was carefully orchestrated to create the atmosphere for this
interview. The moment this occurs to me, the goats in the stable let
loose a chorus of shrill, vein-stiffening screams.

"Ungodly, aren't they?" Živko says, laughing and patting my arm
as he pulls me back down to my chair, from which I have leaped
without realizing it. "No goats in the Nativity, you know. They are
the Devil's beast."

The Balkan vampire consistently arises as a product of hard times.
As so many people in Serbia and Croatia grumbled at me, the reign
of Josip Broz Tito was a time in which the primitivism of ancient
fears had no place. For a region as war-ravaged and unstable as the
former Yugoslavia, it is no wonder that the devastation and disillu-
sion of recent decades precipitated a return to the mainstays of
tradition, and especially to supernatural stories in which evil, if in-
defatigable, is always easily identifiable. Villages overcome their
vampire plagues as they would more secular hardships: the story
becomes in its own way a narrative of hope, a throwback to the
surety of old beliefs, old customs—to tiny, frightening truths that
stabilize a community against the world. The vampire is an agent
of chaos, a self-inflicted spiritual trauma, but nevertheless manifests the Devil in a form that society can, occasionally, defeat.

If we consider the vampire a cultural necessity, an adaptable
product of a society's fears and obsessions, then his role in the
Western world is not so different. Here, too, the story of the vampire offers hope. Refined and beautiful—and stapled into his
obligatory leather pants—he is a far cry from that dirty, bloated
wanderer of graveyards, that product of a people for whom the
desolation of the dead cannot surpass the cruelty of the living. He
is too well traveled now to linger at crossroads, too hygienically inclined to dig his way out of coffins; having spent eternity studying
art, literature, philosophy, he is no longer confounded by a cruci-
fix; as a lover, he has worked hard to overcome his cadaverous loco-
motion, his ungainly south Slavic diction, and his indirect Victorian fumbling, so that the mere sight of his fangs now inspires
young maidens to bare their throats of their own accord. The
Americanized vampire is the ultimate fantasy for a nation in decline: the person who has been able to take it all with him when he
dies, who has outlived the vagaries of civilization itself.

Having abandoned the culture that forged him, moreover, he deceives us into thinking that he has moved beyond what he always has been—a disease. Now the plague he spreads is a therapeutic fantasy in which an embarrassment of wealth and youth and hedonism is acceptable as long as its beneficiary is equipped with the right intentions. We have forgotten to be afraid because as long as he protects his loved ones, as long as he is conscious of his own dangerous nature, as long as he pits himself willingly against others who share his wrath but not his noble motivations, we are willing to believe that a weapon of evil, in the right hands, can be transformed into an instrument of good.

In the early fall, three months after my departure from Croatia, I receive a hesitant e-mail from Veljko. He writes with information he's restrained himself from sharing until my journey was over and I was safely home. The morning of my departure from Otrić-Seoci, he says, he stood by and helped load my belongings into the bus having already learned, from village gossips, that Živko's brother —cheerful alcoholic, generous host, mocking unbeliever—had died suddenly the previous night, a few hours after we left Živko's house. In some ways, as Veljko sees it, the suddenness of the death is a good thing, because liver failure is a slow and excruciating process. But something about it still leaves him unsettled, and he has spent months wondering whether he should tell me about this, weighing anew the consequences of explicit communication. Is it possible that our conversation with Živko loosed some infernal force that night, upset the delicate balance of something unseen, and felled Živko's poor brother as a warning to the rest of us? Veljko isn't certain. But he is, he tells me, entitled to his superstitions.

ANNIE PROULX

A Year of Birds

FROM *Harper's Magazine*

ON MY FIRST DAY alone at Bird Cloud, my ranch near the Medi-cine Bow range in southern Wyoming, a bald eagle sat in a favorite perch tree across the river. It was December 30, 2006. The day be-fore, two of them had sat side by side for hours, gazing down through the pale water sliding over the rocks, waiting for incau-tious fish. This was eagle-style fishing. Sometimes they stood in the shallows, cold water soaking their fancy leggings. Bald eagles are skillful at their trade, and I have seen them haul fish out of the freezing water onto the ice, or swoop down, sink their talons into a big trout, and rise up with the heavy fish twisting futilely. Bird Cloud's construction crew was lucky enough to see one of them dive onto a large fish, lock its talons, then struggle to get into the air with the heavy load, meanwhile riding the fish like a surfboard down the rushing river.

The house at Bird Cloud took two years to build. During that period I tried to identify the habits of the birds in the area and gradually recognized seasonal waves of avian inhabitants. Watch-ing a large number of birds took concentration and time—there was nothing casual about it. The bald eagles were permanent resi-dents. Some hawks stayed and some hawks went south. The great horned owls stayed. The ravens raised families every year and then went somewhere else for the summer to hunt once the young be-gan flying. They came back in autumn to tidy up the nest and poke around, then departed again before the winter storms came. In early spring hundreds of red-winged blackbirds hit the copper-stemmed willows on the island and the cliff echoed their yodeling *aujourd'hui! aujourd'hui!* I put out feeders to attract the smaller birds, but days, weeks, and months went by with no visitors. These wild birds were too naive to recognize feeders as a source of food.

I was impressed that the bald eagles stuck around. The *Stokes Field Guide* stated: "Once a pair is established on a territory, they are very reluctant to move elsewhere to breed." That fit the case. Stokes also warned readers to stay at least a quarter of a mile away from the nest during the "egg-laying to early nesting" period, as alarmed parents might abandon their young. But these eagles hadn't read *Stokes* and tolerated all of us. The house itself was roughly a quarter of a mile from them and they warned us away only if we stood on the riverbank directly across from the nest or got over to the other side of the water and walked near their tree. The bald eagles have raised two chicks every year except one, when only a single chick survived. The books say one surviving chick is the norm, but these eagles have been calm and laid-back—wonderful parents with a high success rate. Whenever a stranger came to the house the bald eagles took turns flying over and scrutinizing them. Anything new—lawn chair, garden hose, shrubs—piqued their curiosity, and they flew over low and slow, examining the object. In fact, they were nosy. It was quite fair. I peered at them through binoculars, they peered back.

The North Platte River runs through the property, taking an east-west turn for a few miles in its course. Bird Cloud is 640 acres, a square mile of riparian shrubs and cottonwood, some wetland areas during June high water, sage flats, and a lot of weedy over-grazed pasture. On the lower portion, about 120 acres, Jack Creek, an important spawning site for trout, comes down from the Sierra Madre, thirty miles distant, and angles through the property to enter the North Platte. Jack Creek is big enough to need a bridge, and it has one, a sturdy structure made from the floor of a railroad freight car. Just below Jack Creek there is a handsome little island, a shady cottonwood bosque, in the North Platte. The bulk of the property, more than five hundred acres, lies at the top of a sandstone cliff, a sloping expanse of sedge and sage. The cliff is four hundred feet tall, the creamy cap rock a crust of ancient coral. This monolith has been tempered by thousands of years of polishing wind, blowtorch sun, flood and rattling hail, sluice of rain. After

rain the cliff looks bruised, with dark splotches and vertical channels like old scars. Two miles west the cliff shrinks into ziggurat
stairs of iron-colored stone. At the east end of the property the cliff
shows a fault, a diagonal scar that a geologist friend says is likely
related to the Rio Grande Rift, which is slowly tearing the North
American continent apart.

On that first solitary day at Bird Cloud, I walked east to the Jack
Creek bridge and looked up at a big empty nest high on the cliff
across the river. It was clearly an eagle nest. Had the bald eagles
used it before moving half a mile west to the cottonwoods? Had it
belonged to another pair of eagles? The huge structure was heaped
with snow. Somehow it had a fierce look, black and bristling with
stick ends. At 4:30 the sun still plated the cliff with gold light. Ten
minutes later it had faded to cardboard gray. I looked again at the
distant big empty nest, then noticed that on the colluvium below
and a little to the west of the nest there were two elk, likely refugees from a big herd that had moved through the property several
weeks earlier when hunting season opened. Twenty or thirty geese
flew upriver high enough to be out of gun range. Dusk thickened,
and then, in the gloaming, I saw a large bird fly into a cranny directly above the elk. Roosting time for someone, but who?

The next day—the last day of the year—the sun cleared the Medi-
cine Bows at 7:45. It was a beautiful, clear winter morning, the sun
sparkling on the snow, no wind, two degrees below zero, and a setting moon that was almost full. As Richard Lassels, a seventeenth-
century guide for the Grand Tour, said of fireflies, "Huge pretty,
methought." By noon both bald eagles were in the trees above the
river, watching for fish below. After half an hour they flew upriver
to try their luck in another stretch of water.

In mid-morning out of the corner of my eye I saw a large bird
flying upriver with steady, brisk flaps, and remembered the one I
had seen the previous evening taking shelter near the big, empty
nest. Was it the same bird? What was it? It was too large to be a
hawk.

New Year's Day was warm and sunny, thirty-two degrees, encour-
aging a few foolish blades of grass to emerge from the snow. A flock
of goldeneyes, diving underwater to forage, dominated a part of
the river that stayed open all winter. I thought there might be a hot
spring there that kept it clear of ice.

At the end of the daylight the bald eagles sat in trees three hundred yards apart, merging into the dusk but still staring into the river. Their low-light vision must be good. At 4:40 a dozen Canada geese flew upstream. An orange ribbon lay on the western horizon. I waited, binoculars in hand. Two minutes later the last sunlight licked the top of the cliff, then was gone. The sky turned purple to display a moon high and full. I did not see the large mystery bird. Perhaps it was an owl and had no problem flying after dark. But I doubted it. I had a strong suspicion that it was an eagle, the owner of the big, sinister nest.

For me the keeping of a list of birds sighted has neither value nor interest. I am more interested in birds of particular places, how they behave over longer periods and how they use their chosen habitats. What the birds did, ate, and raised attracted me. I suppose I could say I was drawn to their stories. But in thinking about all this the next morning I once again missed seeing the big mystery bird. In the fleeting seconds it was in view I saw that its coloring was uniformly dark. The rhythm of its wingbeats was similar to that of an eagle. Could it be a juvenile bald eagle from last year's hatch? Or was it a golden? Maybe.

Days of flailing west wind, strong enough to push its snout under the crust of the fallen snow wherever the hares or I had left footprints, strong enough to then flip up big pancakes of crust and send them cartwheeling east until they disintegrated in puffs. Eagles love strong wind. It is impossible to miss the joy they take in exhibition flying. The bald pair were out playing in the gusts, mounting higher and higher until they were specks, then splitting apart. After a few minutes of empty sky the unknown big dark bird flapped briefly into view before disappearing in a snow squall.

Late in the afternoon, as dusk crept up the eastern rim of the world, one of the bald eagles showed up with talons full of branches and dropped out of sight at the nest tree. Were they redecorating the nest on a cold winter day? The wind swelled and blustered. A solitary duck appeared, blown all over the place. White underside and black head and wings and was that a round white spot on its face?—probably a goldeneye, but for a second it resembled a penguin shot out of a cannon. Half an hour later two more eastbound ducks appeared, clocking along with the wind at about eighty miles per hour. The second bald eagle came into sight fighting the head-

wind, just hanging in the air and flapping vainly, until finally it
turned and in seconds was miles away. The nest eagle rose up and
followed.

The next morning the wind had calmed to thirty miles an hour
with gusts hitting fifty. It was a cold and sunny day, and the bald
eagle team was out flying at 8:00. As I made coffee I saw the big
mystery bird flapping out of sight toward the neighboring ranch.
Why was it so elusive? I wanted badly to get a good look at it, but it
seemed to fly past only when my head was turned. The two isolated
elk stood on a knoll at the west end of the cliff; antlerless, dark
brown necks, yellow rumps, and red-brown body color. At first sight
I could imagine they were the mountain sheep that used to live on
the cliff in Indian times. Their faces seemed rather dished, like
sheep faces. Magpies were busy across the river, and one raven sat
in a tree slightly to the west of its nest site in the cliff. Could the raven, like the eagle, be interested in fixing up its nest so early in the
year?

By afternoon the wind was up again, and at the top of the sky
were three eagle-shaped specks. Three eagles playing in the wind.
Three? Was one of them a juvenile bald planning to nest here, or
was it the big mystery bird? And just how many eagles called this
cliff home?

That night the wind went berserk, terrific shrieking and batter-
ing. In the morning it was still intense and I could see the windows moving slightly in and out. The worst wind yet. I went out
into the driveway to see how badly it was drifted. Huge impassable
drifts. The wind almost knocked me over. A small bird shot past the
kitchen window, but on the far side of the river the two bald eagles
sat calmly in the trees near their nest.

During the nights of high-velocity wind I lay tense and awake in
the dark listening to the bellowing and roar. In the daytime it was
easier to ignore. The television would not work because the wind
had wrenched the satellite dish out of alignment. After four or five
days of relentless howling the wind fell into a temporary coma,
turning everything over to a warm, sunny, and calm day. Temperatures climbed into the forties. But the weather report warned that
another storm was approaching. A friend in town smashed a narrow alley through the drifts on the county road and cleared out the
driveway. I was no longer snowbound. The power company made it
out and realigned the dish.

The daylight hours were lengthening by a few minutes each day. While it was calm I walked down to the east end of the property, and glancing up at the cliff I saw not one but two big dark birds. They were playing in the air, obviously delighted with the calm, with each other, with life in general. Then they both dove into their bedroom niche in the chimney west of the big, empty nest. I could not hear their voices, because a large flock of ducks, more than a hundred, flew over, twittering and whistling. The birds looked like eagles, they flew like eagles, but they were completely dark. They did not have the golden napes pictured in the bird books. Goldens soar with a slight dihedral; bald eagles soar with their wings almost flat. But I was now almost sure that a pair of golden eagles owned the big nest and were preparing to use it.

The next day started sunny but another three-day storm was on the way, and by late morning low, malignant clouds smothered the ranges in all directions. The weather people said it was going to turn very cold. I took advantage of the lull before the storm to get outdoors with the binoculars. A raven was fooling around the cliff face, trying out several niches. Then the big dark birds appeared above the cliff in a tumbling display. The binoculars showed that they did have lighter necks and heads. I had no doubt now. They were a pair of golden eagles and they were courting, planning to fix up the empty nest and raise a family only half a mile from the bald eagles. I felt fabulously wealthy with a bald eagle nest and a golden eagle nest both visible from my dining room window. I wanted to spend the day watching them, but the storm was due to hit during the night so I headed out to get supplies while the road was still open.

January wore on. It was cold, and day after day the snow fell as in Conrad Aiken's story "Silent Snow, Secret Snow," which I read when I was eight years old, thinking it was a story about a profound snowfall. Later, when I learned it was an oblique study of intensifying juvenile madness, I was disappointed. On the frozen river four coyotes nosed around the north shore margins. Upstream the goldeneyes' strip of water was still open but shrinking daily.

On a Sunday morning of flat calm it was twenty-one degrees below zero. The air was stiff. Freezing mist had coated every tree and shrub. The river pinched in, making waists of black water in the ice. There were no birds in sight. The sun struggled up and the mist rose in great humps over the remaining ribbons of open water. The tops of the cottonwoods glittered like icy nosegays, stems wrapped in gauze. Spring seemed very far away, but the bald eagle pair sat side by side catching the first rays. They often sat this way, one great eagle-beast with two heads. As the sun gained height the eagles fluffed themselves out and began to preen. A lone magpie flew over the mist. In the afternoon I skied down to the east end and into the cottonwood bosque. A golden eagle and four magpies were eating the scanty remains of a snowshoe hare. The eagle fled as I came in sight, and the magpies followed reluctantly, sure I was after their feast. It was easy to see what had happened. The hare's tracks zigged and zagged through the brush, but one foot east of the corpse I saw the snow-angel wing prints of the attacking eagle.

Wyoming was once a haven for eagle killers. In the bad old days of the 1960s and 1970s in this valley many men who are now cattle ranchers raised sheep and firmly believed that bald and golden eagles carried off young lambs. If you raised sheep you killed ea-gles—bald or golden, but especially goldens, though both birds were protected by law—by poison (thallium sulfate was popular), or by shotgun from rented helicopters and small planes, or by rifle from an open pickup window. Eagles were killed in other states, especially in the West, but Wyoming became notorious to the U.S. Fish and Wildlife Service, to the Audubon Society, and to news-paper readers across the country as the home ground of the most ignorant and vicious eagle-killing ranchers. Chief among them was the wealthy and powerful sheep rancher Herman Werner, ex-president of the Wyoming Stock Growers Association. He and his son-in-law were called "the Wyoming helicopter monsters" after they used a hired helicopter to "sluice" eagles.

Nathaniel P. Reed, an assistant secretary of the interior under Richard Nixon, made stopping the killings a primary goal. In 1971 the FBI set up a sting. An agent who had been raised in the West posed as a ranch hand and got a job on Werner's spread, where, in the bunkhouse, he heard about dozens of dead eagles. Because this was hearsay, a federal judge would not issue a search warrant. But two Audubon Society members who had been monitoring the eagle killings were out at the airfield one day and happened to no-tice someone working on a nearby helicopter. They could see a shotgun and empty shells in the craft. They had a camera with them and they used it. The man working on the helicopter realized he had been photographed. Weeks later the anxiety-ridden helicopter pilot showed up at the Department of the Interior in Washington. He said that if he were granted immunity he'd tell about the eagle killings, and so he did, telling a Senate subcommittee that he had carried eagle-hunting shooters into the Wyoming skies, that Werner was one of the air service's best customers, and that the gunners had shot more than five hundred bald and golden eagles. *Time* reported that the Wyoming dead-eagle count was 770 birds. Despite "national outrage" the department was still not able to get a search warrant for Werner's land. But the U.S. Air Force flew a surveillance plane over the ranch, and an infrared camera picked up a pile of decomposing flesh. That finally got the search warrant and led to the discovery of a great number of eagle carcasses. As Dennis Drabelle reported in *Audubon* magazine:

> There was still a hitch. The U.S. attorney for Wyoming balked at bringing a case against the rancher because he was sure that Herman Werner would never be convicted by a Wyoming jury. Werner . . . made a surprise visit to [Nathaniel] Reed's office. "He simply bolted in," Reed remembers, "a wiry man wearing a Stetson hat. He said he was going to get me. I said quietly, 'Before you get me, please tell me who you are.' He said, 'I am Herman Werner, the man who protects his sheep by killing eagles. And you don't know anything about eagles.'"

The tough alternative newspaper *High Country News* took up the cause and public opinion began to quiver and shift. The U.S. attorney general pressed for prosecution. But Werner never came to trial. A few months before the court date, he was killed in a car wreck. In Wyoming, as the wool market declined and sheep men turned to cattle, as the fine for killing eagles greatly increased, as ranchers began to learn that the Department of the Interior had sharp teeth and that bald eagles were interested in carrion and fish, not lambs, the killings mostly stopped.

A very Wyoming touch to the whole affair is in the Werner Wildlife Museum at Casper College. The museum includes "an extensive bird collection."

Finally, after weeks of swinging in the wind, the bird feeder attracted a clientele—around fifty gray-crowned rosy finches. Rosies started coming in from everywhere. Chris Fisher in *Birds of the Rocky Mountains* put it well: "During the winter, Gray-crowned Rosy Finches spill out of the attics of the Rockies to flock together at lower elevations." So they were likely coming into this valley from both the Sierra Madre and the Medicine Bows. They rose into the sky for no reason I could ascertain, paused, and then returned to the feeder. There were no birds of prey in sight, no humans, no dogs or cows or snares, the wind was calm and the day sunny. Did they all fly up to spy out the land for distant threats? Or to reassert a (to me, invisible) hierarchy? Sometimes they flew to the trees near the river for a few minutes, then back to the feeder. I had to refill the thing several times a day.

The beautiful days had grown longer. One morning I watched one of the bald eagles dive toward an open stretch of water off the island, and I ran madly upstairs with the binoculars just in time to see it heave a fish onto the ice. It ate part of the fish and then flew to the nest. At ten past five the sun still gilded the top fifty feet of the cliff. One bald eagle was in the nest tree, the other flying down-river. The cliff turned the color of a russet apple, and I enjoyed the rare deep orange sunset smoldering under the edge of a dark dirty-sock cloud.

I bought a telescope and set it up in my bedroom, which has a grand view of the river and the cliff. The eagles weren't in sight but one of the elk was. Oddly, it seemed to be wearing a canvas jacket, different and lighter in color than its neck and haunches. Was it a trick of the light? It looked like a boulder in the middle. After an hour the elk stood up and disclosed the second elk lying close be-hind it. With the telescope, details leaped into prominence. The first elk pulled some tufts of hair from its back, then nibbled on sage or rabbit brush. The second elk became invisible again. There looked to be well over a hundred rosy finches at the feeder. I tried to walk along the river but the golden eagles became so agitated that I turned back. One golden angrily escorted me all the way to the house. I had once thought of inviting bird-watchers onto the property but I knew then that was impossible. The goldens had to have privacy.

A few days later I went for an evening walk on the old property-line road, keeping a quarter-mile distance between myself and the goldens. They came out but did not call, just flew along the cliff, watching me. Near the end of the property another pair of goldens appeared, silent and flying rather low as though also checking me out. Suddenly the nest pair came roaring east along the cliff and drove the strange pair away. I could see the new goldens settling in a tree to the east. Perhaps they were nesting there. Six eagles in three pairs in the space of a mile.

The next morning one of the bald eagles and a prairie falcon had a sky-filling quarrel, the falcon darting, the eagle swooping. The falcon disappeared suddenly. At noon the wind began to rise and in an hour it was lashing the cottonwoods. One of the bald eagles sat on a branch above the river watching for fish. The branch moved vigorously to and fro. With each lurch the eagle braced its tail against the branch like a woodpecker, and for some reason I found this endearing. Sometimes I thought of these birds as Evan Connell's Mr. and Mrs. Bridge. The falcon flew around near the goldens' part of the cliff. The big birds were not in sight. Something about the falcon's busybody day bothered me. Was it looking for a nest site? In previous years they had nested at the far eastern end of the cliff near another pair of prairie falcons. Every bird the falcon came near seemed agitated.

Chickadees were rare at Bird Cloud. At my first Wyoming home, in Centennial, dozens of mountain chickadees came to the feeder on the lee side of the house every day, but I almost never saw them at Bird Cloud. Of course, Centennial was close to the forest and Bird Cloud was surrounded by open grazing land. The prevailing weather at Bird Cloud had, as its basic ingredient, a "whistling mane" of wind from the northwest. It built concrete snowdrifts in winter. In summer it desiccated plants, hurled sand and gravel, and dried clothes in ten minutes. The eagles, falcons, and pelicans loved windy days and threw themselves into the sky, catching updrafts that took them to mad, tilting heights. Why was it so windy at Bird Cloud? With the top of the cliff checking in at a little more than seven thousand feet above sea level the wind was almost never flat calm, and often like a collapsing mountain of air. The cliff directed the wind along its stony plane face as boaters coming down the river knew only too well. And because vast tracts of land to the west were heavily grazed cow pastures unbroken by trees or shrubs, the wind could rush east unimpeded. And this, I found, rereading Aldo Leopold's *Sand County Almanac*, was deadly for chickadees.

I know several wind-swept woodlots that are chickless all winter, but are freely used at all other seasons. They are wind-swept because cows have browsed out the undergrowth. To the steam-heated banker who mortgages the farmer who needs more cows who need more pasture, wind is a minor nuisance . . . To the chickadee, winter wind is the boundary of the habitable world.

He adds "books on nature seldom mention wind; they are written behind stoves."

Fresh snow fell overnight and the rosy finches were fighting over the woodpecker picnic mix as rich suet held the seeds together. I wondered if something was dead at the top of the cliff. The goldens were up there, rising and falling, and the balds were there as well. I remembered several years earlier in Centennial when a deer got into our small herb garden, got panicked by something, tried to squeeze through a six-inch space between fence slats and got its broad chest wedged in, and was unable to escape. Whatever had frightened it tore out its heart, leaving the body still jammed in the fence. We dragged the carcass down into the willows. A pair of goldens found it within hours and in three days had eaten the entire deer. Now I hoped that whatever attracted the eagles was not one of the elk. I had not seen either for about a week. A little later one of the balds was back in its fishing tree and half a dozen whistler ducks flew over the house with one of the goldens right above them, maybe trying for a feathered jackpot.

As March came in the river deepened and widened. I could hear the water gurgling under the ice from the house. As I knew they would, red-winged blackbirds took over the bird feeder. Their main meeting place was the willow thicket on the west end of the island where hundreds jammed into the same clump of trees, sang and sang, flashed their epaulets, then all flew away only to return and sing and flash again. The prairie falcon cruised back and forth in front of the cliff, its color so like that of the pale rock it was virtually invisible. A marmot showed up from somewhere—a leftover pile of lumber—and took up a station beneath the bird feeder, happy with the seed that the redwings dropped. Walking down at the east end of the property in a light rain I saw a large marmot on the top of the cliff, peering down. A few hundred yards east I caught a glimpse of a large coyote as it ducked out of view. Both were oversized. With hindsight I later thought the marmot was really a mountain lion cub and the large coyote probably its mother, as I saw both cats at close range later in the spring.

One lovely warm afternoon the goldens were sunning themselves on the cliff top above their nest site. They flew outward, wheeled, and returned to a projecting rock they favored. When they flew, their shadows also flew along the cliff and it was not easy to sort out the birds from their shadows. The larger golden sat on the rock while the smaller, darker eagle did some fancy wingwork, glided down to his lover, presented her with something to eat, then mounted her. I had never seen a pair of eagles mate before.

Every day Bird Cloud showed remarkable changes. The dull mud was inescapable. A few pale green rushes sprouted at the end of the island. The river grew larger and faster. One of the elk reappeared after a two-week absence. It, or they, may have been feeding on the back slope, which could not be seen from the house. In mid-month a little burst of warm days cleared most of the ice out of the river. Falcons, ducks, geese, hawks, and eagles sped in all directions, coming and going. I counted twenty mountain bluebirds and knew there was a housing shortage. But the ravens, harassed mercilessly by the prairie falcons, abandoned their old nest site. I was left with only the memory of the previous year when four young ravens teetered, flapped, and finally pushed off from the home nest late one afternoon to try their wings. It had been Memorial Day weekend and one of the season's first thunderstorms was moving in. The young ravens fluttered and hopped, clung and dropped, flew short distances, always close to the cliff face with its thousand crannies. We watched them with pleasure, but their hopping and unpracticed flying also attracted the attention of every other bird in the vicinity. The bald eagles, red-tailed hawks, and falcons circled or chose high perches suitable for diving attacks. The great horned owls hooted from the island. The storm arrived, dropping first a few splattering drops, then sheets of cold rain that drowned our campfire. I was sure the young ravens were done for. They could not seem to get back to the nest ledge and huddled on narrow shelves or exposed knobs of rock. With sadness we went inside, dreading what the morning would bring. Would any of them survive the waiting predators? Would the storm batter them?

The dawn showed off one of those fragrant, polished days so

rare in Wyoming, windless and fresh-washed. We all rushed to the cliff with binoculars wondering whether any of the young birds had survived. "I see one!" someone called and then another came into the sunlight from its hiding hole, rather damp and bedraggled. The last two joined them from some cranny, and there they all were, preening in the sun, smart and sassy and very much alive. They spent the day practicing evasive flying and I didn't worry about them any longer.

An early-morning walk on the island brought me face to face with a great horned owl in a willow thicket. So strange. The left eye was brilliant yellow, the right one a rusty brown, very likely from an injury. It fled into a cottonwood and stayed there all day. Now migrating birds flew over constantly, following the river. One afternoon there were six golden eagles on their way somewhere else but unable to resist playing in the air currents above the cliff. Mallards, mergansers, and dippers arrived, then black scoters, a pair of northern flickers, a northern harrier, and a single western meadowlark. The river, fed by rapid snowmelt, continued to rise, and on March 19 it was high enough to lift the bridge and swing it onto the island shore, cutting it off from the mainland. The warm days continued, worrisome because everything was drought dry. A forecast for rain brought nothing. When it finally did fall it made the roads into an icy, slippery mush.

One of the Canada geese, no doubt thinking itself clever, built a nest high up on the east end of the cliff, not far from a peregrine falcon nest. I wondered if this was the same foolish goose that had built a nest the year before in the top of a tall tree and open to the sky between the golden eagle nest and the prairie falcons. She and her mate lost all their chicks to predators and had to try again, this time with a nest on the ground beneath the tree and the male standing guard.

In late March a winter storm moved in for a day and a night. Despite the snow and wind a flock of horned larks gleaned seed among the sage and rabbit brush. The prairie falcon roared down out of nowhere and the larks exploded into fleeing rockets. Other carnivorous birds, especially the bluebirds, sat dejectedly on the fences waiting for spring. When the storm sailed away it left a foot of fresh snow. At the cold sunrise there was a heavy fog over the river that expanded and blotted out the sun. Beneath the snow the ground was wet, half-frozen mud. Just to have somewhere to walk I drove the truck back and forth in the driveway, flattening the snow. The snow turned the black metal ravens on the gateposts into magpies.

April came in windy and warm. On a walk to the east end I found a dead osprey on the ground, its gray feet curled in an empty grasp. There was no way to tell what had brought it to its death. There were so many jealous and territorial birds around that any one of them might have seen the osprey as an interloper—within half a mile two pairs of goldens, red-tailed hawks, and a pair of peregrine falcons, and a little farther west the raven family and the prairie falcons. Spring is the time for death. A calf carcass washed up on the island to the delight of the magpies and perhaps the eagles.

I was not sure of the timing of the bald eagles' family life. They had started fixing up their huge nest in December, a task that can go on for several months. It looked to be more than six feet across. But I suspected there were young in the nest the first week in April, mostly because I saw one of the bald eagles determinedly chasing a red-tailed hawk near the nest. The hawk had been patrolling the western section of the cliff for several days. That would put the eagles' egg-laying in the last week of February or the first week of March. The female lays two or three eggs over a period of about a week. Both eagles take turns brooding the eggs. Though the females do more of this duty than the males, both have a brood patch on their bellies: bare, hot skin that rests directly on the eggs. Whoever is not on the eggs rustles food. On a warm, sunny day both parents can have a little break. Incubation takes thirty-five days, more or less. Once the eaglets have hatched, exhausting work begins. If the weather is still cold one of the parents stays with the babies and keeps them warm. When the spring sun beats down hot and fierce the parent eagles transform themselves into wide-wing umbrella shades. In the early days the male was kept busy finding and bringing food to the nest, four to eight times a day. After the first few weeks the female hunted as well, and in the late stages of rearing a nestling the mother did most of the hunting.

By the third week in April the American pelicans had arrived, big knobs on their beaks showing it was breeding time in their world. The pelicans were fabulous fliers and on windy days put on astonishing exhibitions of soaring and diving. Fishermen in Wyoming shoot pelicans because they believe the birds eat all the fish, leaving nothing for them. That first spring at Bird Cloud I was appalled by all the big, fluffy white carcasses that floated down the river.

In May the weeds came and I spent hours pulling evil hoary cress and trying to claw out the prolific white roots. The air was stitched with hundreds and hundreds of swallows. Several persistent rough-winged swallows tried to build nests in the house eaves. To reduce the number of possible spots for porcupine dens I started piling up dead wood and fallen branches on the island, planning to have a bonfire on a rainy day. There was plenty of undisturbed room for them on the other side of the river. A tiny, dark house wren had found the wren-sized birdhouse on the island and was moving in, carrying wisps of dead grass and minuscule twigs not much larger than toothpicks.

It was a big thrill when I saw a white-faced ibis near the front gate where there was irrigation overflow. The ibis stayed around for weeks. A few days after this sighting I was sitting near the river and saw two herons fly to the bald eagles' fishing tree. They were too small to be great blue herons and did not really look like little blues. A few minutes with the heron book cleared up the mystery; they were tricolor herons, the first I had ever seen. By the end of the month American canaries were shooting around like tossed gold pieces despite another cold spell.

Suddenly it was mid-June and noxious weeds grew everywhere — leafy spurge, cheatgrass, Canada thistle, and more hoary cress. Nests were full of young birds, and the predator birds, who had hatched their young earlier, had rich pickings. Even a raiding great blue heron flew over pursued by smaller birds. I hadn't dared go near the fence across from the big nest for fear of forcing the goldens to abandon, but I could see now that they had two big chicks in the nest. And June marked the appearance of an insect I had never seen before — *Eremobates pallipes,* a.k.a. wind scorpion, a resident of deserts and the Great Basin. It is straw-colored, about three quarters of an inch long, and very much resembles a scorpion although it is not poisonous. It will bite if disturbed. It feeds on smaller insects, so I caught it and put it outside, hoping it could catch mos-quitoes. More likely it made a snack for the myriad hungry birds rushing around outside.

On a hot, dusty Fourth of July, I walked down the road to the east end, pleased not to be cursed by the parent goldens. One of their chicks had found a narrow shelf with an overhanging ceiling not far from the nest, and there it sat, harassed by—who else?—the prairie falcon. But even young goldens are tough, and the falcon departed. When I got back from my walk I found some bird had dropped the corpse of a large nestling on the deck, white downy feathers, wings not fully fledged, the head gone. I thought it might have been the chick of a great blue heron or sandhill crane. The drought was bad, very hot and dry day after day and no rain for a long time. The grass cracked and broke when stepped on and it was too hot to sleep at night. Wind scorpion weather.

A hard, hot wind blew incessantly, drying out the lettuces in the garden, tearing petals off any flowers not made of steel. But the young eagles, both bald and golden, loved this hot wind. They and their parents were all soaring and zooming, trick flying, mounting high and then rolling down the air currents. At one point I could see seven eagles flying above the cliff at various altitudes, some so high they resembled broken paperclips.

A few mornings later a bird with an ineffably beautiful song woke me. I had no idea what it was and it was not visible from the high bedroom windows. I tried to identify it from birdsong CDs without success. It was the harbinger of a nasty little frost, a complete surprise that killed the tops of my tomato plants and beans, scorched the zucchini and cucumbers. I didn't realize it but the surprise mid-August frost would be an annual event at Bird Cloud, striking just when the garden was approaching high ripeness.

On the first of September, making coffee in the kitchen, I glanced up at the cliff and saw the big tawny-red mountain lion walking along the top. It descended to an area of outcrop above and to the right of two huge square stones balanced almost on the edge. Three weeks later, just before dark, I glassed the cliff and the colluvia below and noticed a large round rock on the debris pile that I couldn't remember having seen before. The telescope revealed it as a dead deer that had apparently fallen from the top of the cliff. Falling off a cliff was not something even the most addlepated deer would do. I surmised the lion had chased the panicked deer over the edge, and until dark I kept peering through the telescope, looking for the lion come to claim its kill. But the lion did not come. The next morning two ravens were on the carcass. As I made coffee I noticed that the ravens were gone, replaced by thirty magpies and two coyotes. It took the coyotes half an hour to break through the hide. The bald eagles perched nearby, waiting for their chance, and several ravens also waited. One of the coyotes departed. There was no sign of the lion. By mid-morning the remaining coyote, bloody-muzzled and gorged, waddled away. The magpies moved in. The most cautious diners were the eagles and ravens, who waited until after eleven for a turn at the deer. The first coyote returned with two friends and all three began to tug the carcass toward the edge of the colluvium, a drop-off of about ten feet. By afternoon the carcass was no longer in sight, now fallen into the brush below where perhaps the lion would claim it. The renegade thought occurred to me that perhaps the neighbor's cow that had fallen off the cliff the year before had been chased to its death by the lion.

The prairie falcons left, and the next week the ravens were back. A lesser goldfinch flew into a window. I left it on the deck and in the morning it was gone—I hope because it revived. Many birds knock themselves out and then come back from apparent death rather groggy and confused, but alive. The big, handsome northern flicker is an aggressive bird that often hurls itself at its reflection, falls like a stone, lies on its back with its feet curled up for a while, opens one eye, gets shakily up, and staggers through the air to a nearby branch, where it spends an hour or two thinking black thoughts—and then flies into the window again.

By the end of the month most of the migratory birds were gone. I remembered an earlier September when some friends and I had camped at the top of Green Mountain where we could look down at the Red Desert and make out the old stagecoach road and a few bunches of wild horses. We hiked around, noticed quite a few hawks, and by mid-morning realized that the hawk migration was in full spate. Hundreds of hawks flew over us that day, swiftly, seriously intent on getting away. Also intent, not on getting away but on filling up great pantries with pine seeds, were gray jays. They would cram seed after seed into their pouches and then take them to their secret caches. One smart gray jay, trying to pack in more than his crop could hold, hopped (heavily) to a little pool of water in the top of a boulder, took a few sips to wet down the seeds, and resumed gathering.

By mid-October most of the birds had gone south. The meadow-larks were the last to leave. The golden eagles were somewhere else, though probably in the area. The bald eagles were involved in a major undertaking—the building of a new nest in a cottonwood closer to the river and closer to our house. One eagle flew in with a double-talon bunch of cut hay, likely swiped from a cattle ranch's bales. This new nest, unlike the old one, was highly visible. I worried about people who floated the river in summer. Of course, this eagle pair had shown that they were more interested in river traffic and what we are doing around the house than in privacy and isolation. As with humans, in the bird world it takes all kinds. For weeks they hauled materials in, mostly sticks and a dangerous length of orange binder twine that could tangle young birds tramping around in the nest. They took breaks from the construction and went fishing at the east end of the cliff, something they would not do when the goldens were in residence. But were the goldens really gone? There were a few days of rain and wet snow that made the county road a slithery mass of greasy mud.

On the first of November I walked along the river fence line in the evening, and as I came abreast of the big nest, the scolding "GET AWAY, FOOL!" call came from the cliff. The goldens were in their bedroom niche.

Colder and colder the days, clear and windless, the kind of days I have loved since my New England childhood. A rough-legged hawk, a stranger in these parts, came hunting over the fields. The bald eagles did something unusual—they chased it furiously, asserting their territorial rights. The hawk fled. The new nest looked large and commodious. The day after Thanksgiving a Clark's nutcracker appeared briefly. It looked a little like a gray jay but had dark markings on its face like a small black mask, and the body and wings were utterly Clark's. I saw it for only a few seconds before it sprang away, but it seemed that very often I saw birds that were subtly at variance with Sibley's illustrations.

Near the end of the month a little warm wind pushed in a bank of cloud. A northern harrier coursed over the bull pasture, just barely skimming the grass, floating on and on in lowest gear, then landing in the distance, hidden from me. It rose again, higher, using the wind. One morning one of the bald eagles brought a hefty stick to the new nest. It was long and awkward, and to get it in place the bird had to circle behind the nest and trample it in from the back with the help of its mate. It was a really big nest. A few hours later a bold raven came and sat on the west branch of the bald eagle's fishing tree, about twenty feet away from the male eagle. They both seemed uneasy. The raven pretended unconcern and stretched his wings. The eagle shifted from one foot to another as if muttering, "What is this clown doing in my tree?" The big female eagle came in for a landing and sat beside her mate, and as she put down her landing gear the raven took off.

In the afternoon the wind strengthened after four days of calm and the goldens enjoyed it, rising into the empyrean until they seemed to dissolve in blue. It was like one of the *Arabian Nights* tales in reverse, the tale in which someone fleeing looked back and saw something the size of a grain of sand pursuing, and a little later looked again and saw something the size of a lentil. Later still the pursuer resembled a beetle, then a rabbit, and finally a slavering, demonic form on a maddened camel. But to my eyes the goldens shrank first to robins, then to wrens, then hummingbirds, and finally gnats or motes of dust high in the tremulous ether. Just before gray twilight the northern harrier returned but strayed into enemy airspace above the cliff, and suddenly there were four ravens chasing and nipping. The extra pair of ravens came from nowhere, like black origami conjured from expert fingers. As darkness swelled up from the east a full moon rose and illuminated great sheets of thin cloud like wadded fabric drawn across its pockmarked white face.

November fell through the floor and December began with the tingling, fresh scent of snow. Seven or eight inches fell. I had hoped this month would be snow-free, but that hope was dashed. Getting the mail or supplies was chancy. Usually I could put the old Land Cruiser in low and smash through the snow, but in places the wind had packed the snow into unsmashable drifts and I got well and truly stuck on the county road. I tried to barrel through a five-foot drift that looked fluffy, small in comparison with the big piles that would come later in the winter, and ended up high-centered on a solid pedestal of snow, all four wheels off the ground. It snowed again just before Christmas, deep and beautiful snow that lay quiet in a rare calm. The hero sun came out for a quarter hour, then fell as though wounded. Eagles and goldeneyes were the only birds around. At dusk I skied down to the Jack Creek bridge. Mist rose from the river and the cliff seemed to be melting, the top floating on quivering froth.

I made it down to the last days of December. It was fifteen below zero and the snow squealed when I walked on it. Late in the morning I saw the pair of golden eagles flying high over the cliff, playing in the frigid air. It began snowing again and I decided I would try to get out the next day. The lane was half choked with snow. If I didn't go the next day I knew I could be isolated for a long time, jailed at the end of the impassable road. I packed the old Land Cruiser and fled to New Mexico.

GARY SHTEYNGART

Moscow on the Med

FROM *Travel + Leisure*

"MY HANDS ARE COLD, but my heart is warm," a tanned young
Israeli girl coos to me in broken Russian at a Tel Aviv nightclub as
we nod along to an incomprehensible ska beat. "Do you think I'm
pretty? Are you a Russian billionaire? I only want to marry an oli-
garch. Like Gaydamak."

That would be Arkady Gaydamak, the Israeli Russian billionaire,
aspiring politician, owner of the right-wing Beitar Jerusalem soccer
squad (its fans famously refused to heed a moment of silence in
honor of slain former prime minister Yitzhak Rabin), noted philanthropist, and fugitive from French justice for alleged illegal
arms trading to Angola and the less glamorous crime of tax eva-
sion. No book or screenplay has yet been written about Gaydamak's
fantastical life, an omission that may soon have to be corrected. "I
am the most popular man in Israel," Gaydamak once proclaimed
(at least one opinion poll said as much), marking him as the most
stunning representative of an immigrant group that has peppered
the omelette of Israel's politics, society, and culture since the
1990s, when the Soviet Union collapsed and more than a million
Russian speakers showed up in the Holy Land.

In Tel Aviv, Israel's Mediterranean business and cultural capital,
I meet the young, freckled, redheaded Masha Zur-Glozman, a freelance writer and Israeli-born daughter of immigrants from Russia
and Ukraine. "The Russians are now perceived to be cooler, more
cosmopolitan," Zur-Glozman tells me. "They have connections to
places like Moscow and Berlin [a city also home to a large Russian
community] that the native-born Israelis do not."

Zur-Glozman has written about the ten stereotypes of Russian Israelis. Among her menagerie: the bad-tempered veteran who puts
on his World War II medals on Victory Day, can't let go of his memories, and constantly toasts "Death to our enemies!"; the quiet, intelligent one with very specific interests like Greek pottery or Na-
poleonic campaigns who speaks shyly with a heavy Russian accent;
the very bitter former-Soviet-bureaucrat-cum-third-grade-sports-
teacher who drinks too much, terrorizes his family, and is forever
torn between over-patriotism and hating Israel; and the sexy
math teacher with a white-collared blouse, spectacular cleavage,
and leather skirt who abuses her students, ignores the girls, humili-
ates the physically weak, and openly cheats on her poor schmo of a
husband.

Walking down Tel Aviv's Allenby Street I seem to run into all of
the above and more, the Russian language muscling in on the spit-
fire Hebrew and the occasional drop of English. "Worlds *colliiiiiid-
ing!*" Zur-Glozman does her best Seinfeld imitation with a comic
flourish of the arms. Allenby, like many streets leading in the direction of a municipal bus station, has something not quite right
about it. The street exudes its own humid breath, its faded buildings sweating like pledges at a Southern fraternity. When the sun
goes down, darkened nightclubs with names like Temptation and
Epiphany entice the passersby. Russian pensioners, some sporting
the beguilingly popular "purple perm," sing and play the accor-
dion for shekels. Hasids try to snare male Jews with the promise of
phylacteries.

At 106 Allenby the Mal'enkaya Rossiya (Little Russia) delicates-
sen has everything you need to re-create a serious Russian table in
the Middle East. There's vacuum-packed *vobla,* dried fish from the
Astrakhan region, which is perfectly matched with beer; marinated
mushrooms in an enormous jar; creamy, buttery Eskimo ice cream
—a Leningrad childhood favorite of mine; tangy eggplant salad;
chocolate nut candy; glistening tubs of herring fillet; and a beautiful pair of pig legs. "Israelis love these stores now," Zur-Glozman
tells me, and the pig legs may be just one of the reasons. Russian
speakers, Jewish or not, have an abiding love affair with the piggy,
and it was the influx of former Soviet immigrants that brought a
taste for the cloven-hoofed animal to Israel, much to the dismay
of the country's religious conservatives. The wildly successful and

ham-friendly Tiv Taam chain of luxe food stores came along with the Russian immigration; the aforementioned Gaydamak tried to purchase the chain and turn it kosher, but even his billions couldn't temper the newfound Israeli enthusiasm for the call of the forbidden oinker.

Farther down on Allenby, the Russian-language Don Quixote bookstore — the Russian nerve center of Allenby Street — is full of curious pensioners and boulevard intellectuals feasting on a lifetime's worth of Isaac Asimov's science fiction, Russian translations of the kabbalah, and an illustrated Hebrew-Russian version of Pushkin's *Eugene Onegin,* which is presented like a Talmudic text with sweeping commentaries crowding the words. "To Nineteen-Year-Old Gaga — so that he won't be stupid," an old tome is helpfully inscribed.

A few blocks down the street, the Little Prague restaurant is full of Russian boys hitting on Israeli waitresses, and young Russian women pretending to eat. Little Prague exults in a wonderful version of the Czech classic *veprove koleno*—a marinated and slow-roasted pork knuckle with a hint of rye, which in the hands of the chef is flaky and light. There is also a heroic schnitzel and excellent Staropramen and dark Kozel beer on tap. The interior is gloomy Mitteleuropean, but outside a nice garden deck beckons, fully populated by drunk, hungry people as late as 3 A.M. and at times bathed in the familiar sounds of the theme song to *The Sopranos.*

Allenby saunters into the sea, where pale ex-Soviets take to the beach like it's their native Odessa and florally dressed babushkas offer me advice: "Young man, take your sneakers off, let your feet breathe." A right turn at Ben Yehuda Street leads to the Viking, a languorous, partly outdoor restaurant that joylessly specializes in dishes like *golubets,* a stuffed cabbage peppery and garlicky enough to register on the taste buds. As I tear my way though the *golubets* and lubricate with a shot of afternoon vodka, a mother in one corner softly beats her son, who is wearing a T-shirt that says READY WHEN YOU READY. Crying, beaten children, along with sea breezes and heavy ravioli-style pelmeni swimming in ground pepper, complete the familiar picture, which could have been broadcast live from Sochi, Yalta, or some other formerly Soviet seaside town.

Off the Allenby drag, Nanuchka is what Zur-Glozman calls a neo-Georgian supper club, a place where one can order a cool pomegranate vodka drink, featuring grenadine juice from Russia and crushed ice, or a frozen margarita made with native arak liquor, almonds, and rose juice. The decor is mellow and cozy like a shabby house in Havana, complete with gilt-edged mirrors, portraits of feisty, long-living Georgian grandmas, and many charming rooms stuffed with sumptuous divans and banquettes in full Technicolor. The highlight of the crowded and raucous bar is a photograph of the former prime minister Ariel "The Bulldozer" Sharon staring with great unease at a raft of Picassos. At its more authentic, the Georgian food can really shine. Try the tender *chakapulu* lamb stew with white plums and tarragon, or *setsivi*—a cool chicken breast in walnut sauce, bursting with sweetness and garlic. Pinch the crust of the *cheburek* meat pie and watch the steam escape into the noisy air.

On the same street as Nanuchka, the club Lima Lima hosts a popular Sunday night showcase for Russian bands called "Stakanchik," or "little drinking glass." Amid luxuriant *George of the Jungle* decor, young, hip, and sometimes pregnant people in ironic CCCP and Jesus T-shirts shimmy and sway by the stage. A young singer wearing an ethnic hat begins a song with the words "Now it has come, my long-awaited old age," a sentiment somehow both Jewish and Russian.

I end my tour of Russian Tel Aviv at a much stranger place, the cavernous Mevdevev nightclub, located a stone's throw from the American embassy but occupying, until its recent closing, a space-time continuum all its own. As the evening begins, a birthday boy in his forties, dressed in a plaid shirt and sensible slacks, is paraded onstage by the MC and forced to sing seventies and eighties Russian disco hits.

A young woman in a skimpy plaid schoolgirl outfit dances around a SpongeBob birthday balloon as the nostalgic Russian music, along with a detour into the early Pet Shop Boys, bellows and hurts. My friend Zur-Glozman meets an armed, cigar-chain-smoking Ukrainian, a graduate student of the History and Philosophy of Science and Ideas at Tel Aviv University who now lives in the occupied territories, as do many ex-Soviet immigrants. He invites Zur-Glozman and some of our friends for a ride in his car, which is the size of a school bus. We negotiate the gleaming white curves of Bauhaus Tel Aviv, looking for a nightcap. Over at Little Prague, the inevitable Israeli political argument breaks out between the right-wing Russian-speaking settler and some of my liberal Israeli friends. "You probably think our houses are built of Palestinian babies," the settler huffs.

"Well, you're the one with the gun," an Israeli woman tells him.

I worry for the sanctity of the evening, torn between geographical kinship with the formerly Soviet settler and political kinship with the progressive Tel Avivians, but as mugs of Kozel beer are passed around and the nighttime temperature falls to bearable levels, the passions cool. "As you can see," an Israeli friend tells me, "we aren't killing each other."

WILLIAM T. VOLLMANN

A Head for the Emir

FROM *Harper's Magazine*

A BARE BULB WAS GLOWING from the ceiling of an olive-brown tent outside the city limits of Khanaqin, in the place called Mulik Shah Camp; and cigarette smoke and kerosene smoke were bitter on the tongue. Three little children sat in a row beside three men, the smallest child, a girl, watching me, her hands on her knees. They were Feyli Kurds from Baghdad. It was not safe for them anymore.

And coming back late at night on the chalky road from the beleaguered camps of various transnational Kurdish insurgencies in the Qandil Mountains, hoping to avoid the checkpoints set up specifically to catch journalists, we saw the sadly glowing boxes of many refugee tents: Kurdish families who had fled Turkish shelling. Not far away, on the other side of Rania, were many more tents, longer established, testament to the earlier intentions of Turkish and Iranian fighter planes.

All of these places hinted that Kurdistan, like a sunken land diked all around against high and hostile seas, might not last forever, which was why my fixer said that he would kiss the boots of any American soldier. He imagined that if Hillary Clinton had won the election, she might have built a military base to turn Kurdistan into a "second Israel"—the Kurds' best hope, he thought. The interpreter, who agreed with him that the Kurds had no friends other than the Americans, was more realistic about my nation's fidelity to her friends. For him the only comfort was that wherever else America went—Iran, for instance, or Somalia—terrorism would follow.

The interpreter told me the tale of the three Kurds who, driving home from Baghdad, bearing atop their car the corpse of one of their fathers, whom the doctor had failed to save, reached the checkpoint of a certain militia—Sunni or Shia, the interpreter did not know—and were informed that one of them must yield his head to their prince, their Emir (this was the word used, as if the story were a fable). Money and persuasion finally impelled the highwaymen to behead the father's body; the Emir would never know the difference. But when they came safely back into Kurdistan, the mother was angry with the son who had permitted this.

I wondered whether Kurdistan itself could be preserved by means of some similarly painless sacrifice, or whether Kirkuk must be given up, and who knows what else. What would be enough?

Sulaimaniya was safe, and the fixer said: "Here in my city I don't take care for you. Why? Because even in market at two, three o'clock morning is no problem. But in Kirkuk I must watch for you." Indeed, Kirkuk was not especially safe, although it was safer than Mosul, where I could perhaps have manipulated the fixer into taking me had I not minded the possibility that I might then be informing his wife and children that he had been murdered for the sake of a few photographs.

In Sulaimaniya, in a refugee camp for Arabs called Camp Qalawa, one was surrounded by blocky tents, laundry, and garbage, and across the highway dusty houses smeared into semi-invisibility in the bad air. We were standing next to a water tank from which the refugees shared a metal dipper; the tank leaked and the mud stank. The air smelled of manure from the cattle that came grazing there, human urine, and sweat: of the many people all around, the closest man, in sandals and striped shirt, squatting. The women were in a row at the rear, some in striped headscarves, a few of the younger ones naked-haired and even blonde with reddish highlights.

They seemed to live by begging in the market, and perhaps (said the interpreter) by prostitution. A gray-bearded man said: "For what we do? Begging. Nobody like to do this, but what is the suggestion? I want to work. In Sulaimaniya the cold was very hard and we lived a horrible day. The Kurdish governor, he don't want anything to do with refugee here."

"Why did you leave Baghdad?" I asked a man in a white headscarf, who answered: "Because of the violence between Sunnis and Shias. The Shia militia killed fourteen members of my family. All of the families here have same problem."

He did not much like Americans, as you might imagine. I asked about George W. Bush's actions, and he replied: "When he come to Iraq, some things true and some things lie. If he say America come to make a good thing for Iraqi, now it is six years and there is nothing happen, no good thing!"

"Should the Americans stay or go?"

The gray-bearded man answered: "If he come just to make free, now Iraq is free. Better that he going. Why the soldier although he have a family in America he stay here until now?"

I told him of a friend's son whose military tour in Iraq kept getting extended and extended. He said in an ugly tone: "This is not an answer."

They all wanted money. I asked one man to take a few steps away with me so that I would not be mobbed. One of the younger men came regardless. When I reached into my wallet they all lunged, and an old woman spread the wings of her robe, shouting: "Money, money!" I gave the man twenty thousand dinars (not quite twenty dollars) and he spread his hands in angry disgust, pointing to all the members of his family. The fixer finally gave him twenty thousand more.

Being a Kurd, the fixer disliked them; he thought they should be resettled outside the city.

I asked a man what he thought about Kirkuk, and he said: "It is not my problem. I don't stay in parliament. I am simple person and I don't care if Kirkuk stay in Kurdistan or not."

"What is America doing good for Iraq?" he shouted, and the crowd around him buzzed threateningly.

"Maybe Kurdistan," I said. "As for the south of Iraq, I don't know what to tell you."

Sometimes the dust was so thick in the air as we came down into the valley of Kirkuk from the second-to-last checkpoint that the world ahead became as dead white and blanked out as sea fog in Monterey; dust pricked my eyelashes and I breathed in the chalky smell. Then one day it rained, making the desert a trifle greener and the air clean enough to reveal a few red and blue tints in the pale dirt hills; and when we began to descend toward the last checkpoint, we could actually distinguish ahead, against the tan dirt darkly flecked with rubbish, Kirkuk's blue-gray sprawl. In spite of such variations, the drive always felt the same.

To separate the safe from the unsafe, the Kurdistan Regional Government had in its wisdom established nearly half a dozen checkpoints between Sulaimaniya and Kirkuk. Each checkpoint possessed its own character. Some installations were elaborate, such as Tasluja Checkpoint on the hill above Sulaimaniya; some were humbler, such as the traffic island in Sulaimaniya, where a soldier in a dust-colored camouflage uniform stood beside a concrete column. Across the street, a girl all in black walked beside a girl whose hair swung free.

At every checkpoint our experience was the same: since the fixer's car bore license plates from Erbil, the capital of Iraqi Kurdistan, and because the fixer knew so many soldiers, we rarely needed even to raise our documents to the window and already the sentry was waving us through, which is to say waving *at* us, sweetly.

Taxis crammed with bearded Arabs or private cars with plates from outside Kurdistan got swept with a pole mirror. Occasionally we would see a car pulled off to the side in order to be more thoroughly searched, the driver and passengers standing in the road. If an Arab wished to come into Sulaimaniya, he had to wait at Tasluja until a Kurd arrived to vouch for him in person, and very likely it was such measures that had kept Sulaimaniya safe: only a couple of bomb blasts in the past two years.

Aside from the checkpoints, there were other points of interest along the way, such as Chamchamal, near the thirty-sixth parallel, the southern border of Kurdistan, which at the end of the first Gulf War America had amputated from Saddam's zone of control. Some of the most ancient relics of humanity in all Iraq were found near this spot. The interpreter preferred to describe Chamchamal as "the front line between Kurdish and Iraqi forces before 2003." Kirkuk lay beyond, in the region Kurds referred to simply as "Iraq."

It was ninety-four kilometers from Sulaimaniya to Kirkuk. Wherever there were roadside settlements there would be vendors with their rows of jerry cans yellow and red, the red being Iranian gasoline, which was stronger than the yellow Iraqi gas. The fixer liked to fill his hundred-liter tank with a "cocktail" of the two. The dust settled on the jugs, and on the fixer's windshield. The best sources of brightness amid the dust were women, who occasionally wore colorful clothes; the nearer to Sulaimaniya we happened to be, the more brightly clad were the women. The owner of a women's clothing boutique in Kirkuk explained to me: "Usually people here wear the veil for their own security. Since the old time it has been like that. It has not much changed until 2003. After that, more people are wearing the veil. Here and in Erbil, the majority of people put on the veil. Sulaimaniya is more like Europe." He had many slinky dresses of Turkish make, but those were for parties; in Kirkuk, women were well advised to cloak themselves before going out in public.

So we came down the hill into the hot dry valley of Kirkuk, where entrepreneurs sometimes sell people to kidnappers.

Kurdistan is an idea, or a series of ideas, encompassing parts of Iraq, Iran, Turkey, and Syria. My Turkish taxi driver in Vienna sternly said, upon learning where I was headed, that Kurdistan does not exist. The Kurds I met in northern Iraq thought otherwise. Of the four countries just listed, all but the first lack, and intend to continue lacking, autonomous Kurdish regions. Many Arab nationalists in Iraq would likewise do away with the Kurdish Regional Government if they could. My interpreter's father, who had been a member of the National Assembly in 1997, said: "Maybe there is a chance that Arabs will suppress us again, since they consider us second class. If it happens, I don't think that Kurds will be able to fight back. Let us hope there will not be another Saddam."

By the half accident from the first Gulf War that brought the KRG into existence, Kurds are some of my country's few remaining friends. I felt almost young again to be in a place where "America can do everything." When I got home, I told my neighbors about it, and they said: "Kurds, Shias, Sunnis, I can't keep them all straight."

Kirkuk's various fortresses of officialdom express their character with prudent literalness. In perhaps the most glorious of them all, Brigadier Sarhad Qadir, chief of police of Kirkuk districts and subdistricts, had agreed to receive us. The fixer threaded his incredible six-cylinder vehicle through a pinball machine of gates and concrete slabs. A blue-clad policeman met us and slowly inspected the underside of the car with a pole mirror, then waved us through. We traveled along corridors with armed escorts. Sarhad's office was typical of such places: a long, spacious, air-conditioned room with half a dozen matched chairs and sofas along the side walls, a television shining and softly babbling at the back wall, and then in front a grand desk with a uniformed man beside it. A young man brought tea in narrow-waisted glasses.

Sometimes when an official wished to create an informal impression he would come and sit in one of the armchairs beside me; then he would gaze across the room at the interpreter while I politely craned my neck. Sarhad, however, sat at his desk. Three silver stars shone on each shoulder of his black vest. His hair was cropped; his mustache was dark. Behind his chair hung photographs of him in the company of various dignitaries. I spied a framed memento of Operation Iraqi Freedom. Miniature Iraqi, American, Kurdish, and Kirkuk Governorate flags flew beside the telephone. Nor should I omit the framed certificate from an American official, the framed appreciations of an American combat team, or the framed article from an American military newspaper: "Iraqi Police Uncover Major Weapons Cache." The uncovering had been one of Sarhad's triumphs.

About the situation in Kirkuk he said: "In comparison with last year there is a big difference, a big improvement, not 100 percent but more than 60 percent. Last year, there were daily explosions of nine vehicles. But now in one week one cannot even find one explosion."

When he seized the weapons cache in Kirkuk's Hawija district, he also found dossiers on various party members and journalists, and on himself. "You cannot imagine how accurate was this information. It was like your friend or your wife had provided the information."

In the same fortress I was now escorted to the office of one of Sarhad's subordinates, Major General Jamal Taher Baker. He wore blue and a gun at his hip. He said that "the security here is good, but not *very* good; we have some problems with IEDs they put on the road." I asked to know the reason for improvement, and he explained: "They will kill children, women, old men, and destroy schools and other places. And now the people know this, and sometimes they give us information." On the day we spoke, he had

393 persons in custody, either twenty-three or thirty-three of them women (the interpreter was inconsistent). Their cases had not yet been tried. I asked if I could interview any of them, and that was how I met Colonel Khorshid, who was, so the interpreter wrote in my notebook, the "prison and holding director."

The colonel called in a prisoner for me. His name was Basim Mahmood, and the police told me that in 2007 he had been caught holding the controller in a huge explosion in Kirkuk that killed eighty-six people and injured two hundred more. He was thirty-two. He came from Basra. He had entered Kurdistan two days before the crime.

"Did you take part?" I asked him.

"Under torture I confessed to this."

"In Basra, what do people think about the Americans in Iraq?"

"The British are there, not the Americans."

"All the same, what do they think about the Americans?"

"I don't know."

He was smiling mournfully, with his hands behind his back. He was a big man with an almost babylike face. I asked him whether he had anything he would like the Americans to know, and touching his belly he replied: "I want to say that I am innocent, and until now my family doesn't know where I am."

They took him away, and when I asked the colonel for his comments he said: "I want you to know that when the terrorists are captured, first of all they confess everything, but later on, when they have spent some nights here, they change their minds."

I asked his opinion of human nature: Did he think that most people lacked integrity? Perhaps the interpreter did not understand or properly convey the question; he was always better with quantities than with the abstract. In any event, the colonel replied: "I think most of them are liars."

On my second visit to Kirkuk, departing Sulaimaniya and passing the gypsum factory (and near Chamchamal a row of dusty metal-shuttered concrete cubes, a few with people sitting in them, then a bus of schoolgirls off to the mountains, the girls in rainbow finery, some of them dancing), we saw an auto accident, the shattered vehicle surrounded by silent people, and then cleared Bani Maqan Checkpoint, exempted from waiting in that long line of petrol trucks, where a crouching donkey brought up the rear. We rolled down the hill into Kirkuk, waving to a yawning soldier, and then at the city limits the checkpoint soldier saluted me slowly. The fixer and the interpreter did not appear very tense. An old woman in a black robe spread the wings of her back, toiling up a dirt hill.

I asked the fixer to telephone Azadi Hospital to see if there were any new casualties. We drove there in the hot tan afternoon, into the lighter tan of the entrance portico in whose shade two soldiers, one in concrete-colored camouflage, the other more darkly dressed, peered into each arriving taxi or private van, while other visitors stood waiting in an unmoving crowd for their turns to pass by the soldier in desert camouflage who sat beside his AK-47 in the lobby. This we also did, accompanied by another soldier (who said that for his own safety he always changed out of uniform before he went home), and after ascending dim flights of stairs were ushered behind a half-drawn curtain where a young policeman lay: Heman Abdullah, born in 1981. His neck was bandaged, and a tube was in his bandaged arm. In a dreamy moaning voice he said: "A car was exploded near my house. They have located an IED near my house. I have been shot two times before but survived . . ."

As gently and briefly as I could, I went over the tale with him. "It was a trapped car," he said, holding his forehead. "I suspected that it would happen, but I was not able to protect myself. It was a Volkswagen taxicab. I stopped the car, and the driver started running. I shouted, but no one heard anything. I am blind in one eye and my head is damaged. I was unconscious for two days after the explosion."

His brother sat next to him. He was also a policeman. He said that this morning three other IEDs had already been found. "The terrorists, they are now chasing those people who are working," he said.

The wounded man was saying: "My brother told me they are suspicious about a car outside. There is a crowd gathered outside. I asked the crowd to step back . . ."

He grimaced and licked his lips. He said that the terrorists had attacked him in one form or another six or seven times. He could not say which group was after him, or even if it was the same group.

I asked the policeman what color the explosion had been, and he answered that it was a dusty brown light.

*

On my third visit to Kirkuk, when we had nearly arrived at the checkpoint by the checkpoint just before the city gate, which is to say the narrow spot with the waist-high caltrops and sandbags and the burly soldier in sunglasses who stood beside the overhang, I asked the fixer to telephone the hospital again. He reported that there had been one new casualty, but the patient's injuries had been sufficiently mild to justify release. It was now noon; the bomb, a small one, had detonated in the city center at ten that morning. Did I want to see the place?

We were all of us a bit silent as we made our way there, the car rushing past the open doorway of a shop that sold women's dresses, then a field of cornlike weeds not much larger than my hotel room, a very crowded cemetery on a sand hill, the narrow headstones practically touching, a sidewalk suddenly occupied by uniformed schoolgirls going home for lunch, soldiers and policemen whose trauma plates on their black bulletproof vests were light and cheap over their hearts, a mosque's verdigrised onion dome, a bread factory through whose open door I could see one man punching the pallid dough while another brought the warped, bubble-pocked *naans* out to a table on the sidewalk; and I had a slightly sick feeling in my chest, wondering if we might arrive just in time for the next explosion. But the Turkish proverb the interpreter once smilingly quoted to me—*All my luck is black except for watermelons, and then it is white*—could not be true of me since I was an American. The barbed wire here, by the way, was of a simpler type than I am used to in the American West: small single points like thorns. Tables of secondhand books were propped behind wire on the sidewalk.

The fixer always insisted on going out first in such situations. I was his guest, even if his paying guest; moreover, he liked to take charge. Already trotting down the street, he motioned to me over his shoulder. As I opened the car door, the interpreter told me to take care. The fixer had asked him to stay with the car.

The place was a small alley. The blast was indicated by broken glass, shards of concrete the size of small boulders, a bit of rubble, a few men ringed around—always the indication of catastrophe: a ring of people gazing inward.

The proprietor of a neighboring shop kept repeating that he could not understand anything, that he had just inserted the key in the lock to open the steel shutter of his photocopy establishment when the explosion happened and he could understand nothing; eight people were wounded and one killed; he'd seen a human leg go flying. He was a Turkmen named Shad Adi. His shutter was warped now and someone was trying to pull it up from within while all of us men pushed at its convexity until it clicked back into its riding grooves. The target, two stores down, had retailed military clothing and supplies. The IED had been hidden on one of those wheeled carts so prevalent in the shopping districts; so another spectator explained to me, gesturing with a bottle cap. Here the grating had caved in more severely; but the owner's brother, Shirwan Samad, who had been working inside, had, peculiarly enough, remained safe — never mind that he had been deafened; he could speak to us but did not know how to read our lips. "It was a very, very loud explosion," the man with the bottle cap said. A few rags of military camouflage lay in the dirt or hung from crevices in the wall of shop shutters. The owner vowed to make another shop "by tomorrow." It was, all considered, a trivial explosion. No one you or I know was affected. As I stood there in the alley, the fixer several lonely meters away, making his own interviews, I was sweating with anxiety, knowing how conspicuous I looked, wondering if the person who had detonated the cart was watching us. The other men kept flicking their eyes uneasily from side to side. When we returned to the car, I saw that the fixer was also shaken; then we returned to work, and those men we had interviewed continued their own dangerous lives.

Why was Kirkuk so much more dangerous than, say, Sulaimaniya? Because it was not inside Kurdistan; because it remained ethnically mixed; because it was contested.

In 616 B.C. Kirkuk was on the front line between the Assyrians and the Babylonians.

Ahmed Mohammed Hassan, the ward nurse at Azadi Hospital, said that he and his colleagues "just come out of home directly to the hospital and back. We try to avoid crowded places." He stayed in at night. Meanwhile, the proprietor of a clothing store for women opined: "Maybe I feel safer at night. Most of the operations take place at daytime." He had seen one car bomb, then another; he reckoned them up; perhaps he had witnessed four. There had been two bombings so far this week in Kirkuk, he thought; he considered his life to be improving. This person, a Turkmen, perceived no betterment in the ethnic situation. All the same, he was the only resident of Kirkuk who ever told me it was the best place in the world.

The fixer's niece expressed a more typical opinion, cynically, bitterly giggling as she said it: "I have seen nothing good in this city. I have got nothing from this city. You see, there is discrimination. When the teachers are Arab and you are a Kurd, we cannot write in Kurdish or we will be punished." Her throat was pulsing above the hijab.

"In this Kurdish area I have no fear," she said. "But my college is in an Arabic area."

Her father remarked that from 2003 until perhaps 2005 or 2006, Kirkuk had been fairly safe, but then the occupiers failed to guard Saddam's old munitions. "That was the Americans' mistake. But even now it is much better here than in other provinces."

"How many times have you seen explosions?"

"So many. Every time you go to the market, you must expect it."

"When was the last time you experienced one?"

"Within the last few days. It was in a restaurant, at seven or seven thirty in the morning. It was a mortar shell. There were not so many casualties."

"Can you explain about the mortar shell?"

"Usually the terrorists set up mortars on traps at night and time them to be exploded in the early morning."

He had two daughters, one in a red, the other in a lavender headscarf. Both wore ankle-length dresses.

The young woman in the red hijab was a pathologist. She said: "We are not certain when we are going out that we will come back." Terror victims were often taken to her hospital, of course, and once when "an explosion killed so many people" she slept poorly for two weeks, "because of all the dead bodies and the blood." She saw bomb casualties once or twice a month.

The daughter in the lavender hijab praised her city lovingly, with her knees always together, her bare feet always touching. She studied history at Kirkuk University, which, as she said, lay in the Arab district. "You cannot feel safe," she said. Once, when she was on her way to an examination, a bomb went off, "so I forgot everything."

I asked the family whom they blamed for the terrorism, and the mother, the fixer's sister, said: "Most of the operations are committed by former Baath Party members. But sometimes they catch some people from Pakistan or Sudan or other countries. I am surprised why they come here and do not do it in their country."

"So what is the best thing to do with the former Baathists?"

"I believe according to my opinion they will never return to be good people. So the best solution is to push them out of the city."

We never stayed overnight in Kirkuk, because that would have been reckless. Pointing out the hotel that was now closed because the proprietor kept arranging to have his guests kidnapped, the fixer had detailed the proper procedure for the city: Arrive in late morning, leave by three or four, and remain in certain neighborhoods no longer than an hour. Refrain from carrying any bag or backpack into a restaurant; that way, perhaps they will not recognize that one is a stranger. (I look up from the table and catch a man's eye, and look quickly back at my plate.)

The fixer used to go more frequently to Kirkuk and to Mosul and even to Baghdad, but, as he pointedly said, journalists always pushed and pushed, so that he started to wonder why he was doing this. In Baghdad one sometimes had to sleep at the office for four or five days if something bad was happening. Now he avoided working there. As for Kirkuk, I pushed and pushed, even though the fixer assured me that my work there was finished.

No, he preferred not to keep driving to Kirkuk. He wanted even less to go to Mosul, where he estimated the chance of being murdered at about 90 percent, and regarding this he invariably said he wouldn't mind if his head were cut off, since that must not be painful, at least not for long; but he had a horror of being killed with a heel or shovel blade to the neck. I told him that if they killed me he could take all my money and if they killed him I would take his money, and then we both laughed, and the next morning we drove with the interpreter to Kirkuk for the fourth time.

There had been no explosions so far that day. Gazing at the long flatbed trucks full of cement bags in the traffic jam before the final checkpoint (manned by that same soldier in sunglasses), I wondered whether something would detonate. Two boys kicked a blue metal drum down the street. A tiny black-haired girl followed a man in sweaty garments who was pushing a wheelbarrow of wet cement along the sidewalk. And now came the Kurdish restaurant whose food had declined since it was first blown up, and now the low concrete houses of Kirkuk. Driving rapidly through the shopping district, where so many bombs had been detonated (TNT in plastic bags, the fixer said) that the store owners no longer permitted cars to park in front of their premises, we arrived at the Syrian Christian church called Mar Ghorgis, whose wall shrugged behind feeble caltrops and almost casual loops of barbed wire, across the street from an ice cream shop and a small restaurant with a rotisserie. A headscarfed old cyclist slowly pedaled by. The late morning reeked of smog. I asked the interpreter whether it was dangerous for the owners of the two food establishments to be situated so close to a Christian church, and he said: "Of course." We were all feeling anxious, and when an orange and white taxi rolled up slowly, a huge metal tank lashed to its roof, and stopped level with our vehicle, I felt a bit sick. The taxi departed.

The deacon's name was Johnu David Israel, and he was thirty-five or thirty-six years old. His family had been Christian for as many generations back as he could tell. He was born here, in the quarter called Arafa, which means something like "wetland." About his childhood he said, as they always did, that it was "very great," without discrimination—and, by the way, although the interview took place in Arabic, he considered himself neither Arab nor Kurd nor anything but Syrian Christian, an identification he reiterated almost defiantly. "I never heard, 'This is a Kurd, this is an Arab,' like that." His favorite activity had been soccer.

Ethnic differentiation began in 1982, he said. Although Deacon Israel did not mention him specifically, one of Saddam's most hated henchmen, the infamous and recently executed "Chemical Ali," set up shop in Kirkuk in 1986, when the Anfal campaign against the countryside began. Like Kurds, Syrians could not get jobs unless they changed their official nationality. In the course of their Arabization program, the Baathists constructed about two thousand houses for Arabs in Arafa alone. I asked about religious discrimination, and Deacon Israel remarked that even now there stood in Mosul a church built by Saddam at his own expense, with his name engraved into every brick.

"So would you say that he was not so bad concerning religion?"

"You cannot measure his goodness or badness by what he has done," replied the deacon in a rising voice, rapidly shifting the blue beads of his rosary.

His brother had been a member of a secret political organization. He was arrested in 1985 and held incommunicado for two years.

"Was he well treated?"

"Very nice," laughed the deacon. "They just gave him biscuits all the time. They tortured him and pulled out his fingernails . . ."

The deacon had a round head. His eyes glinted at me through rectangular spectacles. The neat zone of stubble on his chin matched his mustache. He wore a gold watch, well-worn shoes, and a slightly rumpled suit.

"Have many Christians been killed since 2003?" I asked.

"In 1997 there were 810 Christian families; I performed the census myself. That number has fallen by half now, so many have fled."

"Who was the latest Christian to be killed?"

"He was an oil engineer. Last year they knocked at his door and they shot him."

"Do they catch these people?"

He laughed with the same bitterness as when he had spoken of his brother. He spread his hands. He said: "No. This is why the Christians say it is better to flee."

We ventured into the Kurdish zone of the city to get something to eat, because, as the fixer said: "I cannot come in Arab district now, because we are coming in Kirkuk about five times" (actually, it was only four) "and in same car." Later he mentioned his Erbil license plates once again, and the interpreter was quiet, and the fixer said: "Did you finish your work? Because I don't care about ourselves, but I care about you." In the restaurant, when the lights failed for a moment, some of the diners immediately looked to us because we had eaten there several times and thus without a doubt been *noticed*. Not long after lunch, when I finally agreed that we could go, the fixer floored it, and once we had passed through the checkpoint at the city limit, he and the interpreter were embracing each other and singing in happy relief.

We had done interviews in the Arab quarter on two previous

occasions, and if I have not related them before, it is because the
spiraling complexity of Kurdistan seemed sufficiently complex already; and before introducing you to the two sheikhs, I should
remark that these men, being at least minimally cordial to the fixer,
and agreeable to entertaining an American journalist, must almost surely have been in comparison with their compatriots pro-
Kurdish.

The al-Haidi clan has fifteen or twenty thousand members in
Kirkuk Province, more in Mosul. Sheikh Ismail al-Hadid was born
in 1957 a few hundred meters from the quiet, luxurious house he
lives in now, which stood behind caltrops and concrete barriers;
his father was also born in Kirkuk. A bodyguard led us in. The
sheikh had a rectangular face, thinning gray hair, and a gray mustache. When he received me, in a marble-floored room with a *bis-
millah* and many hangings on the wall, he was wearing a blue-black
suit with a striped tie and shiny narrow-toed shoes. The servant
brought black coffee that had a lemony taste.

"I believe that Arabs are newcomers," he said. "The people of my
clan are old dwellers of the city. Others are more recent. The people of Kirkuk, they are lovely. They have no problem with each
other." Raising his hands to his heart, he assured me, as so many
Kirkukians did, that ethnic differences had scarcely existed in his
childhood, that there continued to be intermarriage even now,
that his neighbor on the left was a Turkmen and on the right a
Kurd. "My ancestors built in this area. So of course most of the
people here were Arabs. Here were so many great parks, for gardens and picnics. We were not afraid about our females, our daughters, whether they would be kidnapped. Now we are very much
afraid about our girls, that they could be kidnapped or raped."

He considered Kirkuk to be unsafe now because "the law is
weak."

"I believe that the Iraqis and the Americans are both responsible
for what is happening now. The Americans came to Iraq as libera-
tors, but later on they mistreated the situation and turned into occupiers. Maybe it was our fault that we did not advise the Americans," he said tactfully. "Each faction, they were trying to get the
largest share of power at that time. We did not cooperate at that
time; that was our biggest mistake. The Americans disbanded the
Iraqi army; this was very bad."

"Should the Americans leave Iraq?"

"I believe that withdrawal is in the interest of the Kurds."

"Which groups are directly to blame for the terrorism?"

"I believe that many terrorists come from Turkey, Iran, Syria, more than from Iraqi Arabs. They are all the time plotting against the Kurds."

When the subject of ethnic cleansing came up, he remarked that some discrimination against the Kurdish majority had begun in the 1960s. "Later on, we discovered even before Saddam that all were treating Kurds with cruelty in order to Arabize Kirkuk City. Now when we hear there are some campaigns against the Arabs, we are not surprised. But on the other hand, we don't want it to be repeated, for the Kurds to repeat the acts of the former Iraqi regime."

Sheikh Ahmed al-Ubaidi, also known as al-Hamid, was secretary-general of the Iraqi Kirkuk Front. To meet him we headed for Hi-al-Wasadi district, "an Arab area, not so safe," advised the fixer. The feeling of fear was getting very tiring. Passing the city council office, we whirled down hot, uncrowded streets, the fixer watching left and right. Here was an auto repair shop, then we entered the Shia Turkmen area, then left behind a vacant lot with rubbish heaps and polka dots of rubbish, a car empty in the dirt, everything silent, a figure sitting knees up on a wall ledge, police at a concrete island with sandbags, then a walled compound with caltrops, followed by the Academy of Kurdish, the Academy of Police, and the sheikh's office, where we were greeted by bodyguards.

He was a big man with a husky voice, balding and graying, not distinctive, with the exception of his long, delicate fingers. "The Arabs are forming one third of the population—one third!"

Regarding ethnic differences, he said: "We did not think about those things, but unfortunately after the arrival of the occupier, the situation changed."

"Where would you like to see the border of Kurdistan?"

"As it exists now, according to the determination of Paul Bremer."

He demanded to know why an Arab with an out-of-town license plate must be checked if he goes to work in Erbil.

The fan was slowly turning. On the desk was a small red, white, and green flag with stars. "I see you looking at the flag. This is the old Iraqi flag. We consider this the flag of our party. It contains three stars symbolizing unity between Iraq, Syria, and Egypt. We in the Front would like to have the same unity on our side."

He was formerly an officer in the Baathist army, but he too had been arrested.

I raised the subject of the violence and he stared at me through half-shut eyes, saying: "The problem is an Iranian conspiracy through the Shia in the south of Iraq. They are sticks in the hands of Iranians." He saw Iraq as a cake layered with petrol.

But the security situation of Kirkuk was now "very good"; recently he had gone to visit some friends in a formerly dangerous place and did not even bring a knife! "The improvement took place due to the participation of all groups," he said meaningfully. "Maybe Turkmens or Arabs would not inform the police about terrorism, since police are Kurds. But now we feel the city is for all."

Even so, he considered himself underrepresented in the city council. Right now there were twenty-six seats for Kurds, nine for Turkmens, only six for Arabs.

"Why should we consult the Kurds?" he asked me. "After all, if something happened here, the people of Sulaimaniya do not care. Kirkuk is the mother of troubles. Kurds are ruling themselves. Turkmens are supported by Turkey and Syria. So, we need Arabs outside to support us." If the city council could come to consensus, "Kirkuk will turn into heaven."

The fifth time we went to Kirkuk, we grew a trifle silent as usual after Bani Maqan Checkpoint, speeding down from the dry hills into the valley of Kirkuk, the dust-dome of sky higher and broader today, the air better to breathe. The gray city began to spread before us, its hordes of concrete stumps truncated by the dust. Here came the final checkpoint's familiar stop sign, the left-hand lane of the highway blocked off by concrete slabs and three caltrops, the fourth caltrop in the right shoulder. The soldier was different today. Gray cinder-block houses burst silently out of the dirt. From a billboard a lovely young girl gazed out hijabed and smiling, decently covered from the throat down. Here came the roundabout, one sector of which had been closed off with barbed wire, and then we arrived at the Kirkuk Security Directorate—one of two, I should say, for each of the main parties maintained its own office, which in

America might have seemed redundant or worse; but the inter-preter, who was a member in good standing of the Patriotic Union of Kurdistan (PUK), approved, explaining that adherents of one party might decline to phone in terrorism tips to any branch of the other. So we came, as I can now more properly put it, to the Kirkuk Security Directorate of the Kurdistan Democratic Party (KDP), whose entryway was studded with spanking-new yellow caltrops. A machine-gun bearer in desert-gray cammies and a green cam-ouflage facemask over which glared dark sunglasses greeted us. I could see part of his mustache and teeth through the round breath-ing hole. He wore one light trauma plate in front and another be-tween his shoulder blades. All in all, he seemed dressed for the weather of Kirkuk, whose meteorologists must sometimes report light showers of lead, steel, or concrete fragments.

Our way now wove between concrete blocks painted absurdly with water scenes and peace doves. We entered another gate, rolled slowly down a concrete-walled alley where machine-gun-carrying camouflaged soldiers stood smoking; and a small girl and a small boy toddled among them, holding hands. Presently we found our-selves inside an air-conditioned carpeted office. There was soccer on the television and a light machine gun propped up behind the desk. The white and tan drapes were drawn, and the sun of Kirkuk glowed soothingly through them.

Our amiable interpreter said that he had learned his English from television; he spoke with a trace of a midwestern accent, and I wondered whether he might have been in contact with troops from Kansas or Missouri, perhaps assisting them in interrogations. Also present was Salar Khalid Kamarkhan, deputy-in-charge. As such people so often are, he was youngish, cheerful, and fit. I flattered him that he must be an excellent shot, and he smilingly agreed that he was.

The reason I had asked to meet the deputy was that everybody kept asserting that Iraq, and Kirkuk specifically, was being destabi-lized by neighboring countries, especially Iran. Since similar claims about Iraq had been one of our twin pretexts for invading that country, I guessed I might feel happier if and when we bombed Iran into democracy to know that Iranian materiel had indeed been employed by terrorists.

In Khanaqin, a colonel who declined to be interviewed had de-

scribed IEDs as olive-green metal boxes about the length of a man's
hand. He did not know what was inside them, because he simply
phoned the Americans, who came and took them away, but he
called the devices "well organized," meaning well constructed, "not
something made at home. Maybe some company makes them."

As soon as Mr. Salar referred to the meddling of neighbor countries, I seized the hint, and asked what IEDs in Kirkuk might look
like.

"Mostly they are homemade," he said, thereby confirming the
fixer's account of TNT in plastic bags. "The terrorists connect the
wires. They differ in shape. Yesterday's was two rockets, you know,
artillery bombs, connected by a wire, and there was detonator cap-
sule."

I mentioned the IEDs of Khanaqin, to which he replied: "Maybe
there are such kinds of things over there, which is closer to the Iranian border, but here they cannot pass all the checkpoints. Even
here you can find some Iranian thermal bombs, but most are hand-
made."

Now it was time to visit the operations room just behind the
door. The wall-size aerial photograph of Kirkuk had not been par-
titioned, but the deputy and his interpreter pointed to a certain
long boulevard that ran west to southeast across town, and they
said that below this were the two southern sectors, "the hot places,"
which were mostly Turkmen and Arab in their composition; the
southwestern sector was hottest of all. I was quickly informed that
just because those zones were hot did not imply that the Kirkuk
Security Directorate was out of control down there, and I replied
that I had never doubted it.

The previous night, terrorists had launched a rocket from the
Khasa River, whose name means Good River. In that season it was
very low between its sloping concrete banks, like the Los Angeles
River; insurgents often staged such attacks from the riverbank, especially in the southeastern sector, since few other people went
there. The launchers, said Mr. Salar, were of local manufacture;
but he showed me a photostat of the markings of three 107 mm
rockets (eighteen-kilogram payloads) that he believed to be Iranian. Last night's rocket had struck the Kurdish neighborhood of
Azadi. There had been no casualties.

He said, without exactly giving it, that there was evidence not only of Iranian IEDs and rockets but also of "Turkish backup to the Iraqi Turkmen Front" in Kirkuk, a group that Brigadier Sarhad had not mentioned.

And what can I say about the Turkmens?

The few I interviewed wished without exception for the withdrawal of American troops. The Kurds never did.

On one of our first drives into Kirkuk, before our license plate had been too frequently seen, we had entered the Turkmen district and arrived on a silent bright street occupied by a gutted car, a cyclist, an old woman in fluffed-out black robes, and a hijabed young woman whose eyebrows were so black they glittered. It was, said the fixer, a dangerous place. He got out of the car and began knocking on doors, trying to find a Turkmen for me to speak with. He went from house to house. "All of them afraid!" he reported. We swung around the traffic circle, whose center was nothing but sand, and then he parked and went to try again. To you, this will sound quite dull, especially since nothing happened to us who waited in the car; certainly we felt vulnerable as we sat there in that brightness, hoping not to get kidnapped, blown up, or shot. The fixer had several faults, but cowardice was not among them.*

He finally persuaded an old Turkmen to invite us in (later the interpreter said bitterly that the man had agreed only because his mother was Kurdish). He had lived all his life in this house, which was two hundred years old, with a horseshoe-arched ceiling, arched white walls inset with niches for cups and saucers and a clock, and two huge whatnots in the far space, holding a television each, one of which was on. Daylight came in through the curtained doorway.

---

* When the Turks began shelling the border—which happened on a Friday, the Muslim Sabbath, family day, hence a paid holiday for the fixer—he roared off to photograph the damage for the newspapers, having declined to invite me. Perhaps he was jealous because I had accepted the interpreter's invitation to picnic with his family beside a river with lovely frogs that quacked like birds, ladies in bright, sparkling, many-layered gauzy skirts, willowlike trees, an ancient cave-cliff tomb dating perhaps to Assyrian times and now brought up-to-date with graffiti, and lamb guts floating in the water like balloons. Shortly after I left Iraq, the fixer was caught in a suicide bombing in downtown Kirkuk. He escaped injury but was attacked afterward by an angry mob who mistook him for a Turkmen and beat him so badly the doctors later thought the metal embedded in his face was shrapnel from the explosion.

In the corner sat a younger woman, probably his wife, looking stiff and sad, covering her mouth with the end of her hijab.

He said: "Life is beautiful if there is no explosion, no violence. Whenever my children go out, I just think: Will they come back?" It had been this way for about three years. He blamed neighboring countries who were "playing" in this area, specifically Syria. Not surprisingly, he did not accuse Turkey.

"What do you think about Kurdistan?" I asked, and he said: "I don't care. We as Turkmens don't care to whom Kirkuk belongs." He spoke in a deep, rather stern voice. His gestures were always various and beautiful.

"In general, do Turkmens get along better with Kurds or with Arabs?"

"Relations between Turks and Kurds are stronger than between Turks and Arabs," he said, "because in old times Arabs had a small existence in this city. But now Arabs are infiltrators."

Like everyone else in Kirkuk, he had bad memories of the conscription and discrimination under Saddam. In those days he had been barred from acquiring land. His brother-in-law was imprisoned for seven years because he had prayed in a mosque. The last five of those he passed in a place whose hideousness was perpetuated by American torturers: Abu Ghraib. The Turkmen said: "You cannot imagine how many young people were inside those prisons and kept there for nothing."

The sixth and last time we went to Kirkuk, when there was no reason to go there at all and the fixer simply passed through the city out of childish bravado, he undid my seat belt; he thought that made me less conspicuous.

We drove past black car skeletons crumpled into the dirt from an explosion eight months before at a car show; one of the twenty-odd murdered was a thirteen-year-old cigarette vendor whose corpse, said the fixer, they finally discovered on the roof of the tall building across the street. I wanted to take a photograph, and as I stepped out of the fixer's vehicle alone a white car pulled up slowly beside me and I looked into the driver's face, my hands already sweating. He appeared to be a family man; he was not going to kill me.

I got back into the fixer's car, and we drove around a trifle longer in the Kurdish area, the Arab quarter being now too hot for us (the interpreter had asked the fixer to drive a different car today for safety's sake; the interpreter even volunteered his own car, but the fixer refused, fearing an argument about gas money). Barbed wire guarded walls with nothing but scrap behind them. We passed a market—wheeled stalls of shoes on the sidewalk—and men crossed the street between taxis, carrying big plastic bags. Kirkuk threatened us with a trio of women in black, with men lounging beside a cigarette stand. What might have been sanitation workers, all in blue, stood in a crowd on a truck bed; one of their faces was masked by dirty mummy wrappings, and he turned toward me and reached inside his clothes, but it must have been only to scratch; then came two bank entrances piled shoulder-high with sandbags, guarded by machine-gun men in dark sunglasses; beyond these, on a stretch of dirty wall, someone had written KURDISTAN.

EMILY WITT

Miami Party Boom

FROM $\mathcal{N} + 1$

Villa Vizcaya

DATE: JULY 2005
VENUE: VILLA VIZCAYA
LIQUOR SPONSOR: FLOR DE CAÑA RUM

THE VILLA VIZCAYA is one of those Gatsbyesque single-family mansions that have been converted to event spaces. The new owners installed an industrial kitchen to accommodate catering companies and an HVAC system to dissipate the warmth generated by large groups of people. They removed the permanent furniture so gilt chairs could be trucked in for weddings. Guests still had the run of the extensive gardens, but there was no longer anything particularly Gatsbyesque about the place, just a rental tab of $10,000 for a weekend evening.

The Vizcaya was still a very nice event space. From the parking lot, a jungle of banyans and broad-leafed foliage obscured the house. At night, when picking one's way down a path lit with honeycomb floodlights around the ground, there was a feeling of tropical intrigue, followed by awe when the coral mansion finally emerged from the fronds and the vines, a floodlit beacon in the night. This used to be a Xanadu, a neo-Italianate castle built before Miami was even a city, before Miami Beach was even solid land. Where one person saw a mangrove swamp, the mind behind the Vizcaya saw greatness. Thus the first real estate boom began.

Now another real estate boom was happening, here in Miami,

where I had just settled (in the gravitational rather than pioneer-ing sense of the word: for several years I had been sinking in a southerly direction, like the pulp in a glass of orange juice). This was my first party. I don't remember much—not even what the party was intended to celebrate—and I took bad notes. The mos-quitoes were formidable. I was plastered in sweat. The night was thick and hot and the concrete steps in back descended into still, inky water. The moon hung over all of it: the bay, the stone barge, the topiaries. Corporations were the sponsors. They hung banner ads promoting Clamato; girls in miniskirt uniforms served free mojitos with Flor de Caña rum. I picked up a free copy of a maga-zine called *Yachts International.* A real-life yacht was moored to the dock out back, and its passengers were drunk and tan.

I stood with my friend Krishna, watching fireworks explode over Biscayne Bay, over the girls serving rum, over the maze hedge and the moss-covered cherubs and the coral gazebos. We sipped our drinks and scratched our mosquito bites. He gazed at the explo-sions and said, "The fireworks were so much better at the condo opening I went to last weekend."

Spa Opening

DATE: JULY 2005
VENUE: HOTEL VICTOR
GIFT BAG: YLANG-YLANG-SCENTED BATH CUBE,
    THONG UNDERWEAR

I moved to Miami from Arkansas to work at an alt-weekly news-paper. My first order of business, after finding an apartment, was to make friends. I appealed to a girl from work to rescue me from loneliness, and she sent me an e-mail about a spa opening at a new boutique hotel on Ocean Drive, steps away from the mansion where Gianni Versace had met his violent end.

I walked up from my new apartment past the deco and neon, past Lummus Park and the homeless people and mounds of malt liquor bottles beneath the stands of palm trees. It wasn't yet dark —this was an early weeknight party. My co-worker checked us in with the tan girl at the door with the clipboard. From then on there would always be tan girls with clipboards. We were led to an eleva-tor past tanks filled with pulsing jellyfish lit a glowing indigo. The elevator went down to the basement area where the spa was, and when the door slid open an impossibly tall drag queen greeted us, dressed only in white towels except for the diamonds that twinkled from her earlobes.

Petrova, a woman with a thick Russian accent, stepped in front of the towel-bedecked drag queen and handed us champagne glasses. She said they contained cucumber martinis, but I think it might have been cucumber and 7Up. "Welcome," murmured Petrova. She took us on a tour that was like a ride at Disney World. Curtains were pulled aside: behind one was a naked man on a slab of heated marble. Behind the next was a woman having her breasts gently massaged. "Ew," said my co-worker. We stayed twenty minutes, then collected our gift bags, which contained thong underwear and an effervescent bath cube. I didn't have a bathtub.

Hurricane Katrina

DATE: AUGUST 2005
VENUE: MY APARTMENT BUILDING, SOUTH BEACH
LIQUOR SPONSOR: MY NEXT-DOOR NEIGHBOR BRETT
PHARMACEUTICAL SPONSOR: IBID.
FOOD: FROZEN PIZZA
ATTIRE: SWEATPANTS

Maybe nobody remembers now that Hurricane Katrina hit Miami before New Orleans, but it did, as a baby hurricane. Then it crawled over to the Gulf of Mexico and turned into a monster.

On the afternoon of Katrina I waited too long to wrap my computer in a trash bag and leave work, and the outer bands of the storm were laying into the city by the time I drove across the causeway from downtown to Miami Beach, my car shuddering in the wind. I understood I was to buy nonperishable food items.

The grocery store was chaos, and I was completely soaked from the trip across the parking lot. While I considered the selection of almonds, the power went out. A dramatic hush fell upon us. One minute the store was all beeping scanners and fluorescent lights, the next darkness and total silence but for the wind and rain. I ate some almonds. In the darkness someone broke a wine bottle.

We were told to move to the front of the store. Minutes passed. Rain pounded, wind howled. Suddenly a generator turned on, creating just enough electricity to bathe the store in low-key mood lighting, enough for us to grab bottled water and get out but not enough to forget that the hurricane was something to be taken seriously.

Outside, Biscayne Bay, normally tranquil, was a mountainous expanse of gray and white in extreme motion. Plastic bags flew through the air. The high-rises looked exposed and frail, the dozens of cranes in Miami's skyline like toothpick structures that would come crashing down with the first gust of storm. Once safely home, I put on my pajamas and uncorked a bottle of wine. I opened my door to a blast of wind, rain, and sand that filled my apartment with leaves. I ran across to my neighbor Brett's place, on the other side of the stoop. He opened his door and his apartment filled with leaves.

A friend in Miami once referred to Florida as "America's funnel," and that's what I'd thought of when I met Brett. He was in his mid-thirties and had dyed black hair, stained teeth, and a permanent sunburn, and was almost always smoking on our building's stoop and drinking from a bottle of Tequila Sauza. His apartment was draped in fabric of different psychedelic patterns. He had been looking forward to Burning Man. He had played in an early-nineties grunge rock band of some repute—they had toured with the Smashing Pumpkins—but things hadn't worked out very well. In a moment of idle gossip one afternoon, my landlord Dave told me that Brett had woken up one morning after a night of substance abuse in New York and found his girlfriend dead next to him. So he took their cat and moved to Miami, and now the cat was in its waning days and Brett was selling boats on the Internet, supposedly.

Once I left him my rent check to give to Dave, since I was at the office most days. The next morning Dave, a tan surfer type from Boca Raton who never seemed upset about anything, knocked on my door. "Um," he said, embarrassed. "Don't give your rent check to Brett."

But Brett was the social nexus of our building, which was a low-rent holdout in a neighborhood at the bottom tip of South Beach that had gotten much, much fancier since Brett moved in. Our building was funny—the walls of most of the apartments had variously themed murals: underwater scenes, jungle scenes, and, my favorite, in the studio behind mine, hot-air balloons and clouds. My guess is that the landlords originally painted the murals as a sort of spell against the crack-addicted undead that were said to have ruled the neighborhood in the early nineties. The building even used to have some kind of tiki setup on the roof, but the door to the roof was padlocked when the rule of law finally arrived, sometime around the turn of the century. My apartment was painted the colors of a beach ball and included sloping wood floors, bamboo shades, and a mosaic tile counter. It was a one-room studio and a total dump, but it had beach style.

Our two-story baby-blue building was surrounded by towering new condominiums of gleaming white stucco, one of which had a helicopter landing pad. I saw a helicopter land exactly once in the two years I lived there. Rent was month-to-month, which meant I was the only person in the building with a salary.

Upstairs lived a call girl with whom Brett was good friends. She would come down sometimes in her evening finery and ask Brett if he would "do her," meaning would he please fasten her black lace bustier to maximize the lift of her fake breasts. Brett would flash his tobacco-stained teeth, hook her into her corset, pat her bum, and reassure her that he would do her anytime. They were fond of each other.

She didn't like me, with good reason. She lived above me, in a jungle-themed studio. Once, when I was sitting on my couch on a Saturday morning, a thin stream of amber-colored liquid began to patter steadily on my windowsill from somewhere upstairs. Fuck this, I thought. I went upstairs and banged on her door, asking why somebody was peeing out the window. It was that kind of building. She said that she had spilled a cup of tea. "Peeing out the window!" she yelled. "What kind of trash do you think I am?" I apologized, but the damage was done. Later she moved back home to Michigan, leaving in a sweatshirt, with no makeup on. But that was much later, when everyone was leaving.

Brett's friends were always hanging around, none of them model citizens, but I would regularly cross our foyer to chat with them, because being alone at the end of the day sometimes felt unbearable. Two months in, my friend-making campaign was going only so-so.

The night Hurricane Katrina hit Miami, Brett had a pizza defrosting in the oven—the power wasn't yet knocked out—and he dispensed Tombstone, Percocet, and beer. This combo hit me quickly, and I soon staggered home. It was raining so hard that a puddle had seeped under my door. As the streetlights flickered and the eye of the storm passed over the city, I slept.

I woke up the next morning and drove to work. I assumed that the rest of the city still had electricity, but it turned out that almost nobody did—some wouldn't get it back for two weeks. Downtown Miami was deserted. The stoplights were out. The only movement was that of a tribe of vagrants deeply concerned with the transportation of fallen palm fronds scattered across sidewalks and intersections. I arrived at the *New Times* building. Its parking lot was empty except for palm fronds. I sat there for a full minute, engine idling, before turning around and driving back down the Biscayne Corridor. Even the windows of the Latin American Café were darkened, the spy shop shuttered, the sidewalks damp and empty but for the Sisyphean struggle of man versus palm frond. You wouldn't think electricity makes that much of a difference during the day, but it makes a world of difference.

The MTV Video Music Awards

DATE: AUGUST 2005
VENUES: PAWN SHOP LOUNGE, THE REDROOM AT SHORE CLUB, BACK
   SEAT OF A POLICE CAR, LA CARRETA 24-HOUR TAKEOUT WINDOW,
   HIBISCUS ISLAND, SOMEONE'S YACHT
LIQUOR SPONSORS: VARIOUS
FOOD: EMPANADAS, ROAST SUCKLING PIG, CIGARETTES
ATTIRE: COWBOY BOOTS
CELEBRITIES: KANYE WEST, CARMEN ELECTRA, JESSICA SIMPSON,
   BLACK EYED PEAS
GIFT BAG: ONE SLIM JIM, ONE SLIM JIM T-SHIRT

Brett was closing on a big Internet boat deal "with some Mexicans" the weekend of the MTV Video Music Awards, and the one party I'd been invited to was canceled because of storm damage. The publicity buildup for the awards had been extensive. I kept seeing press releases on the fax machine at work that said things like HO-TEL VICTOR LANDS A SPACE IN THIS YEAR'S MOST COV-ETED GIFT BAG. P. Diddy had flown in to a local marina wearing a rocket pack and a white linen suit to announce the nominees. I couldn't go outside without returning with souvenirs like a free

Trick Daddy Frisbee handed to me from the trunk of a Louis Vuitton–upholstered muscle car. But my lack of party invitations made me feel sorry for myself. When an event happens in Miami and you have no parties to attend you start to doubt your own self-worth, even if you're a pale myopic person with the salary of a rookie civil servant who has no business at any Miami party, let alone the fancy ones.

Then a friend called from Los Angeles to see if I would go out with his friend, who was in town for the awards. This friend was a Jewish rapper in a hip-hop group called Blood of Abraham, who also co-owned something called a "lifestyle store" in Miami's Design District. The Design District, much like the Wynwood Arts District, was more of a semiotic hypothesis than a reality. Most people still knew it as Little Haiti, and in spite of skyrocketing housing prices it was one of the poorest urban zip codes in America. Average T-shirt price at the store, which closed down within the year: $70.

This friend of a friend, whose MC name was Mazik, picked me up with a cousin or two in a shiny white Land Rover. He was wearing a pink polka-dotted shirt and a green sweater vest. He announced that Kanye West was performing downtown and that we were going to see him. I was wearing cowboy boots and a dress I'd bought at a Savers in Little Rock, but somehow Mazik and the cousins and I managed to talk our way into a pawnshop-cum-nightclub through leggy models in stilettos. Kanye West showed up for five minutes and then Carmen Electra performed a choreographed dance with four anemic-looking girls in spangled costumes. The free drinks tasted like lemon drops and when we left we were presented with a gift bag containing a Slim Jim and a Slim Jim T-shirt.

We continued on to the beach, to a hotel called Shore Club. Mazik again was on the list. Outside, under a cluster of Moroccan lanterns, I saw Jessica Simpson sitting on a bench looking lonely. She was very small—midget-size, almost, tan and tiny. In the VIP room I saw a member of the Black Eyed Peas get into a fight. My new friends got peripherally involved, in a drunken inept way, but at least they didn't take off their shirts. Somebody else did, at which point Jessica Simpson was whisked away by what looked like a bodyguard detail dressed up as county sheriffs. We left. The following night, Suge Knight would be shot in the kneecap in that very spot.

Miami is connected to the island of Miami Beach by a series of

causeways. The General Douglas MacArthur Causeway, I-395, is the
main artery into South Beach, the palm tree–lined promenade
that Crockett and Tubbs were always driving down on *Miami Vice*. I
drove back and forth across the causeway almost every day of my
time in Miami, and it never lost its air of serenity. Because of Florida's flatness, the sky is bigger there; the clouds pile into endless
stacks of white Persian cats and mohair bunnies. The MacArthur is
bordered on one side by the port of Miami, where massive cruise
ships and freighters come and go. When I was heading toward the
beach, the view was of glittering white condominiums and yachts.
When I was heading toward the city, it was of downtown: luminous
skyscrapers growing up from a rickety forest of cranes, half-finished
high-rises, and canvas-draped rebar skeletons.

At night sometimes the moon would rise large and yellow over
the water and packs of scarablike motorcyclists on Yamahas would
whir around my car, occasionally doing wheelies. Even when traffic
was bad, the environment was glossy: the shiny surfaces of moonlight on the water, of streetlights on freshly waxed cars; the palm
fronds rustling and the revving of German motors and the glow of
LCD screens through tinted windows showing pornography.

At the end of the night, inside the marshmallow-white Land
Rover, I clutched my Slim Jim gift bag. A row of blue lights flashed
behind us. We pulled over and a group of police cars somehow
screeched into formation around us, cutting us off in front, reduc-
ing traffic on the causeway to a single lane, and leaving our car
with two thirds of the highway and a very wide berth on all sides.
I'd lost count of how many lemon-drop cocktails I'd had, but I
was drunk. We were all drunk. I can say fairly confidently that the
driver was drunk, and that all the other drivers on the causeway
were drunk too. It was 4:30 on a Saturday morning, and now we
were going to be arrested.

The police had their weapons drawn, and emerged from their
cars shielded by bulletproof car doors. They yelled into a loud-
speaker and we followed their instructions. I stepped out of the car
and held my hands in the air. I walked backward, a breeze rippling
the palm fronds and my dress, my eyes on the asphalt where normally cars speeded and now all was quiet. I knelt, gazing up at the
soft, purple sky. Then I was cuffed and put into the back of a police
car next to an empty pizza box, where a lady cop began demanding
information about our firearms.

I was suddenly a lot more impressed with the people I'd been hanging out with. They had weapons? I quickly confessed that there had, in fact, been a fistfight. But then it emerged that no, the police had simply confused our car with another white Land Rover. Someone in *that* Land Rover had fired shots at a police officer. We were sheepishly released, our drunkenness apparently not enough to merit attention from the law. We drove to Little Havana and ate empanadas.

There was one more party that weekend, on Hibiscus Island. We were transported by boat, and the theme was sort of luau-meets-Vegas: tiki torches, roasted suckling pig, and girls in uniform carrying around piles of loose cigarettes on silver platters. I think American Spirit sponsored the party, but maybe it was Lucky Strike. We removed our shoes and climbed onto a yacht moored against the mansion's back dock. Out in the gulf, Katrina was growing and New Orleanians were preparing to flee, but the Atlantic was quiet now. It was pretty, with the lights and the palm trees and the views of South Beach, and a little rain that would fall for a minute and stop.

Driving Brett and Andy to the Airport

DATE: SEPTEMBER 2005
VENUE: TOYOTA COROLLA
PHARMACEUTICAL SPONSOR: BRETT
GIFT BAG: A VERY SMALL ZIPLOC

Brett and a friend of his, an Australian male model named Andy, were going to Burning Man. I agreed to drive them to the airport. Their flight left early, and when I knocked on his door Brett emerged baggy-eyed and smelling like a mildewed sponge soaked in tequila. We picked up Andy at his girlfriend's. She was also a model, tawny with dark brown eyes and a minimalist figure. As they said good-bye they were orbited by what seemed like a dozen teacup Chihuahuas but might only have been two very light-footed teacup Chihuahuas.

We merged onto the highway. Brett, in the back seat, began emptying his pockets, pulling out bags of pills and empty mini-Ziplocs coated in a residue of white dust.

"Should I put those pills in a container?" asked Andy.

"I guess. I don't know. You think?"

"I guess."

Brett passed a baggie of prescription pills to the front seat and Andy put it into an orange case with a prescription on it.

"But what about the cocaine?"

"The cocaine?"

"The *cocaine?*" I shouted.

"Somebody gave me all this coke last night. I can't bring it?"

"Don't bring it on the airplane."

"*Really?*"

They decided there was only one thing to do with the cocaine. As I nervously pulled up to the airport, Brett put what remained in the well next to the gearshift. He looked at his nostrils in the rearview mirror and took a Percocet. I quickly put the baggie in the glove compartment. Off to Burning Man! We waved to each other. I drove to work feeling lonely.

Hurricane Wilma

DATE: OCTOBER 2005
VENUE: TED'S HIDEAWAY, SOUTH BEACH

Wilma hit Miami in the middle of the night, and by the time I woke in the morning the city was silent, void of electricity. The air felt a way that it would never feel again in Miami: crisp, dry, and cool like a New England fall day. I walked to the beach. Men with surfboards ran past me to catch the only surfable waves there would ever be on South Beach. The wind was still blowing and pelicans loitered miserably, too worn out to flap their wings even when the surfers barreled toward them. Somebody spoke up for the pelicans and ordered everyone to leave them alone while they were tame like this, docile with exhaustion.

People wandered the streets with cameras, taking photos of smashed cars under fallen trees. One parking lot between two buildings had formed a wind tunnel. The cars had piled up like leaves. This was a popular spot with the photographers. My trunk, which had been stuck shut since a British woman in a gleaming chrome SUV rear-ended me, was suddenly open and filled with the branches of a nearby ginkgo tree.

A curfew was called for nightfall and the city forbade driving after dark. My neighborhood bar was crowded and candlelit, but outside the strange autumnal chill remained. My neighbors picked their way through the darkness, stepping over fallen trees. They held flashlights and lanterns and the landscape seemed odd, like they were going to a Halloween party in Sleepy Hollow. The stars were bright over the darkened city.

Some parts of the city were without electricity for weeks, but my place regained power after three days. Miami Beach with its tourists is always a priority. For the remainder of the time I lived in Florida, skyscrapers had plywood over the places where windows had broken. In poorer neighborhoods blue tarps covered damaged roofs for years. But the significance of Wilma didn't register at the time. Now people say that was the moment when the manna curdled in Miami, when the fragility of its physical location started to affect property values, when the logic of building taller and taller high-rises in a natural disaster–prone peninsula started to seem suspect. Wilma wasn't even a real storm, it wasn't an Andrew or a Katrina–in–New Orleans, but it was enough.

Art Basel Miami Beach

DATE: DECEMBER 2005
VENUE: MIAMI BEACH CONVENTION CENTER, MY APARTMENT
CELEBRITIES: JEFFREY DEITCH, DAVID LACHAPELLE (RUMORED),
   MADONNA (RUMORED), SOFIA COPPOLA (RUMORED)

Art Basel Miami Beach is perhaps the only time each year when New York aesthetes bother with Miami. The art fair is an offshoot of Art Basel in Switzerland, and it attracts a lot of very wealthy people. These were a different sort of wealthy people from the banana-yellow-Hummer-driving, highly leveraged "rich people" who were always cutting each other off on I-95. Suddenly my neighborhood hamlet of fake tans, silicone breasts, and hair gel was invaded by pale androgynous people with Italian glasses. The first rule of fashion in Miami was that you wear nothing that might make you look androgynous or poor. These people all looked like shit, but wonderfully so, expensively so.

I spoke with my friends on staff at various hotels, who told me that Sofia Coppola had been spotted at the Delano, and that Madonna was at the Visionaire party last night, and that David

LaChapelle's poolside installation at the Setai had a live transsexual made of silicone lounging naked in a glass house in the middle of a swimming pool.

New Year's Eve

DATE: JANUARY 2006
VENUE: THE DELANO HOTEL
FOOD: SURF AND TURF
LIQUOR SPONSOR: DOM PERIGNON
CELEBRITIES: BILLY JOEL, SNOOP DOGG, JAMIE FOXX, LUDACRIS

I ended up at Jamie Foxx's album release party on New Year's Eve because I accepted an invitation from a man twenty years older than me who was the local correspondent for a prominent celebrity tabloid. "You're the only person I know who is superficial enough to actually enjoy this," he said, kindly.

I decided I would enjoy myself. The problem was that as soon as I stepped into the lobby of the Delano, with its gossamer curtains and high ceilings, and as soon as I was served champagne by models dressed in silver angel outfits, and primal hunter-gatherer food (fire-blackened meat, stone crab claws, oysters, caviar, lobster tails) by a waiter dressed in tennis whites, I was overwhelmed by a profound sadness.

But 2006 was going to be a good year, or so promised Jamie Foxx when his press handler escorted him over to us. He was covered in distracting surfaces—mirrored sunglasses, diamond earrings, polka-dotted shirt—and graciously shook our hands.

"An excellent year," he promised, and I believed him.

Then he performed the song "Gold Digger" against a backdrop of more gossamer curtains and dancing angels and pewter candelabras, while we watched from the lawn around the pool, where the grass was cut short like a tennis lawn and tiny white edelweiss-like flowers sprouted. I held my glass of Dom and my high heels sank into the soil. Snoop performed, looking shy and grinning goofily, then Ludacris, and then fireworks exploded over the Atlantic Ocean and a new year began.

I ended the night without my escort, at a bar called Club Deuce. In Florida, unlike in Brooklyn, the dives are really dives: neon lights shaped like naked ladies, wrinkly alcoholics, obese bartenders, all in New Year's crowns, blowing horns and throwing confetti. I was in a cab heading home alone by 4 A.M., my gold shoes somehow full of sand.

My Twenty-fifth Birthday

DATE: APRIL 2006
VENUE: STAND OF PALM TREES, KEY BISCAYNE BEACH
LIQUOR SPONSOR: BYOB

I celebrated this birthday with my friend Krishna, who made close to six figures a year as a waiter at the most expensive hotel in South Beach. Krishna had grown up in a yoga ashram in central Florida and then gone to Brown. The son of his ashram's guru was now a big-time real estate broker in Miami Beach with a boat and a BMW and an apartment in the Mondrian. Krishna was gay and surrounded himself with down-to-earth, interesting people. He was a real friend, not a fake friend. Things were changing for me. For example, I started taking tennis lessons. I started hanging out with people I actually liked. I stopped shooting the shit with Brett. I would nod on my way out the door, when he was sitting there having a cigarette, but I didn't go swimming with all his friends in the evenings, and their parties got so depressing. One night, I agreed to drive one of them to "pick something up." I was just trying to be neighborly. On the way, the guy failed to warn me about a helpless animal crossing the road. I know that as the driver I was technically at fault, but he saw this animal, this doomed raccoon, and he just let out a slow "Whoa." Then I ran over the raccoon. In the rearview mirror I watched the raccoon drag itself toward the curb. I hadn't even properly killed it. I was furious. I was furious at this poor creature for trying to live on Miami Beach, at myself for having maimed it, and especially at this guy for being too much of a stoner to stop me. It wasn't quite fair, but that's how I felt. From then on, when Brett's drug-dealer friends offered cocaine when I stepped out of my apartment in the morning I would be outright rude. At some point Brett had lost his job selling boats.

My relationship with Miami changed. I went to fewer parties at hotels. The gift-bag influx slowed. I stopped being around so many people who sold real estate, who picked me up in luxury vehicles, who drank lychee martinis and said things like, "Well, I was talking about this with John Stamos at Mansion the other night." I still pursued unlikely friendships out of curiosity—I went on a date with a paparazzo who had netted his fortune from a single portrait of Paris Hilton with her tiny dog. The funny thing was that this paparazzo had a tiny dog of his own that would nuzzle and burrow under your arm when you held it, like a little cat.

I stopped writing e-mails to my friends in New York about my mirth at outrageous Floridian real estate nonsense. The billboard advertising a condominium project on I-95 that was simply a photo of a man's hands unhooking a woman's bra was no longer delightfully symbolic of everything that was wrong with the real estate boom, just depressingly so.

To live in a place like Florida is to destroy the earth. I watched snowy egrets and great blue herons picking their way through drainage ditches outside Costco. I covered county commission meetings where the merits of building suburbs in the Everglades were proclaimed and posters of digitally rendered high-rises were offered in exchange for slackening of the zoning laws. I went to the Everglades and saw anhingas flitting under the boardwalk, their tails expanding like fans in water stained brown like tea. I thought about how in Florida, a bird like the anhinga was useful only insofar as it provided local color in the names of housing developments. The names of new housing developments grew more and more offensive. I started keeping a list. The idea was to make some sort of game out of it, like that Internet game that generated Wu-Tang names. I thought I could make a Florida subdivision name generator.

Here is an excerpt of my list: Villa Encantada. Gables Estates. Old Cutler Bay. Journey's End. Hancock Oaks. Cutler Oaks. Pine Bay. Deering Bay Estates. Old Cutler Glen. Cocoplum. Saga Bay, Serena Lakes, Lakes by the Bay, Three Lakes, Cutler Estates. Swan Lake. Arabesque. Arboretum Estates. The Sanctuary at Pinecrest. Gables by the Sea. Tahiti Beach Island. Snapper Creek Lakes. Banyans by the Gables. Coco Ibiza Villas. Kumquat Village. The Imperial. The Moorings. Trocadero in the Grove. Gladewinds. Killian Oaks Estates. The Palms at Kendall. Poinciana at Sunset. Villas of Briar Bay. Las Brisas at Doral. The Courts at Doral Isles. Porto Vita. The Terraces at Turnberry. Lychee Nut Grove. Flamingo Garden Estates. L'Hermitage. The Palace.

Nightly Barbecue, Guantánamo Bay

DATE: MAY 2006
VENUE: LEEWARD DORMITORIES, GUANTÁNAMO BAY NAVAL BASE
LIQUOR SPONSOR: NAVY PX

A senior reporter at the paper quit, and they sent me in her stead to report on the detention facilities at Guantánamo Bay. Cuba fell under our purview as a Miami newspaper, even if Gitmo was four hundred miles away. Before I left, I watched *A Few Good Men*, the basic-cable mainstay about a military cover-up at Guantánamo. When Demi Moore and Tom Cruise visit the island to look for evidence, Demi, in curve-hugging Navy whites, accuses a flippant Tom of goofing around. "Are you going to do any investigating," she demands, "or did you just come here for the tour?" I came for the tour.

I flew Air Sunshine. A lawyer, a frequent flyer on Air Sunshine propeller planes, had told me that taking the airline's shuttles from Fort Lauderdale to Guantánamo Bay was like traveling in a "minivan with wings." The nine-seater's decor was peeling blue pleather accentuated with protruding bits of orange foam. A front-row seat afforded a detailed view of the cockpit, since one sat practically inside it. The windows were pockmarked and scratched. The engine thrummed a steady bass vibrato. The air smelled acrid with fumes. As the plane tilted to land, a container of shoe polish rolled across the floor.

I spent ten days at Guantánamo, most of it by myself on the deserted leeward side, where I rented a bicycle from a Jamaican contract worker and went swimming on a rocky beach overseen by Marine guard towers. The detention facilities were on the windward side, where we could go only with military escorts. I toured the camps twice, going through the motions of journalism. The tour was a farce. We saw the prisoners only from a distance. The cells they showed us were stocked with "comfort items" like soap, the "interrogation room" furnished with a plush armchair and an espresso machine. The troops we spoke with told us about their scuba-diving lessons. They lived in a suburb devoid of a city, like an amputated limb with a life of its own, with Pizza Hut and Ben & Jerry's and outdoor screenings of *The Hills Have Eyes 2*. When inside the camp, the military personnel removed the Velcro name tags attached to their uniforms and emphasized that detainees have been known to make threats. On one of the tours our guide was Naval Commander Catie Hanft, deputy commander of the Joint Detention Group. Commander Hanft's previous job was commanding the naval brig in Charleston, South Carolina, where José Padilla was jailed in an environment of almost total sensory deprivation, never allowed to see the faces of his captors, until his transfer to a federal prison in Miami. Hanft had short hair and a tan. When one of our escorts accidentally called her by name she smiled and interrupted: "Colonel, don't say my name in the camp, please." The mood curdled slightly.

Most nights we would pick up some meat and alcohol at the Navy PX before they escorted us back to the deserted side of the bay. Then we would drink alcohol and grill meat, "we" being an assortment of human rights lawyers, Pashto translators, and journalists. Joshua Colangelo-Bryan, one of the lawyers, told of walking in on his Bahraini client, Juma Al Dosari, as he attempted suicide during a bathroom break the previous year. Dosari, who had made twelve serious attempts, had cut one wrist and tried to hang himself. On this visit, although Colangelo-Bryan noted a couple of new scars, Dosari seemed in better spirits.

On the night before I left, there was a bigger group than usual at the barbecue. Around midnight, when everyone was slightly drunk, a plane came in to land on the base's runway, which was also on the deserted side of the bay. Sleek and floodlit against the night sky, the plane gleamed white and bore the green insignia of the Saudi royal family on its tail. The Saudis had come for some of the prisoners. In the morning the plane was gone.

NBA Finals

DATE: JUNE 2006
VENUE: STREET IN COCONUT GROVE

The Miami Heat had had a good season, and as the team advanced to the playoffs people actually started going to Miami Heat games. Everybody in the stands wore white to these games. Later I was informed that the entire sports blogosphere made fun of Miami for doing that. The Heat beat the Mavericks in the finals. I went to an outdoor screening of the last game and watched Dirk Nowitzki run backward chewing his mouth guard with an increasingly frantic air of frustration. Lots of Miami players seemed to be wearing special injury-preventing compression kneesocks and sleeves. After the team won, a friend who was visiting observed the cheering hordes in white on the street. "The most hard-core Miami Heat fan is like one of those girls who wears a pink Red Sox shirt," he said.

Fidel Puts Raúl in Charge

DATE: AUGUST 2006
VENUE: CALLE OCHO

Everybody wanted to be in Miami when Castro fell. The *Miami Herald* supposedly had a plan, or rather *the* plan, for the moment of Castro's death. Then nothing turned out as planned. Castro showed up on television in an Adidas tracksuit, looking ill. Then he made his brother president. The streets outside Café Versailles were full of people honking horns and waving flags, but Fidel wasn't really dead. *Fidel Castro was no longer president of Cuba,* he was attached to a colostomy bag and being fed through a tube, but the Berlin Wall moment everyone in Miami expected didn't happen. For the first time, it seemed possible that it might not ever happen. Then again, he's not dead yet.

Dinner with a Psychic

DATE: SEPTEMBER 2006
VENUE: THE HOME OF UNIVISION'S MORNING SHOW'S VISITING
   PSYCHIC

I was writing about the first homosexual love triangle in an American-made Spanish-language telenovela. One of the actors, who was straight (it was unclear whether the show's tolerance extended into telenovela casting practices), invited me to dinner at the house of a Spanish-language television psychic named Frances. I had a friend of a friend in town so I invited him, too, thinking he would enjoy the cultural experience. He did not enjoy it. The evening ended with Frances waving a wand around a warbling vibratory instrument called a meditation bowl and ordering the friend of a friend to hug a palm tree. "I'm an atheist," he kept repeating, his face pressed against the palm tree. The next week I got an e-mail inviting me to a gathering at Frances's with some Tibetan monks. I have many regrets, but few loom so large as my decision not to attend.

Weeknight Shindig at Brett's

DATE: SEPTEMBER 2006
VENUE: OUR APARTMENT BUILDING

This year Brett came back from Burning Man with an announcement: he had fallen in love. Kellie, an eighteen-year-old from Truckee, California, arrived shortly thereafter. She immediately found work as a cocktail waitress and started supporting him. I gave her my old driver's license so she could get into bars. We had other news as well: our building was going condo.

Art Basel Miami Beach

DATE: DECEMBER 2006
VENUE: SHORE CLUB

This year I went out a little more at Art Basel. I went to a *Vanity Fair* party. We got rubber bracelets, like Lance Armstrong testicular cancer bracelets, but hot pink and stamped VANITY FAIR. My aunt, who lives in southwest Florida and paints pictures of children on beaches flying kites, came to see the art, but what excited her most was watching someone write a $400,000 check in a particleboard boothlet.

A Celebration of the Jade Collection of Thi-Nga, Vietnamese Princess in Exile

DATE: FEBRUARY 2007
VENUE: THE SETAI, COLLINS AVENUE

The paper assigned me an investigative piece: discover the true identity of Princess Thi-Nga, a Miami Beach philanthropist and supposed member of the exiled imperial family of Vietnam. She was on the board of the Bass Museum of Art, where the parties were always sponsored by Absolut Vodka. Her collection of ancient jade sculpture was on display at the Bass at the time, which some people saw as a conflict of interest. My editor thought she might be a fraud. I failed to uncover much evidence of this. I failed to uncover much evidence at all, actually. It appeared nobody was paying close attention to the lineage of the former royal family of Vietnam. I too didn't really care.

I met Thi-Nga at the Setai, the hotel where my friend Krishna worked. A room at the Setai cost upward of $1,000 a night. Its bar was inlaid with mother-of-pearl and its couches upholstered with manta ray skins, or something like that. According to Krishna, when a guest of the Setai arrived at Miami International Airport, he or she had the choice of being chauffeured in a Bentley or a Hummer (a question of personal style). In the car was a wide selection of bottled water brands and an iPod.

Thi-Nga was launching her jade sculpture exhibition with an elaborate party at the hotel. I met her there for breakfast the day before the party. I ate a $12 bowl of muesli. It was the most delicious bowl of muesli I have ever eaten.

For her party, Thi-Nga had rented an elephant named Judy. Adorned with gemstones, Judy led a parade down Collins Avenue on Miami Beach that also included dancers: Thai ones with pointy golden hats and splayed fingers and a Chinese lion that batted its paper eyelashes to the rhythm of cymbals. The princess rode in a silver Jaguar convertible behind them, seated next to the mayor of Miami Beach, waving to confused pedestrians who tentatively waved back. Then all her guests went to the Setai and ate salmon.

Brett Moves Out

DATE: APRIL 2007

This party is in fact only theoretical. My neighborly relationship with Brett had deteriorated to the point of mere formality, so I'm not sure if he had a good-bye party or not. I hope he had a big party, where the lava lamps oozed and the cigarette butts accumulated and the dollar bills were dusted in cocaine. Our building was depopulated now. The call girl was gone; the dumb stoner who had been my accomplice in the murder of the raccoon was gone. The

apartments upstairs had sold for phenomenal amounts of money.
My apartment had been purchased by a tennis pro, who informed
me that I could consider him a landlord upgrade. I took him at
his word and purchased the air-conditioning unit with the highest
Consumer Reports rating, paid the alcoholic handyman who hung
around the neighborhood to install it, and deducted the whole
production from my rent check. Going condo was amazing.

Unless you were Brett. Things weren't going well for Brett, who
was still unemployed and being supported by his teenage girlfriend. He and Kellie had recently been arrested for driving someone else's car that happened to have a felony-size quantity of crys-
tal meth in the glove compartment. I encountered them on our
stoop after they had been released on bail. Apparently everything
would be all right; they had agreed to rat on some drug dealer. But
still, this on top of moving. They were heading up to 8th Street, a
part of South Beach that remarkably had retained its seedy character, and whose apartments, though as expensive as everything else
in Miami, were terrible to live in. I'd had a friend who lived on
Brett's new block; her floor was often inexplicably littered with mil-
lipede exoskeletons. She would gamely sweep up the hard brown
shells and claim that they were harmless, but I vowed that I would
draw the line of shitty-apartment-living at mysterious worm infesta-
tions.

Then one day Brett was gone, and the landlords were happily
ripping out the interior of his apartment. One of them, Dave, told
me it had been a relief.

"You should have seen the bathroom. Drug addicts. It's dis-
gusting."

Very stupidly, I had never thought of Brett as an *addict,* just as a
guy who did drugs. A certain kind of Miami guy who liked to party.
But now Brett was gone. All traces of him were replaced, in a matter of weeks, with granite countertops and track lighting.

I saw him one more time that summer, on 5th Street, when I
knew I would be leaving Miami. I was walking home from the gym
when I was waylaid by a torrential downpour, the kind where I
could see the violent wall of water approaching from across the
street. I waited under an overhang, staring at nothing, until it retreated. In the dripping aftermath, the sidewalks gray and clean,
the palm trees still quivering, I encountered Brett on a street cor-

ner. Brett wasn't a pessimist. Everything was going great, he said, the new apartment was fantastic. Later, when the recession came, I took comfort in knowing that, like me, Brett was probably all right, because Brett owned nothing.

That was the thing about boom times that later became clear: We now know that boom times don't feel like boom times. They feel like normal times, and then they end. Particularly if one is not a direct beneficiary of the excess wealth and one's salary is measly to nonexistent, boom times are just the spectacle of other people's reckless spending. Their gluttony was my gluttony of course — only a bore would have abstained from the festivities — but their downfall was little more than an abstraction from the vantage point of one with no assets.

Our downfalls would not involve grand narratives of repossession or foreclosure, just a steadily diminishing ability to keep some fundamental part of the city at bay. In heady days, we conquered Miami, carving out the mangroves, digging up the ocean bottom and slathering it on a sandbar, molding concrete into skyscrapers, pumping refrigerated air through miles of metal windpipes and over glass coffee tables and white couches. But here, now, as those with no assets fled to low-rent holdouts, inland from the beach to paved-over swamps, recession only meant a slow infiltration: worms burrowing through the floor and dying, spores drifting through vents, and terracotta roof tiles uplifted by the autumn winds.

My Last Day

DATE: AUGUST 2007

The Corolla was packed up, and as I was about to leave, one of those terrific summer rainstorms hit. I lay next to my boyfriend on his bed (for by then I had a boyfriend), watching the rain pound against the windows, the palms lean into the wind, and the cat purr between us. Of the whole tableau, the only thing I anticipated missing was the cat. The relationship was ending, my job was ending, and the real estate boom had already ended. I had gotten ornery in the last months in Miami. If another interviewee told me, as we drove in his golf cart through a maze of pink stucco on top of a leveled mangrove grotto, that he "lived in paradise," I thought I might wrestle the wheel from him and plunge us both into the algae blooms of a fertilizer-polluted drainage canal. So I left the place where baby sea turtles mistake the floodlights of condos for the rising sun, where the dogs are small, the breasts are big, and the parties are ornamented with drag queens in bubble baths.

When the rain stopped I drove past suburbs until I hit the Everglades, then emerged into suburbs again on the other side.

Contributors' Notes

Notable Travel Writing of 2010

Contributors' Notes

André Aciman is the author of *Out of Egypt: A Memoir* and the collection of essays *False Papers: Essays on Exile and Memory*. His latest collection of essays is *Alibis: Essays on Elsewhere* (2011). Aciman has also co-authored and edited *The Proust Project* and *Letters of Transit*, and has written a novel, *Call Me by Your Name*. Born in Alexandria, he lived in Italy and France. He received his Ph.D. from Harvard University and has taught at Princeton University and Bard College and is currently the chair of the Graduate Center's doctoral program in Comparative Literature, CUNY, and the director of the Writers' Institute there. He is the recipient of a Whiting Writers' Award, a Guggenheim Fellowship, and a fellowship from the New York Public Library's Cullman Center for Scholars and Writers. He has written for the *New York Times*, *The New Yorker*, the *New York Review of Books*, *The Paris Review*, and *The New Republic*.

Ben Austen is a contributing editor of *Harper's Magazine* and writes as well for *The Atlantic*, *Bloomberg BusinessWeek*, *GQ*, *Popular Science*, and *Wired*. Born in Chicago and raised there, he currently lives in Tennessee.

David Baez is a freelance writer and a graduate of Columbia Journalism School currently working on a book about his recovery from alcoholism and his relationship with his Nicaraguan father.

Mischa Berlinski is the author of *Fieldwork: A Novel*.

Christopher Buckley is the author of fourteen books, including *Thank You for Smoking* and *Losing Mum and Pup*. His awards include the Thurber Prize for American Humor and the Washington Irving Prize for Literary Excellence. His novel *They Eat Puppies, Don't They?* will be published in May 2012.

Maureen Dowd, winner of the 1999 Pulitzer Prize for distinguished commentary, became a columnist on the *New York Times* Op-Ed page in 1995 after having served as a correspondent in the paper's Washington bureau since 1986. She has covered four presidential campaigns and served as White House correspondent. She also wrote a column, "On Washington," for the *New York Times Magazine*. Ms. Dowd joined the *New York Times* as a metropolitan reporter in 1983.

Porter Fox was born in New York and raised on the coast of Maine. He lives, writes, teaches, and edits the literary travel writing journal *Nowhere* (nowheremag.com) in Brooklyn, New York. His fiction, essays, and nonfiction have been published in the *New York Times Magazine, The Believer, Outside, National Geographic Adventure, Powder, Narrative*, and *The Literary Review*, among others. He was nominated for Pushcart Prizes in 2008 and 2010 for fiction and nonfiction and was a finalist for the 2009 Robert Olen Butler Fiction Prize. Last summer he completed a two-thousand-mile sailing voyage along the Maine coast and he is working on a travel narrative based on the trip. He is also a member of the Miss Rockaway Armada and Swimming Cities art collectives and collaborated on installations on the Mississippi and Hudson rivers, Venice Biennale (2009), Mass MoCA (2008), and New York City's Anonymous Gallery (2009).

Keith Gessen is a founding editor of the magazine *N + 1* and the author of *All the Sad Young Literary Men*, a novel. He was born in Moscow and has traveled extensively in the former Eastern Bloc but has never been to Cairo or Mexico City, where, it is said, the traffic is even worse.

Tom Ireland is an editor with the Office of Archaeological Studies in Santa Fe, New Mexico. His most recent book is *The Man Who Gave His Wife Away* (2010).

Verlyn Klinkenborg was born in Colorado in 1952 and raised in Iowa and California. He graduated from Pomona College and received a Ph.D. in English literature from Princeton University. Mr. Klinkenborg joined the editorial board of the *New York Times* in 1997. He is the author of *Making Hay, The Last Fine Time, The Rural Life,* and *Timothy; Or, Notes of an Abject Reptile*. His work has appeared in many magazines, including *The New Yorker, Harper's Magazine, Esquire, National Geographic, Smithsonian, Audubon, Martha Stewart Living,* and *Sports Afield*, among others. He has taught literature and creative writing at Fordham University, St. Olaf College, Bennington College, and Harvard University and is a recipient of the 1991 Lila Wallace–Reader's Digest Writer's Award and a National Endowment for the Arts Fellowship. He lives in rural New York.

Ariel Levy is a staff writer at *The New Yorker*, where she has profiled the South African runner Caster Semenya, the director Nora Ephron, the lesbian separatist Lamar Van Dyke, and the conservative politician Mike Huckabee, among others. Prior to joining *The New Yorker* in 2008, Levy wrote for *New York Magazine* for twelve years. Her work has been anthologized in *The Best American Essays* and *Sugar in My Bowl: Real Women Write About Real Sex*. She is the author of *Female Chauvinist Pigs: Women and the Rise of Raunch Culture*.

Jessica McCaughey is a writer and adjunct professor at George Mason University and Northern Virginia Community College, where she teaches writing, literature, and English as a second language. She earned her B.A. in English at Mary Washington College (now the University of Mary Washington) and both an M.A. in English and an M.F.A. in creative writing at George Mason University. Her work has appeared in *The Colorado Review, Silk Road, Phoebe*, and elsewhere. She is currently at work on a book examining fear from both a scientific and personal perspective. Jessica lives in Arlington, Virginia, and can be found on-line at jessica@jessicamccaughey .com.

Justin Nobel covers science and culture for magazines and pens a blog about death for the funeral industry and another where he sits for hours in one New York City spot. He lives in Blissville, a sliver of forgotten New York.

Téa Obreht was born in 1985 in the former Yugoslavia, and spent her childhood in Cyprus and Egypt before eventually immigrating to the United States in 1997. Her writing has been published in *The New Yorker, The Atlantic, Harper's Magazine, Zoetrope: All-Story,* the *New York Times,* and the *Guardian,* and has been anthologized in *The Best American Short Stories* and *The Best American Nonrequired Reading.* Her first novel, *The Tiger's Wife,* was published in 2011. She has been named by *The New Yorker* as one of the twenty best American fiction writers under forty and included in the National Book Foundation's list of 5 Under 35. She lives in Ithaca, New York.

Annie Proulx is the author of eight books, including the novel *The Shipping News* and the story collection *Close Range*. Her many honors include a Pulitzer Prize, a National Book Award, the Irish Times International Fiction Prize, and a PEN/Faulkner Award. Her story "Brokeback Mountain," which originally appeared in *The New Yorker*, was made into an Academy Award–winning film. Her memoir *Bird Cloud* was published in 2011. She lives in Wyoming.

Gary Shteyngart was born in Leningrad in 1972 and came to the United States seven years later. His debut novel, *The Russian Debutante's Handbook*, won the Stephen Crane Award for First Fiction and the National Jewish Book Award for Fiction. His second novel, *Absurdistan*, was named one of the Ten Best Books of the Year by the *New York Times Book Review*, as well as a best book of the year by *Time*, the *Washington Post Book World*, the *San Francisco Chronicle*, the *Chicago Tribune*, and many other publications. His novel *Super Sad True Love Story* was published in 2010. He has been se-lected as one of Granta's Best Young American Novelists. His work has ap-peared in *The New Yorker, Esquire, GQ*, and *Travel + Leisure*, and his books have been translated into more than twenty languages. He lives in New York City.

William T. Vollmann is the author of seven novels, three collections of sto-ries, and a seven-volume critique of violence, *Rising Up and Rising Down*. He is also the author of *Poor People*, an examination of poverty worldwide through the eyes of the impoverished themselves; *Riding Toward Every-where*, an investigation of the train-hopping hobo lifestyle; and *Imperial*, a panoramic look at Mexican California. He has won the National Book Award, the PEN Center USA West Award for Fiction, a Shiva Naipaul Me-morial Prize, and a Whiting Writers' Award. His journalism and fiction have been published in *The New Yorker, Esquire, Spin*, and *Granta*.

Emily Witt is a journalist currently based in New York. She has been a staff reporter at the *New York Observer* and the *Miami New Times* and has pub-lished essays, articles, and reviews in *N + 1, Foreign Policy* on-line, the *New York Times*, and *The Nation*. She was the recipient of a Fulbright fellowship to Mozambique and has also lived in Brazil, Chile, and England.

Notable Travel Writing of 2010

Selected by Jason Wilson

Phyllis Barber
The Knife Handler. *Agni*, vol. 71.
Elif Batuman
The Memory Kitchen. *The New Yorker*, April 19.
Summer in Samarkand, Part II. *N + 1*, Spring.
Frank Bures
The Roads Between Us: A Journey Across Africa. *World Hum*, April 19.

Eric Calderwood
The Road to Damascus. *New England Review*, vol. 31, no. 3.
Sebastian Copeland
Alone Across Greenland. *Men's Journal*, December/January.

John D'Agata
What Happens There. *The Believer*, January.
Avi Davis
Creatures of Other Mould. *The Believer*, November/December.
Marcia Desanctis
Strangers on a Train. *New York Times Magazine*, July 16.
Bill Donahue
A Pilgrimage to SkyMall. *World Hum*, January 26.

Brian T. Edwards
Watching *Shrek* in Tehran. *The Believer*, March/April.
Ethan Epstein
Staring at North Korea. *Slate*, October 7.

Ian Frazier
On the Prison Highway. *The New Yorker*, August 30.

A. A. GILL
Loch, Stalk, and Burials. *Vanity Fair,* January.
AARON GULLEY
Shaken. *Outside,* October.

ERIC HANSEN
Steamed. *Outside,* August.
PETER HESSLER
Go West. *The New Yorker,* April 19.
MANNY HOWARD
Sauvage Grace. *New York Times Magazine,* September 26.

PICO IYER
Forever Foreign. *Smithsonian,* June.
Istanbul, City of the Future. *National Geographic Traveler,* October.
Lover's Moon. *World Hum,* March 15.

ROWAN JACOBSEN
Heart of Dark Chocolate. *Outside,* September.
The Spill Seekers. *Outside,* November.
MARK JENKINS
The Forgotten Road. *National Geographic,* May.
ALDEN JONES
The Burmese Dream Series. *Post Road,* vol. 19.

JOHN LANCASTER
Pakistan's Heartland Under Threat. *National Geographic,* July.
ANTHONY LANE
Only Mr. God Knows Why. *The New Yorker,* June 28.
JESSICA LEVINE
My Two Weeks as a Fellini Extra. *The Southern Review,* Fall.
GREG LINDSAY
Triumph of the Air Warriors. *Condé Nast Traveler,* February.

CHADWICK MATLIN
30 Airports in 30 Days. *Slate,* November 12.
ANDREW MCCARTHY
L.A. Dreamin'. *National Geographic Traveler,* November/December.
EMILY MEEHAN
The Humanitarian's Dilemma. *Slate,* June 25.
JONATHAN MILES
A Chowhound's Caribbean Cruise. *Food and Wine,* October.
SHANE MITCHELL
Out Islands Bahamas. *Travel + Leisure,* June.
J. R. MOEHRINGER
Winner Take All. *Smithsonian,* October.

JOYCE CAROL OATES
  Going Home Again. *Smithsonian*, March.

ANN PATCHETT
  As American as Cherry Pie. *New York Times Magazine*, May 19.

APRIL RABKIN
  A Visit to the Shrine of Afghanistan's National Hero. *Slate*, September 9.

ALEXIS SCHAITKIN
  Living Relics. *Ecotone*, Spring.
LIESL SCHILLINGER
  Confessions of a Soukaholic. *New York Times Magazine*, May 19.
JOHN SEABROOK
  The Last Babylift. *The New Yorker*, May 10.
DAVID SEDARIS
  Standing By. *The New Yorker*, August 9.
ELLEN RUPPEL SHELL
  Capsized. *New York Times Magazine*, January 24.
ROBIN SHULMAN
  World Cup Travels in Post-Apartheid South Africa. *Slate*, July 2.
JEREMY STAHL
  "It's Like a Safari and We're the Zebras." *Slate*, September 21.
KAYT SUKEL
  Chet of Arabia. *The Atlantic*, March.
THOMAS SWICK
  A Walk Through Old Japan. *Smithsonian*, October.
  Venice in Three Acts. *Afar*, September/October.
PATRICK SYMMES
  The Beautiful and the Dammed. *Outside*, June.
  Thirty Days as a Cuban. *Harper's Magazine*, October.

DAMON TABOR
  If It's Tuesday, It Must Be the Taliban. *Outside*, December.
HANNAH TENNANT-MOORE
  The Sexual Lives of Sri Lankans. *World Hum*, December 17.
GUY TREBAY
  Going Postal. *Travel + Leisure*, February.
CALVIN TRILLIN
  No Daily Specials. *The New Yorker*, November 22.
  Some Like It Hot. *Condé Nast Traveler*, November.

JOHN WASHINGTON
  The Local to Mexico City. *The Smart Set*, October 7.
JOHN WRAY
  Acquired Taste. *New York Times Magazine*, February 28.